COUPLES
GROUP PSYCHOTHERAPY

SECOND EDITION

COUPLES
GROUP PSYCHOTHERAPY

A CLINICAL TREATMENT MODEL

SECOND EDITION

JUDITH COCHÉ

Routledge
Taylor & Francis Group
New York London

Routledge
Taylor & Francis Group
711 Third Avenue,
New York, NY 10017

Routledge
Taylor & Francis Group
27 Church Road,
Hove, East Sussex BN3 2FA, UK

First issued in paperback 2014

Routledge is an imprint of the Taylor and Francis Group, an informa business

ISBN 978-0-415-87304-8 (hbk)
ISBN 978-1-138-87268-4 (pbk)

Library of Congress Cataloging-in-Publication Data

Coché, Judith.
    Couples group psychotherapy : a clinical treatment model / Judith Coché. --
2nd ed.
        p. cm.
    Includes bibliographical references and index.
    ISBN 978-0-415-87304-8 (hbk. : alk. paper)
    1. Marital psychotherapy. 2. Couples therapy. 3. Group psychotherapy. I.
Title.

RC488.5.C62 2010
616.89'1562--dc22   2009037537

Visit the Taylor & Francis Web site at
http://www.taylorandfrancis.com

and the Routledge Web site at
http://www.routledgementalhealth.com

DEDICATION

…with deep appreciation to five generous and courageous couples who shared their treatment to benefit others.

CONTENTS

SECTION II Psychotherapy With Couples in Groups

ix

SECTION III   Integrating Theory, Research, and Treatment for Couples in Groups

SECTION IV *Appendices*

FOREWORD

Falling in love is easy. But remaining in love is difficult. Where else is a decision made that is contracted "until death do us part?"

Once the glow of novelty is gone, living in an intimate, committed relationship requires hard work on the part of both partners. This is especially true in modern Western civilization, where notions of romantic love enter the equation.

There are certainly historical instances of love that are more akin to modern romantic love. Pliny the Younger left us a series of romantic letters dating from the first century, A.D., indicating that romantic love was alive and well in ancient Rome. The *Song of Solomon* also documents that such notions of love have been around quite a while. Nonetheless, historically, *falling* in love was not the norm.

Historically, marriage served more pragmatic purposes. Marriage was an institution designed to assist in passing property and to guarantee children; in other words, marriage was to accomplish some important societal roles. This included even political purposes because marriages have served to solidify or establish relationships between countries. In much of the world, arranged marriages were (and in some cases remain) the norm in which older and presumably more mature individuals chose whom one would marry.

In modern Western society, there is an imperative to "couple" on the basis of romance and love, and this imperative is rather new. The Romantic Period did not appear until the late eighteenth century, parallel to Freud's life. Indeed, Freud's theories of the unconscious, free association, and the power of dreams all needed the ideals of the Romantic Period to flourish.

Adding the elements of romance and love has immeasurably complicated the concept of marriage (or any other committed coupling). Little girls hear of Prince Charming and modern media portray couples as forever intensely sexual—even if not with their partners.

Today's couples often turn to psychotherapists to assist in the task of keeping relationships alive and exciting and to repair broken relationships. I have had the opportunity to know Dr. Coché over the last 20 years. I have seen her design this model and then go on to develop it clinically in practice as well as offer it in academic training for colleagues.

In this book, I was especially interested to see the elaboration and extension of the first edition. This volume, a sizable expansion that incorporates new methodologies but keeps the solid psychodynamic foundation of the earlier work, serves to unite group and family therapy in a practical and academically viable model. Judith Coché presents a comprehensive approach to working with couples therapeutically—an approach that represents 20 years of clinical work and evidence-based practice. It is a solid approach that incorporates individual, group, and couple sessions along with extended sessions and destination retreat work.

This entirely practical volume walks practitioners through steps in how to establish group psychotherapy for couples, according to the model that Dr. Coché has created, developed, and perfected. For those of us who are committed to working with couples, this is an invaluable book. As Dr. Coché says in this work, recent research informs us that couples therapy is effective, group therapy is effective, and couples group therapy is effective. Even if one does not adopt the entire system that Dr. Coché presents, spending time with her approach serves to solidify the level of understanding of the therapeutic processes at work needed to help couples deepen and strengthen their relationships.

J. Scott Rutan, PhD
Senior Faculty
Boston Institute for
Psychotherapy

ACKNOWLEDGMENTS

In a marriage, each person is like a member of a mountain climbing team. The team can go places together that neither can go alone.

—Erich Coché, PhD

I intended my first marriage to be my last marriage. I thought that one would be plenty. Yet, as I complete this second edition of *Couples Group Psychotherapy,* my second husband, John Edward Anderson, is installing a stained-pine cathedral ceiling in our tiny marsh-front cottage located near the Coché Center's Stone Harbor offices. The cottage overhaul is our 15th wedding anniversary gift to one another. I was a one-man woman until my luck and my future faltered: Cancer took Erich Coché at age 49, 3 months after the publication of *Couples Group Psychotherapy* in 1990. Fortunately, life has a way of introducing opportunity as a handmaiden to cataclysmic disaster.

The later years of my marriage to Erich Coché, PhD, ABPP, are intertwined with the early years of designing and reporting about couples group psychotherapy, and Erich's wisdom glimmers through selected text in this edition. I began to sketch the model conceptually in 1985 from my training in family, individual, and group therapy. Erich integrated a research component, literature review, and assessment. Together, we selected clinical examples and finalized the first edition just short of our 25th wedding anniversary. During these years of 1985–1990, I would frequently come home, after biking, with a new idea for how one could help couples build working marriages. Regardless of how outlandish my idea sounded in its preformed state, I could count on Erich to say, with that sparkle that made the corners of his eyes crinkly, "Well, let's think about that."

I have been thinking about couples psychotherapy ever since. Year after year, I have tinkered with the model in this book, inching toward an attempt at a personal best. Because interpersonal puzzles captivate me, understanding the principles of married love has engaged my curiosity for as long as I can remember.

Of course, one might argue that I had little choice. After all, I grew up in a clan that knew it had to keep its wits about it. Leaving a successful business and affluence behind, my grandparents fled the Ukraine during the 1904–1908 pogroms against the Jews. They spoke no English. To make matters worse, my grandfather died of cancer at age 42, shortly after establishing a jewelry business for his new family in the New World. His oldest son, my father, was 14 at the time. On his deathbed, my grandfather passed on a family legacy along with his treasured gold watch: Lou Milner was to support the others in any way he could for the rest of his life.

Gifted in humor, language, and philosophy, Dad had a life dream of teaching graduate English at the University of Pennsylvania. Instead, to support six fatherless siblings and a mother who spoke only Yiddish, Dad plowed through pharmacy school and started his own pharmacy at age 19. Holidays were simply an extension of the legacy, so, like it or not, Dad's sense of responsibility determined that we spent each Jewish holiday with this clan. As a result, I fell victim to large-bosomed hugs and garlicky kisses from well-meaning aunts in ample print dresses. Plates piled with brisket and great good humor, the clan mixed noodle kugel with gossip and psychological insight at gigantic family dinners each fall and spring.

I got great family therapy training from my Dad and my Uncle Joe, the heads of the clan. They were part of my everyday life as a young girl and I assumed everybody was as smart as they were. I made it my business to sit silently at the top of the steps in my small Philadelphia Main Line home and eavesdrop night after night. Lou and Joe Milner continued to take their father's request seriously and felt bound to help all the brothers and sisters with their lives at all times. By the time I was 15, I understood family clans from the inside out. No matter how I would go on to earn money, I would do it armed with deep expertise in family intervention.

As I added formal interpersonal systems training to the boot camp of growing up in my family clan, it seemed obvious to me that the highly individualistic framework of classic psychoanalysis in the 1960s trained us to practice psychotherapy as though individuals can exist in a vacuum. But individuals cannot thrive in a vacuum. Neither could I, so in my quest for mentors, intellectual playmates, and likeminded compatriots, I actively sought stellar and modest colleagues: Carl Whitaker, MD; Olga Silverstein, ACSW; Harry Aponte, LCSW; James Bugental, PhD; Scott Rutan, PhD; Zygmunt Piotrowski, PhD; Erich Coché, PhD, ABPP; and Juliette Galbraith, MD, were there for me. I have thanked you all in many ways.

The heroes and heroines of my story are five couples: Diane and Dwight, Robyn and Spencer, Margaret and Michael, Antonia and Patrick, and Holly and Trevor. These are the names chosen for the very real couples in these pages. Five couples volunteered their trust in 2006 to help educate readers about this model. They joined four couples who had made the same decision in 1988 for the first edition of *Couples Group Psychotherapy* and the training tape for colleagues. These nine couples, as well as the hundreds of couples who have worked with me clinically, have influenced the marriages of the thousands of couples treated by the professionals who have worked with this model. I thank them on behalf of us all. Their courage and generosity of spirit in inviting us into their hearts and lives is a great gift to the reader and to me.

One of Dad's best one-liners was a brief and gentle admonition to his only and headstrong daughter. At 16, all legs and frizzy hair, I despaired that anybody would ever fall in love with me. But Dad knew better and casually delivered a one-sentence sermon that has lived inside me ever since. I can see him standing in the tiny hallway of my home as he said, "Judy, be careful whom you fall in love with." The gist of his wisdom was that, once felled, the heart can endure years of servitude to those who have enchained the spirit through emotional bonding. Dad will not get to read the neurobiology of coupling in Chapter 11, but he understood its power and its wisdom decades before we knew to write it. His wisdom, customarily delivered in stories laced with biting sarcasm, lives on in the lives of the couples in these pages.

My daughter, Juliette, (Figure 0.1) grew up in a family business, just like her mother did. The business of her parents was mental health service at the level of outpatient practice and hospital administration. At age 3, though she was not yet big enough to reach the chair arms, she play-acted what she thought I did for a living. Pretending that I was a client, she clambered onto the antique mahogany rocker in my office, set it into furious motion, and said, "I am Dr. Judith Coché. I am a psychologist." I knew no other 3-year-olds whose vocabulary included the word "psychology." At this writing, Juliette (Laura Coché) Anderson Galbraith, MD, has developed into a psychiatrist who keeps her wits about her while her heart remains open. One year, not very long after her daddy died, I found a slim-framed, cross-stitched sentence that has lived with her ever since. It says, "The beauty of love is not seen nor heard but felt from the heart." Thank you, Juliette, for all you bring to our field and to my life.

The "second edition project" engaged a village housed in 800 square feet of working space in Center City, Philadelphia, not too far from the

Figure 0.1 Juliette Anderson Galbraith, MD, and her daughter, Ava Lynn Galbraith, at the University of Pennsylvania, 2008. (Photo courtesy of Dr. Judith Coché.)

University of Pennsylvania mental health think tank that bolsters my conceptual world. Nine contributors require mention:

> The ghost of the first edition is the team of Drs. Erich and Judith Coché, whose original text is included in part in this updated volume. Newer is not always better.
>
> Dr. Juliette Galbraith and I teamed on examples and edits. Fresh vignettes from 50 hours of session transcription bring the clinical principles to life through the treatment of five couples.

During Dr. Melissa Hunt's informal mentorship with me, an evidence-based practice model was begun that Kevin McCarthy helped to execute as part of his PhD training.

Kevin McCarthy and I, with help from then 17-year-old Jill Ahrens, completed the modest evidence-based practice presented in these pages.

Dr. Seth Gillihan and I worked with the literature review update and Dr. Gillihan drafted the section on the neurobiology of coupling.

Dr. Suzanne Cohen and I continue to ponder deeply how to integrate body work into the mind games that coupling creates.

Julia M. Hormes, MA, Stephen Schueller, MA, and I teamed for a period that seemed like it was longer than the actual months of painstaking editing.

Stephen Schueller, MA, graduate student with Dr. Marty Seligman, helped integrate material from positive psychology.

Monika Connolly set her talented eagle eye to a professional edit when I could no longer stomach the text.

Academic authorship is an odd hobby. One works harder for no money than for one's honest wages. A special thanks to Sharon Panulla, who read the first proposal for this book in 1988. She encouraged me not to throw it out when I was certain nobody would read it. She suggested that I "remain creative and write new things" in an era when dollars were short for academic creativity. Again, in 2008, over coffee in New York, Sharon encouraged me to do a second edition despite paltry sales of the first edition. Most recently, Taylor & Francis publisher George Zimmar helped editor Anna Moore support this work with a solid publishing contract and quick turnaround teaming. Thanks to the three of you for the kind of support that money cannot buy.

In 2005, I was invited to coffee in a paper cup with Laurie Abraham. Hunkered in a Manhattan Cosi café, she asked if I would consider letting her sit in on a couples group. Her real interest was in observing the marital drama firsthand. Aware that writing about couples group psychotherapy is no easy task, I quipped, "If you can write it, I can see if we can do it." I was later to learn that Laurie combines a master's in journalism (MSJ) with a master's in law (MSL) and is exquisitely trained for the task she set out to do. Now, nearly 5 rich years later, Laurie has created a stir by writing a cover story about our couples for the *New York Times Magazine*, which also later appeared in *Stella*, the weekly magazine for the *Sunday Telegraph* in the United Kingdom.

Laurie expanded this work and has incorporated our five couples (with different names) into an independent nonfiction book entitled *The Husbands and Wives Club: A Year in the Life of a Couples Therapy Group*, slated for publication by Simon & Schuster in 2010. In January 2009, the American Psychoanalytic Association gave Laurie its annual award for excellence in journalism for her *Times* piece. "Can this marriage be saved?" has added to the public's understanding of what couples therapy really is. Thank you, Laurie, for provoking me into a level of analysis of my work as only you could.

"Percs" sometimes happen serendipitously. As part of the *New York Times Magazine* project, justly famous photographer Nicholas Nixon agreed to shoot our couples without revealing their identity. He and his many-tiered partner, Bebe Nixon, came for a day. It felt like an honor to experience their long-lived marriage as they deftly captured interpersonal dynamics in a split second. Nick and Bebe have weathered life and made it theirs. Nick has shared two of the photos in this text. He captured the dynamics of Antonia and Patrick to the letter and then went on to convey anonymous delight as Trevor places his hand on Holly's home for his yet unborn child.

Among my great personal accomplishments, achieved with the stubbornness that is my birthright, I count nearly 40 years of marriage to two good, smart men. I have indeed been careful about falling in love. In 1966, Erich Henry Ernst Coché, PhD, proposed, with a charming Dutch accent, in a rowboat on a small river in his hometown of Kleve, at the Dutch–German border. In 1993, John Edward Anderson, MA, proposed with characteristic Midwestern modesty, dripping from sweat after running around the Philadelphia Art Museum. John promised to be my "rock" from that point forward. I consider these two men, and marriage in general, to be among my greatest lifetime gifts.

Judith Coché, PhD, ABPP
Rittenhouse Square and Stone Harbor

INTRODUCTION

I can't think of a better group of people to share my heart with.

—A woman, graduating

For much of human history, marriage was considered a permanent, life-long bond between two people for the purposes of procreation and survival of the family unit. In the Middle Ages, for example, marriages were frequently arranged by the elders of the partners for the betterment of their respective families of origin. Within the last century, the goal of marriage shifted. Now, all hanker after deriving personal satisfaction from the bond itself. This shift has created confusion, fear, frustration, and competing models of marriage.

Robyn loved and admired her first husband, Wally. In most ways, he made an enviable life partner by anybody's standards. Tall and straight, funny and brilliant, high earning and faithful, Wally tried to turn himself inside out so that his sexual advances would consistently ring Robyn's chimes. Instead, after sufficient couples work with me to determine that the marriage was not viable for Robyn, the couple sustained a friendly divorce. At this writing, each is in a second marriage to chime-ringing partners who are fully competent adults. Robyn and Wally do not regret the divorce. Both are glad to have combined solid life partners with pure delight.

As long as the model of human partnership was basically survival, communication skills and passion were secondary in importance in the marital hierarchy. Consistency, responsibility, tenaciousness, and mutual support of all family members were primary. In *Fiddler on the Roof,* Tevya, the milkman, after 25 years of marriage, asks his wife if she loves him, only to find her surprised and puzzled by the question. She finally gives him a list of all the tasks she has done (washing his clothes, darning his socks, bearing his children) and says incredulously, "If that's not love, what is?" She thus expresses how alien the other, more emotional concept of marriage is to her.

Today's model is much more complex. Because the goal is one of mutual affection, mutual gratification, and the continuing *choice* of staying together, marriage now requires a set of skills different from and more complex than those needed in the survival marriage. It becomes necessary that the inevitable abrasions and conflicts caused when two individuals bump up against one another be resolved adequately so that the couple can continue to be drawn voluntarily to one another. Therefore, basic skills in human communications, human sexuality, and interpersonal problem solving become essential to the welfare of the relationship. They become a kind of toolbox for marital longevity.

These skills are usually learned informally from one's elders—many of whom, however, had entered marriage under the old contract or some variant thereof. When a child is born into a family, the early learnings in human communications give the child a basic set of interactional tools, which the child automatically carries into subsequent human interchanges. If the family was violent, or silent, or sneaky, or boisterous, or crude, it is only later in life that the child realizes that his family acted as a kind of universe for him and that the way they handled human intimacy was problematic. By then, in adult years, the child will in some way or another have perpetuated the mistakes. It is then necessary to unlearn automatic styles of relating to others and learn new and more successful techniques.

Driven by the pain of lost relationships, abuse, anger, divorce, and addictions, an individual often sets out to learn better relationship skills. Sometimes, there is nowhere in the educational system to turn for guidance. Our school systems offer no courses on human problem solving. Insurance companies will not support classes in emotional learning unless the learner carries the stigma of mental wellness. Popular books teach cognitive principles, but do not give the personal guidance and follow-through necessary for the kind of change based on human experience and on human understanding. Books alone are simply insufficient.

Couples group psychotherapy provides both cognitive and experiential learning for couples. This multilevel learning enables men and women to resolve interpersonal conflicts and to keep the vibrancy in their relationship, hopefully with the result that the partners will continue to choose one another. The group narrows the gaping chasm that exists for many couples between their romanticized, Madison Avenue expectations for a perfect marriage and a perfect spouse and their limited ability to achieve the wonderful marriage for which they long.

I long dreamed of creating a clinical community for couples—a place where people could learn basic human interactive skills in order to grow together for a lifetime of loving. The earlier the education is, the better; it is best done before joining together legally. Ideally, a partner could ask not only whether a mate is sexually safe for partnering, but also whether a potential partner has graduated from the institute of human interaction and is emotionally ready to be a partner. Despite efforts to engage couples in a preventative and educational model, the vast majority of couples still wait until one or both partners are disillusioned about the marriage and in some degree of human pain before seeking relief for their suffering. When they then come for help, much of the treatment process is one of reeducation, within a group setting. In recent decades, change on the horizon suggests that couples may try to prevent trouble before it happens. What a good idea!

THE PURPOSE OF THIS BOOK

This book teaches how to conduct group psychotherapy for couples. It teaches the reader how to conceptualize couples group psychotherapy, how to conduct the meetings, and how to incorporate this form of treatment into clinical practice. In so doing, it teaches how to create a clinical model to foster and treat lifelong marital satisfaction—not perfection, mind you, but satisfaction. That is worth a lot.

This book presents a specific model—couples group psychotherapy—that I have worked with over the course of the last quarter of a century. This model integrates theory and research from individual development, family systems theory, and group psychotherapy and invites practicing clinicians to use this integration in their clinical work. Couples group psychotherapy is an efficient clinical model that treats a number of couples simultaneously with as much power as individual couples work. The structure minimizes time needed for travel because it creates a memorable clinical experience for members to draw on between group meetings.

In order to convey the power of the clinical interventions, I have handled the brief case examples with the voice of a storyteller. Couples tell us their stories as part of their treatment and part of our job is to transform their lives and their stories. Finally, I have provided a way for clinicians to evaluate the success of their treatment and have reviewed our evidenced-based practice on this model.

The model presented here necessitates prior knowledge and training in two separate but related clinical modalities: group psychotherapy in general and psychotherapy with couples and families. It is essential that at least one—and preferably both—of the group leaders conceptualize client change via the psychotherapy process in contextual terms. Human change occurs within an interpersonal context and can therefore happen most efficiently when the psychotherapy process is conducted in a vibrant and interpersonal arena. This arena can be marital or family therapy, group therapy, or—in the case of couples group psychotherapy—couples and group psychotherapy simultaneously. What is central, in my opinion, is the assumption that it takes people to make people sick and people to make people well, as Harry Stack Sullivan knew so well.

This model is a synthesis of two approaches, which are brought together under the umbrella of general systems theory. Although some of the conceptual origins come from the worlds of biology (von Bertalanffy, 1968) and social psychology (Lewin, 1951), their application in mental health services comes from two usually separate but not incompatible sectors: family therapy and group psychotherapy. I hope that this book is a contribution to bringing these two worlds closer together.

I am also pleased to note that since the publication of the first edition of this book, several writers have contributed to the literature on the practice of couples group psychotherapy from a variety of theoretical perspectives. Feld has written cogently on the principles of initiating a couples group (1998), as well as on couples group psychotherapy from an object relations point of view (1997). Donovan (1995) has presented a psychodynamic approach to couples group work (for a concise history of couples group psychotherapy, see Sells, Giordano, & King, 2002). Couples group psychotherapy even meets the Internet age in Sanders's (1996) computer-mediated couples group.

During clinical training in Europe and in the United States, I did my best to avoid the "seat-of-the-pants eclecticism" that I had been warned against by many of my mentors. I believed in the wisdom of combining family therapy and group psychotherapy because they are conceptually compatible. A group sometimes operates like a family and a family has the properties of a group. Both are greater than the sum of their parts and the subsystems of each can be fully understood only through a knowledge of the working of the whole (Spitz, 1979).

The model has been developed in an outpatient setting, where it has been practiced since 1987. It is adaptable to varying populations and settings. It is cost effective, as is group psychotherapy for individuals who are not treated as part of a couple. It is time efficient because considerable changes in the lives of a couple and their children are possible within fewer than 60 clinical hours. The power of the model rests on the combined skill of the leaders in family and in group psychotherapy. Of course, all skill rests on a solid working knowledge of individual clinical treatment because couples and groups comprise individuals. The purpose of the book is to infuse the reader with skills in systems therapy with couples, families, and groups.

This is a book for clinicians, as well as for clinicians in training, who are interested in becoming more skilled in working systemically with couples in a group format. It covers basic concepts in couples therapy and in group therapy only insofar as these concepts are germane to the treatment model presented in these pages. Thus, the book begins at the convergence of thought between these clinical worlds.

OVERVIEW OF THE BOOK

As presented here, couples group psychotherapy creates a model of treatment in which, typically, four couples participate in a group that begins and terminates as a whole. The treatment contract runs for 11 months, with one 6-hour session monthly and adjunctive individual couples or group therapy. Strategies to set up these procedures and their rationales are presented in the appropriate chapters.

The book begins with the principles and concepts by which the model is implemented. Section I describes how to structure a couples group. Chapter 1 discusses how to prepare potential couples for a group experience. Research on the value of good preparation for group psychotherapy is discussed as well as clinical techniques needed to assess when to refer couples, how to answer questions and assist with resistance, and how to negotiate time and money issues. These explanations provide the clinician with the practical tools needed to form a group.

The first chapter also introduces the procedures used to assess strengths and weaknesses in a couple's relationship. These assessment procedures form the basis for goal setting for the couples at the beginning of the group and are used later in the clinical year to assess a couple's progress. They also lend themselves to ongoing clinical research if the therapists so choose. An example of such outcome research using the assessment tools described is presented in the section on evidence-based practice.

Chapter 2 outlines the integration of couples group therapy into an overall treatment package for the individual, family, or couple who first requests treatment. Once a decision has been made to have the couple participate in a couples group, the questions of how to maximize the therapeutic impact and how to integrate the group experience with adjunctive therapy outside the group must be addressed.

Chapter 3 discusses the policies that form the foundation of the structure of the couples groups in my practice. These policies, developed over a 5-year period, are presented together with their origins in group psychotherapy theory and research.

Section II presents concepts necessary for the treatment of couples in a group. Chapter 4 starts with concepts from the fields of marital and family therapy that form the foundation of my work with the couples. Chapter 5 discusses principles in building a cohesive working group because they are adapted to a couples group model.

Chapter 6 follows the evolution of the group over time as it moves from a group with no common past history to an independently functioning group in the adult stage of group development. Chapter 7 introduces the structured interventions. Because these are not "prepackaged" but rather meant to be decided on in response to the group's mood and content, the chapter suggests methods by which meaningful learning experiences can be decided in a short time.

Part 3 outlines the theoretical underpinnings of the practical suggestions made in prior chapters. Chapter 8 presents the cognitive map of the couples group psychotherapist, who decides how and when to intervene clinically at a given moment in time. In addition to the factors of group development and structure previously presented, it shows how the therapist can target interventions at any one of four levels (individual, dyad, subgroup, and group as a whole) at any point in time. Deciding when to intervene at which level determines the power of the group for the leaders and members.

Chapter 9 discusses the procedures necessary to maintain a fluid ongoing group from a structural standpoint. Handling of absences and lateness, fee collection, and physical structure of the group form the framework for ongoing clinical work. Recognizing and dealing effectively with emergencies also ensures that the structure of the group makes possible ongoing work for the members.

In keeping with my long-standing and ongoing enthusiasm for the wisdom of evidence-based practice, Chapter 10 presents an outcome study designed to assess changes in a group over a multiyear time period and to obtain the group participants' views of their experience during that time. Did they change in the ways in which they had hoped to change? What about this clinical experience was memorable for them? Assessments and goals discussed in Chapter 1 form the anchoring points for this study.

I had fun in the last 6 months writing Chapter 11. Assessing recent advances that have proven invaluable for my couples, I allowed myself license to guess at a number of key future directions. A look at the neurobiology of coupling led rather naturally to a consideration of nonverbal couples work and sensory awareness. Two educational imperatives include the world of behavioral finance and positive psychology. Theoretical contributions that proved invaluable include those from relational psychoanalysis and cognitive behavioral psychology.

The appendices give the reader handy tools to use the model clinically in his or her own location. Appendix A has forms that I use in my groups, including group goals and policies. Appendix B gives examples of the structured exercises used in the groups. Appendix C briefly considers how I educate my couples about effective communication. This appendix

Figure 0.2 Judith Coché, PhD, holds the first edition of *Couples Group Psychotherapy*. (Photo by Jonathan Wilson, courtesy of Dr. Judith Coché.)

considers the teaching of four basic coupling skills that are needed for all couples. These include skills in "the intimacy loop" and "the business of coupling." Appendix D provides a brief overview of the couples included in this edition.

The earlier edition of *Couples Group Psychotherapy* (Figure 0.2) was published in 1990 by Brunner Mazel. That edition also had a companion training video of real couples being themselves. This video, *Techniques in Couples Group Psychotherapy*, as well as our four workbook series for coupled and coupling adults, can be purchased through the Coché Center (www.theCochecenter.com) at Suite 410, Academy House, 1420 Locust Street, Philadelphia, PA 19102 (tel. 215.735.1908). The DVD is inexpensive and great fun to watch. Recent groups have enabled us to tape over 80 hours of live interaction. Some parts of the transcripts have been integrated into the book sections that provide the conceptual framework for the techniques taught. The case examples are from the lives of real people. Names and identifying information have been altered within the dynamics of the interpersonal world of each couple. The goal was for each couple to recognize itself, but for no reader to know the identities of the couples.

From the many couples engaged in couples group psychotherapy, I chose to illustrate this edition from the lives of the five couples who were in the couples group between 2006 and 2008. They agreed to be called Antonia and Patrick, Holly and Trevor, Robyn and Spencer, Diane and Dwight, and Margaret and Michael. They spanned ages from mid-30s through early 60s and had been married between 6 months and 23 years at time of treatment. Between them, they cared for seven children and were heading toward a first grandchild. They were in first marriages and marriages after widowhood and divorce. One formed a successful stepfamily. They overcame job loss, miscarriage, infertility, long-distance marriage, sexual incompatibility, eczema, erectile dysfunction, and lesser evils. On behalf of my readers, please know that your all-too-human foibles have provided the substance for your growth and the reader's learning.

In sum, the parts of the book combine to form a model for clinical practice that I hope will add a new and valuable dimension to the effective treatment of couples and the progeny that depend on their mental health.

Section I

Structuring Couples Group Psychotherapy

A couple is the most powerful unit on the planet.

—Judith Coché, PhD

1

Preparing Couples for Couples Group Psychotherapy

I'll do anything to buy 2 weeks of not fighting.

—A man deciding to be in a couples group

INTRODUCTION

It is wise to prepare prospective members for a group psychotherapy experience (Mayerson, 1984; Meadow, 1988; Ogrodniczuk, Joyce, & Piper, 2005; Richman, 1979). The consensus of these articles is that group members who have been adequately prepared for their therapy experience show more desirable group behaviors in the early stages of the group and get on with the therapeutic task much sooner than unprepared members. Moreover, prepared groups become cohesive sooner and have fewer absences and dropouts (Garrison, 1978; Piper, Debbane, Garant, & Bienvenu, 1979; Roback & Smith, 1987). Indeed, the American Group Psychotherapy Association (AGPA) includes group member preparation under its "Practice Guidelines for Group Psychotherapy." Its Web site suggests that benefits of membership preparation include meaningful participation, and treatment compliance.

Other advantages of preparation described in the literature will be pointed out later in this chapter. For now, suffice it to say that solid and well thought-out preparation of the new member couple contributes greatly to the success of the complete group experience. Erich Coché used to remind me that "it is quite similar to preparation for a sailing regatta. Inadequate preparation of the boat and getting off to a poor start frequently doom the hapless sailor to a much poorer showing than would have occurred otherwise." He should have known. He began as a hapless sailor.

Preparing couples for group psychotherapy is complex. First is the problem of selection for the group, including creating a mix of couples who are likely to work well together. Then comes the preparation itself, including telling the new couple about the group and its likely effectiveness. Often there is resistance to group psychotherapy and this resistance needs to be handled tactfully and effectively. This phase also includes the introduction to the group policies (see Chapter 3).

Another part of this preparation is what has been called "role induction" (Garrison, 1978; Mayerson, 1984), meaning that the prospective group member is given a reasonably clear idea as to what is expected from a "good group member." In other words, the person is induced into the role of a cooperative, working group participant before the first group session.

The final focus of group therapy preparation is the assessment of the problem on which the couple needs to work (Figure 1.1). This assessment process involves an initial consultation around strengths and weaknesses in the relationship, and it is followed by more formal assessment (see Chapter 10) in keeping with current ethical and practice standards. Group therapy preparation in recent years also requires that each couple be exposed to learning four coupling skills (see Appendix C). These skills include a feelings primer, active listening, interpersonal problem-solving, and the art of negotiation. Further, each couple is exposed to recent research results from the world of couples expertise, including material on the neurobiology of marriage, emotional abuse, and conflict resolution. A mutual agreement on the goals that the couple wants to reach is a vital beginning for later group processes and effective therapy work. Although proper group preparation requires considerable thought and planning, the resulting payoff is worth the investment (for a review, see Walitzer, Derman, & Connors, 1999).

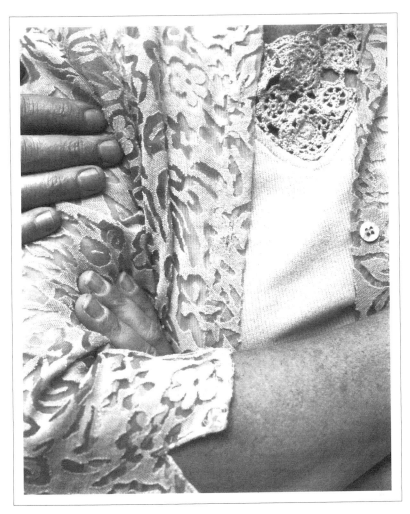

Figure 1.1 *The New York Times Sunday Magazine* captured pillow talk between Antonia and Patrick in its August 12, 2007, issue. (Photograph by Nicholas Nixon. Copyright 2007. With permission.)

INVITING COUPLES TO JOIN A GROUP

Before preparing the couples for their group experience, the leaders have to determine which couples they want to invite into the group. A number of factors are worthy of consideration in putting together a new couples group. Among these are *motivation, homogeneity/heterogeneity,* and *match.*

Motivation

The couples entering a group may or may not be married and have varied motivations. For example, one couple joined the group because they wanted to marry but realized that their ability to use basic communication skills around key issues was so limited that marriage was unwise. They used the group for 2 years to build a foundation of basic skills in communicating anger and in working with competitive struggles between them.

All prospective group members share high commitment to optimizing their relationship and to working out key concerns. There has to be an evident desire on the part of both partners to stay together and work things out when they hit a rough spot. Even though the couple may be in very serious trouble, neither partner has "one foot out the door." Each is not usually threatening the other with divorce or pushing the relationship to the brink of a breakup. In a few cases in which the couple may have been considering divorce, they must agree to work within the marriage contract and not to consider divorce for the duration of the group year. Occasionally, the dynamics of a marriage are such that threats of divorce arise during the course of the group year. The protective blame syndrome and veiled threats are then dealt with therapeutically.

Because of basic marital unhappiness, combined with a religious value system that removed divorce as an option, Antonia found herself choreographing a way to become distant from Patrick while remaining legally married to him. She accomplished this delicate dance through hours spent on career pursuits, statements of Patrick's inadequacy, and general disinterest in making time to be close to him. As long as Patrick remained passive, this pattern of pseudointimacy continued without change. As Patrick became increasingly assertive, a goal set for him by Antonia, he began to ask for more from the marriage. Previously feeble attempts to get Antonia's attention ("It would be so nice if I could take a walk.") changed into clear and declarative statements of marital need ("It is not right that I haven't had sex in 3 months. I deserve a better marriage."). At this point, a period of time ensued in which Antonia refused to consider divorce and Patrick pushed for it. At one point, Patrick said, "If this isn't better in 1 year, I will divorce you." Antonia retorted, "I don't want you to do that." Briefly reverting to the earlier comfort of passivity, Patrick said, "Oh ... okay." However, it was clear that the balance of power had shifted and that Patrick was not about to go back to his old passivity. Either divorce or marital resolution needed to happen. The leader reminded Patrick of his commitment to work within the group toward a better marriage, which firmed up his earlier motivation to keep plugging in the face of difficult marital circumstances. Further therapeutic work considered the difficulty of living in a marriage with a constant divorce threat in the background and the pain of working to improve intimacy when a threat of divorce is present. Other group members offered examples of divorce considerations in their own marriages and encouraged Patrick and Antonia to look more deeply into their selves to resolve the pseudointimacy. With time in the group, Patrick was able to learn to assert himself and his marital rights without the threat of divorce, thereby conveying both strength and commitment to Antonia. Patrick's shift pushed Antonia to balance her own interests and her desire to become more comfortable with sexuality and intimacy in her marriage. Patrick did not allow Antonia to remain disinterested in him, but stated clearly that he did not want to divorce her. He wanted the marriage to work. At the writing of this book, Antonia now asks for sex more frequently than Patrick does, and the couple has approached the seemingly unapproachable goal of marital happiness.

Heterogeneity/Homogeneity of Members in a Group

The couples groups are heterogeneous in relation to the members' ages, diagnoses, and severity of marital problems. Although more homogeneous groups may become cohesive sooner, I have found that, over the life of the group, opportunities for independent growth are richer when the groups are heterogeneous (see Unger, 1989). I have formed groups that included people as old as 75 and as young as 25. I have found that over the life of the group, opportunites for independent growth are richer when the groups are heterogeneous in relation to age, race, cultural background, and economic status. When there is a large age spread, some remarkable, therapeutically useful transference phenomena occur in which the older people relate to the other couples as they might relate to their adult children, while the younger couples get into various aging-parents issues with the older members.

I also prefer groups with variations in the severity of marital problem and/or individual diagnosis. Some couples believe that their marriage is fundamentally solid but that the "spark" has gone out of the relationship; they choose to participate in the group in order to enhance and revitalize the marital foundation. Other members are going through a very serious crisis and actually look at the group as their "last hope." Many have been in marriage therapy before but were unsuccessful. Having both types of couples in the group is encouraging for both: Those with the serious problem find much to learn from the others, and the latter are relieved to learn that they are "not as bad off" as their peers in the group or as they had thought.

In addition to doing the initial consultation, which explores the strengths and weaknesses in the relationship, members of the group are also given individual assessment tools and are assigned a *Diagnostic and Statistical Manual of Mental Disorders (DSM)-IV-TR* diagnosis. Giving a diagnosis is necessary for insurance purposes, but also aids the therapist in determining intervention strategies; it can be done without losing sight of the systems aspects of the work at hand.

Frequent diagnoses are personality disorders, neuroses, learning disabilities in adults, and adjustment disorders. Many clients enter a group with a mild to moderate form of depression, quite a few suffer from serious depression, and many have addictive disorders. I do not invite anyone with an overt psychotic disorder, but I have on a few occasions had one or two persons with a borderline personality disorder diagnosis. I find that these clients require more alertness on the part of the therapists, but they can do well overall in the group if the leadership is skillful.

In direct contrast to Antonia and Patrick, who came in under a thundercloud of potential divorce, Robyn and Spencer started the group in the blissful aftermath of a sudden wedding. Because each had been through a divorce previously, their motivation to join the couples group was mainly to avoid the pitfalls of their prior failed marriages. As each said, "I want this to be my last marriage." Both earlier marriages had been plagued with miscarriages and the emotional carnage that occurs when couples cannot communicate intimately about the loss of an unborn child. The last thing Robyn and Spencer wanted was marital hardship. Spencer had lurking concerns about his own homosexuality, although he wanted a life filled with heterosexual marriage and family. He felt certain that he was "damaged goods" in relation to a wife and was shocked to find that a stately, lively, European woman had fallen head over heels in love with him. Robyn, despite her effervescent personality and huge smile, suffered from moderate depression at least 6 months of every year. Lonely in a first marriage to a British businessman who was "all work and no play," Robyn mustered great courage in initiating the divorce that freed her to fall in love with Spencer. With deep fissures in her self-confidence, Robyn constantly doubted that she could be lovable enough for her new husband. For this reason, Robyn and Spencer, forming a seemingly trouble-free early marriage, were wise to prevent trouble before it started by working with issues at a level deeper than they were able to do on their own.

The heterogeneity of levels of marital dissatisfaction and crisis in the group allows the members to examine their marriages more thoroughly in a new light. Just as Patrick and Antonia could get inspiration from the hopefulness of the young marriage, Robyn and Spencer were forced to deepen their level of work as they helped with Patrick and Antonia's painful work in a seemingly chronic state of marital crisis and unhappiness.

Members joining a group will have different levels of prior experience in a group. Some of the couples are likely to be "returners" who had participated in a couples group previously and are signing on for a second or, occasionally, a third 11-month contract. In other couples, one partner may have been in a prior group experience of a different kind. Finally, some members are likely to be completely new to group psychotherapy. Particularly with these latter clients, pregroup preparation is of paramount importance because pregroup anxiety is likely to be highest in inexperienced group participants.

Diane and Dwight say they may not have been able to remain married without the couple's work that allowed them to enjoy life together. Because this was a second marriage for both partners, each brought old expectations and habits into the marriage with them. They signed on for X contract periods of couples group therapy to build the marriage each wanted. Now, X "rounds" later, they experience greatly diminished anxiety, heightened appreciation of one another, and better sex than either thought the marriage could provide. Although it is very unusual for a couple to remain in a group this long, Dwight and Diane live to benefit from time invested wisely in one another. They both report that the work was worth all the effort. Their happily married children and increasing numbers of grandchildren heartily agree.

The one area in which I plan homogeneity is what is sometimes called "cognitive homogeneity." I screen for couples who are somewhat similar in intellectual and cognitive functioning so that the group can function on a deep level of emotional focus and cognitive skill. The capacity for depth work is needed for permanent internal changes in bonded interpersonal interaction.

Cognitively, members are average or above average in intellectual functioning and have a variety of cognitive styles. They vary in the ways in which they organize their experiences in order to form their own definition of interpersonal reality. Some members are gifted in warm, nurturing ways of thinking about others; others may be cool and distant, yet insightful and incisive. Some members are very concrete and matter of fact, and others are facile in thinking psychodynamically, systemically, or metaphorically. Some are remarkably articulate, but others have great difficulty in knowing and/or expressing how they feel. Most members appreciate humor and enjoy the laughter that is central to the fluidity of group functioning.

In my groups all members are expected to meet certain membership criteria. These are clearly listed on a group description handout and given to prospective members and referring therapists:

- an intimate relationship that is monogamous and plans to be of long duration, with or without marriage;
- marital or couples problems for which solutions have been attempted with insufficiently satisfying results;
- ongoing or previous individual, couples, or family psychotherapy with one of the group leaders or elsewhere;
- an interest in learning from and participating with other adults;
- an intense desire to improve the intimacy and mutual satisfaction in the relationship; and
- previous skill building in two sets of couples skills that are necessary for successful ongoing coupling: the intimacy loop (the feelings primer and active listening) and the business of coupling (interpersonal problem-solving and negotiation skills).

The Matching Process in Group Formation

I have found that four couples is the ideal size for the group. I have run groups with five couples and with three couples and these can work well at times. However, with five couples, some people have complained about insufficient time spent on their issues; with three couples, there may not be enough people to have an active give-and-take and lively exchange of ideas.

Screening couples to join a group is crucial to the treatment success of all the individuals involved. Members will need respect and compassion for the strengths and weaknesses of the couples who are part of their group. Customarily, intelligence, motivation, personality, and humor are considered in forming couples for a group. Placing couples together can also be done on the basis of intergenerational issues: A couple who have lost a child may work well with a couple who have no family of origin nearby. Often, quieter couples are mixed with livelier couples, dual-career couples with those in more traditional roles, urbanites with suburban couples. This kind of variety adds tension and drama as couples learn to be close to people they used to think of as very different in terms of lifestyle, socioeconomic status, or ethnic heritage. Later on, as cohesiveness develops, one hears comments such as, "When I first met you I thought I could never feel close to you; now I feel more at home with you than I do with my own family." The universality of being coupled and of being a person forms the glue in the diversity of selection.

Inclusion can also be on the basis of wanting to avoid the "solo outsider." The concept of the solo outsider states that it is very strenuous for a group to contain a member with a trait that is quite extreme and sets him or her apart from the rest of the group. For example, if the group contains only one person with an addiction, one might find that the rest of the group does not show as much understanding for this person's plight as one would wish. It is better for the group to have at least one other person with a similar problem. The same goes for significant differences in age or severity of diagnosis (e.g., depression).

At times, it is unavoidable to have a solo outsider in the group. Patrick was the only learning disabled adult in one of the groups. With some sensitivity and guidance from the therapist, the group can be helped to deal with such differences constructively. However, if such situations are not handled well, the "outsider" is in some danger of becoming the group's scapegoat.

Homosexual and Heterosexual Couples

I have trained both homosexual and heterosexual couples in psychoeducational couples' skills and have worked clinically with gay and lesbian couples for many years. However, I am only now addressing the need to develop groups for gay and lesbian couples. There is quite a controversy about the wisdom of mixing homosexual and heterosexual couples in the same group. Because sociological and cultural challenges differ enough for the two sets of couples, my own preference to date is to have separate groups for the two lifestyles. I may be incorrect in my assumption, but I am erring on the side of clinical caution in order to minimize risk of mediocre therapy for clients.

Because I have not had a sufficient number of gay and lesbian couples at one time in order to form a group, it has not been possible to start a group with this population. Further, it feels clinically wise to work with a gay or lesbian co-therapist in developing expertise in leading a group of same-gendered couples. I continue to seek the opportunity to team to develop a model for couples group psychotherapy within the gay and lesbian communities. At time of printing, an option is beginning to become available, but for obvious reasons, the following information is primarily applicable to heterosexual couples.

GROUP SCREENING PRINCIPLES

After my 20 years of screening couples for couples groups, the following five guidelines summarize my thinking:

- Couples of average or above intelligence are needed to grasp concepts and apply them to their lives.
- College or the equivalent is typically the educational minimum for couples who choose this experience; however, I have worked with members from hands-on trades with great success.
- A sense of humor really helps to integrate the irony of some facets of committed coupling in a way that allows the commitment to strengthen.
- The vision that marriage can be a lifelong and vibrant enterprise creates goals that later can be reached.
- A willingness to challenge assumptions about what it means to love a partner enables transformational change.

The Screening Interview: Mutual Decision Making

Preparing a couple for group psychotherapy is accomplished in a variety of ways (Garrison, 1978; Mayerson, 1984; Nichols, 1976; Ogrodniczuk et al., 2005). Sometimes, couples come together for skill building and learn to know one another in this psychoeducational arena before working together with couples in a group. This helps them become accustomed to work with another couple and the situation seems less new and foreign. Handouts on group policies and how to be a good group member are sent ahead to elicit questions and concerns before the group begins. Some therapists prefer to do their group psychotherapy preparation in small groups and others in special meetings with the prospective individual or couple. I generally use the latter approach.

Couples Group Preparation

Our preparatory meetings have a number of goals, including changing the "frame" or the way a couple thinks of changing, sparking enthusiasm, explaining boundaries, and inducing effective group behaviors.

Changing the Frame for Change

This seemingly confusing phrase is a concept that is most often found in the literature on strategic family therapy (Keeney & Ross, 1985). Many of the changes that people are able to make in psychotherapy are a product of seeing the world a bit differently than before they entered therapy. The field of cognitive behavior therapy (Beck, 1979) uses this way of understanding change and discusses the power of one's worldview in influencing the way one behaves toward, thinks about, and feels about oneself and someone else. Since the inception of this model in 1987, cognitive therapy has become the world leader in teaching clients how to think. Long a friend of cognitive interventions, the couples group integrates cognitive with existential frames for change. (The positive existentialism described in the earlier edition of this book is now customarily referred to as *positive psychology*.) Both cognitive therapy and positive psychology are concepts useful in the theoretical foundations underlying couples group therapy.

Most couples are embarrassed to speak of their problems in front of anyone else, including a professional psychotherapist. The problems of the marriage or of the individuals in the marriage are a source of shame, and the idea of sharing them with a group of strangers sounds anything but therapeutic. Until couples come to understand that they stand to gain both an emotionally gratifying experience and effective treatment at a modest price from their participation in a group, they are unlikely to be willing even to consider the option. Therefore, the first way in which a couple must be prepared for a group is to accept the value of a group. Often one or both members of a couple need to gain acceptance of the value of psychotherapy and give themselves permission to engage in it.

When Spencer entered psychotherapy with his first wife a number of years before he married Robyn, his attitude toward psychotherapy was largely uninformed and skeptical. Through the assistance he received during the divorce with his first wife and through his individual group work later, Spencer came to see psychotherapy as an important life tool. When he and Robyn decided to marry, each was so determined never to divorce again that they felt both pleased and proud to be invited to join an advanced couples group that was forming. They shared a constructive framework within which to view the psychotherapeutic process. It was only because they were not skeptical, fearful, or defensive that it was valuable to invite them to join the group at the time of their honeymoon. This open attitude enabled them to prevent dragging problems from earlier marriages into this current marriage as well as to work through life issues of great challenge, including anxiety and depression.

Sparking Enthusiasm

This aspect of group psychotherapy preparation may be of concern if it seems to be "selling the group" to the new couple. However, therapist conviction about the wisdom of the approach is valuable. Many couples have to overcome tremendous hesitation and fear before they even come for interpersonal therapy. The idea of a group is even more frightening to them and can approach a level of terror for one of the partners. Frequently, the couple needs to understand how a group can be more effective than marital therapy sessions in which the therapist's full attention is devoted to one couple alone.

Once this point is understood through reading and clarification, however, the potential member can become quite enthusiastic about the invitation to be in a group with other couples. After enthusiasm for the process begins, I inform the couple about the practicalities of group therapy, discuss the advantages within the specifics of the couple's treatment situation, and communicate my genuine belief in and enthusiasm for the group. The therapist's belief in the value of the model becomes apparent to the new couple and can spark the enthusiasm that overcomes their hesitation.

One way to build enthusiasm and overcome hesitations is to elicit the fantasies of the future group member about what goes on in a psychotherapy group. Most people have some preconceived notions about group psychotherapy, frequently derived from the mass media. These notions may have given rise to fears and hesitations. Some people imagine that the group is one continuous ordeal of hard, insistent confrontation (as shown in some shows about drug treatment); others picture a collection of oddballs (as they may have seen in a situation comedy) among whom the couple would be the only sane people there. It is very important to have a sense of what the pertinent resistance fantasies are so that the therapist can deal with the fears and can correct the misconceptions as much as possible.

Michael was willing to join a group because his beloved Margaret had reported how wonderful her individual group at the Coché Center had been. Michael had many hesitations about confidentiality, about who would join a group like this, and about airing dirty laundry, but he managed to agree to sign on for one contract period. Yet Michael was busy and less than completely convinced of the wisdom of group therapy, so he said in advance of joining that he would only do the group for 11 months. I encouraged him to wait and see what was clinically indicated, but he was set. Or so he thought. As the time came to recontract for a second "round," Michael was the first to say that he was on board. He went on to say that his marriage had improved so much in the first year that he could not actually imagine what could happen in the second year, but he knew there was work to do on his anger. At the end of the second year, when Michael and Margaret were ready to "graduate," he stated clearly that the therapy work had so far exceeded his vision of how wonderful his marriage could be and that he would never forget the experience of the last 2 years and was very grateful. The last sentence was said with tears glimmering in his eyes.

Dealing With Resistance

The best way to deal with therapeutic resistance is to begin with the language of the therapist. Classic "resistance" makes therapists anxious unnecessarily. If resistance implies doing something counter to someone's judgment, hesitancy implies moving carefully and slowly. If "denial" implies overlooking something obvious, caution implies taking care of what exists. Thus, it becomes obvious that any couple would be hesitant about a commitment of 11 months that could harm as well as help their marriage. A couple experiencing active distress needs to remain cautious about further disturbing a rocky status quo. If the therapist puts himself or herself in the shoes of the client couple, it becomes much easier to identify with what that couple needs to deal with natural resistance to an unknown therapy experience. I find that couples need

- clarity about the expectations and procedures of the group;
- guidance in choosing to be a member without feeling railroaded; and
- reassurance that the group will act as a "safe harbor" for the couple's pain and as a catalyst for fruitful change.

When preparing a couple for a group, the therapist should avoid any surprises until the group takes over. Therefore, I suggest that questions be answered honestly and that caution and hesitancy be treated with respect. Guidance in how to benefit from the group is very valuable. Because couples have no idea about what they are about to experience, it is very useful for them to hear about who the other couples are, how old they are, which topics will be covered, and other basic information about the group.

Both members of a couple share resistance to the process of internal change. Psychological resistance is *always* mutual, although it may seem implanted in one partner or the other. Frequently, the male carries the resistance for the couple. As Dwight said, "I'm very tired of coming to couples therapy. I want this marriage to be good enough without having to come for help." Men's reluctance to enter therapy seems to derive from their being slower to recognize relationship troubles as well as from their aversion to entering therapy (Doss, Atkins, & Christensen, 2003). However, it is important to note that once they initiate couples treatment, men in heterosexual relationships seem to be as capable as their partners at recognizing and identifying problematic aspects of the relationship (Moynehan & Adams, 2007). My experience with men in couples groups is that they often become the drivers in the couple, urging their female partners to challenge their own assumptions. Once motivation for change begins, the men often become quietly achievement oriented in moving forward.

Respectful inquiry into the nature of the hesitancy, analysis of the function of the hesitancy for the couple, and patient guidance through strategically placed clinical interventions enable a couple to tip the balance of the stability and change scale toward the "change" vector.

Dwight came by resistance to therapy naturally. Growing up in a highly intellectualized, affluent, post-WWII Jewish family, Dwight had learned to move away from difficult emotions and to concentrate on the world of material wealth and intellectual pursuits. After divorcing a wife whom he disliked for many years, Dwight became a confirmed bachelor and was surprised to learn that he wanted to marry a second time. His second wife, Diane, had come from a tragic situation involving the early loss of a husband in a highly intimate, successful marriage with children. Diane was as emotionally hungry as Dwight was emotionally resistant. At times, this combination made it seem almost impossible for the marriage to continue, but the two partners loved one another and were committed to solid marriage and family values. Diane became the driver of the therapy, eventually joined by other group members who pushed Dwight beyond his comfort with intellect to the highly uncomfortable world of raw feelings. This combination of the odd power of the group and the need for a marital partner facilitated needed change.

Role Induction

Role induction is the process of informing prospective group members about the expected behaviors in group therapy. In signing up new members for a couples group, one may assume that they know very little about what kinds of interactions are considered desirable in a group (Nichols, 1976). Without this knowledge, people will guess. They may thus treat the group like a *kaffeeklatsch,* a board meeting, or a religious revival group, depending on which analogy they believe fits best. On the other hand, they may have read about group therapy in the media and try to behave according to what they read there. Even some people who have been in group psychotherapy before may not necessarily interact in a way that fits the couples group. For them, too, some role induction is a good idea.

Teaching Desirable Group Behaviors

Certain behaviors are likely to pay off handsomely for the group member and are therefore worth teaching. The two most important within-group behaviors are self-disclosure and interpersonal feedback. Group members will also benefit from learning how to set appropriate goals for what they wish to accomplish within a single session (Kivlighan, Jauquet, Hardie, Francis, & Hershberger, 1993).

Self-disclosure. Pregroup preparation can significantly increase members' ability and willingness to self-disclose (Palmer, Baker, & McGee, 1997). Research during the last two decades has shown that, for nonpsychotic group therapy clients, the positive therapeutic effect of their group experience depends in large part on their willingness to self-disclose (E. Coché & Dies, 1981). Some depressed couples may get some benefit from being helpful to others without a high degree of self-disclosing, but they are the exception. For most clients, the old rule stands: Your group therapy success depends on your degree of openness to the others in the group.

It is valuable to explain to the new group members that there are two kinds of self-disclosure in groups. One is telling the group about one's life situation, background, marriage, and so forth. The other is of the here-and-now kind—letting the group know how one feels at the moment. Someone who is feeling nervous about being there, angry, joyful, and so on should let the group know about it. This helps members get the idea that "here and now work" will form a valuable part of the group.

Interpersonal feedback. The new group participant is encouraged to give other group members feedback on their behaviors. Providing feedback to other group members demonstrates engagement with the group, which has been shown empirically to result in better group outcomes (Ogrodniczuk & Piper, 2003). It is worthwhile to explain to new members what is meant by giving other members feedback and how they might proceed. There is some debate as to when feedback instruction is best done: Some therapists prefer to have the group get underway and then give instructions for constructive feedback; others see it as an integral part of group member preparation. I do a bit of both, guided to some degree by the gestalt of the members of each group. In a fast moving group, learning about feedback feels safe and interesting. In a hesitant group, feedback instruction is better left until the group has matured to readiness to consider direct feedback.

Month after month, Antonia sat for 6 hours with a pillow on her lap. Often her hands rested on the pillow as she attempted to maintain self-composure in the face of internal unrest. When the unrest got too intense, her hands would fold tightly around her midriff, leaving the pillow perched on her knees. No group member had the courage to mention the pillow for fear of hurting her feelings or angering her. It felt untouchable for many months. As the group deepened, however, Antonia was among those to change most dramatically. She softened a bit, began to dress a bit differently, and began to feel more like a full group member. Only after she began to relax in the group could the group approach her about the role of the pillow on her lap during therapy. The group's giving her feedback about how good it felt to see her more relaxed allowed her to report that the pillow was her attempt to cover her body, not only with large clothing, but with a pillow on her lap.

In feedback instruction, the client is taught to report to others about his or her emotional reaction to their behaviors. What is central is the self-disclosure of a feeling that arose in response to something the other person did. An example would be a comment such as, "When you talk to your wife like that, I feel …"

It is especially important that the client understand that the feedback should be nonjudgmental even though it is laden with feeling. If words like "mean," "terrible," or "obnoxious" are used, the feedback giver is already judging. Such judgments are sure to produce defensiveness and undermine the value of the feedback. In contrast, feedback that is non-judgmental and oriented to feeling gives the recipient of the feedback the information needed to consider doing something about the behavior in question. The recipient may be motivated for change because of concern about the reaction he or she has caused in others, or the recipient may choose to keep the behavior and accept the reaction as the "price to pay" for it. The fact that one has choices in the responses to feedback makes it less threatening to the newcomer to group psychotherapy.

Goal setting. Goal setting has been part of individual and group therapy at the Coché Center since 1978. When I sought a simple way to lead individuals and couples toward measurable behavioral therapeutic goals, Tom Kirusek's scale was already in existence. It struck me as easily adaptable to various client populations and elegantly simple in its presentation. I adapted it when the Coché Center began and have used a variation of it since that time. Asking clients to work toward measurable goals focuses their thinking and enables them to measure their progress. A copy of my goal sheet (Kiresuk & Sherman, 1968) is included in Appendix A-i.

In addition to annual goal setting and periodic progress reports, each session begins with focusing on members' goals for the session. Because many members need help with goal setting, the group leaders facilitate individual goal setting by asking at the start of each session what group members would like to get out of the group meeting. I typically ask, "What do you want to take home with you today?" This procedure encourages members to reflect on their reasons for joining the group and brings their focus into the here and now; research has shown that it leads to greater in-session intimacy as well as better outcomes (Kivlighan et al., 1993).

In the following recent transcript, three couples respond to an invitation to state what their partners' goals are for this group. This exercise can be very useful in many ways. First, by outlining their goals, each couple becomes aware of the top issues for each partner. Second, discussing the partner's goal in the group ensures that each partner has correctly understood tough marital issues from the perspective of his or her partner. Finally, this exercise pulls couples together as they see similarities between themselves and other couples. Here is dialogue to illustrate these points:

Antonia: Patrick would like from this group for things to move forward. To move forward in my relationship this year and not just maintain where we're at to a workable level, but it has to move forward. And the areas that he would want, how he'll gauge if it's successful is the enjoyment; spending time between the two of us; sexual intimacy; seeing me more joyful about life; and ... is there anything I missed?

Patrick: No. That's good. Nothing's missing.

Antonia: I would like just to express myself so that he would fully understand who I am.

Patrick: When I listen, I feel helpless; I'm not making any progress. I get anxious, so I try to fix it. And that's what I've done for the 20 years I've known you.

Antonia: Which means, you don't really know me.

Patrick: Oh, I think I do (in a high, defensive voice).

Robyn: Spencer's afraid that he's going to lose his independence in this relationship, being that this is all very new, because he feels that he sacrificed a lot of what he wanted to do for the sake of his previous partner. So, the main goal for the year is to feel that he can be independent in a relationship and do the things that he wants to do. His goal is to be independent within this relationship.

Spencer: And also how to assert myself so that I don't fall into again … the same trap of just deferring to the other person what their wants are without stressing what I need.

JMC: What would you like to do instead?

Spencer: I would like to learn how to stand up for myself, get my way without being talked out of what I would initially have wanted.

JMC: And Spencer, what does Robyn want?

Spencer: Robyn is very uncertain right now; she's afraid to repeat the mistakes that were made in her last marriage, or with dealing with her parents. And she's also afraid of becoming like her parents. Is there anything I've missed?

Robyn: I've done a lot of work to overcome the parents stuff. I'm not so much concerned about that. I guess I'm concerned about doing the same thing I did in the last relationship.

Spencer: What specifically are you afraid of?

Robyn: Being lonely.

Spencer: Why were you lonely?

Robyn: Because he was there but not attainable.

Michael: Listening to Margaret, Margaret wants to continue on her path to wellness, to be a happier person. She thinks that the happiness will help the whole family be happier and she wants us to enjoy being together as a family. Did I miss anything?

Margaret: No. And Michael's goal is to use his communication skills to help my relationship to grow stronger and to help his relationship with the boys so we can be happy.

JMC: Any special skills, Michael, that seem more important than others?

Michael: Yes. I can get very defensive. I need to deal with confrontation. I need to work things out in such a way that I'm not throwing gas on the fire and be more responsible for my reactions.

This exercise proved to be invaluable as a starting point for the huge growth that followed in the lives of these couples.

Creating Expectations for Successful Membership

These explanations of self-disclosure and feedback take some of the mystique out of the group psychotherapy process, which then begins to seem to the client like something that can be mastered. The client begins to expect that he or she can be a successful group member and can be accepted by others in the group. Having generated this expectation of success, the therapist also communicates the expectation of a successful outcome. I often discuss with the couple which goals are reasonable and which are not, thus providing some guidance in setting expectations that are positive, optimistic, and reasonably attainable.

Preparing a Foundation for Later Group Cohesiveness

As is known from the research (France & Dugo, 1985; Mayerson, 1984; Roback & Smith, 1987), well-prepared groups have fewer member absences and fewer dropouts. By being more consistent in their attendance, members communicate to each other that the group is important to them and that they will go out of their way to attend. Thus, proper group preparation leads to a more cohesive group climate (Santarsiero, Baker, & McGee, 1995) and thereby permits the group to move into the working phase more swiftly and smoothly. Several research studies have shown that group cohesion is a significant predictor of outcome in group psychotherapy (Budman et al., 1989; Joyce, Piper, & Ogrodniczuk, 2007; Marziali, Munroe-Blum, & McCLeary, 1997).

Our couples try to attend all sessions. They travel far and want to be there. When business prevents attendance, it is customary for all to try to reschedule so that all members and leaders can be present. The experience simply feels so important that nobody wants to miss it.

ASSESSMENT: THE FOUNDATION
FOR TREATMENT PLANNING

Assessment of a couple's problem begins long before consideration of the benefits of group participation. It begins with the first phone call and continues through the couple's therapy sessions thereafter. The therapists begin by helping the couple assess the strengths and weaknesses in their relationship, which forms the foundation for setting goals in therapy. For example,

I form hypotheses about the way partners function with each other and with their families, how their balance of power works, and the methods they employ to embrace and to avoid intimacy. In the interviews with the couple, I also ask about techniques the partners have used to date to deal with their problems, either on their own or in therapy elsewhere, and then review results obtained with these strategies. Therapy and skill building begin. Then, when a group becomes open for new members, an evaluation is made whether it is appropriate for this couple to join the group.

Initial Couples Consultation

I begin by setting the stage, answering questions about practice methods, getting needed forms signed, and informing a couple about finances, appointment policies, and other contract issues. It is hard to ask a couple to commit to the process of change if they are confused about the structure of therapy. It feels frightening. I also share the assumptions that underlie the work that I do:

- I assume that a couple is composed of two individuals who choose to stay together over time.
- I assume that each member of the couple is an individual. I request that each person speak for the self, not the couple.
- I assume that partners will disagree, but ask that this be done respectfully.
- I assume blame to be a waste of time and ask that it be left at the door.
- I assume confidentiality of communications directed to me by one member of the couple with the other absent, but report that I may decide to tell the partner about the interchange when we are in session, if I get permission to break confidentiality first. In this way, I avoid collusion without sacrificing individual confidentiality.
- I assume that payment will be at point of service and let them know ways that this can happen.
- I request and therefore assume that each will be as honest as he or she is able to be at any point in time. Should this not be the case, I assume that the therapeutic process is likely to uncover this dynamic.

I want to know what works in this marriage and what needs changing. In a 90-minute consultation, I ask a couple to help me understand the strengths and weaknesses in the marriage as they see them. Typical questions are very simple. I ask each partner for three things that drew him or her to the partner: "What was there about your partner that you feel in love with? How has it stood the test of time?" Partners traditionally mention humor, intelligence, a great smile, great company, and good sex. Each person speaks for himself or herself and I write down what each says. I then summarize: "Here is what you saw in each other and here is how it withstood the test of time."

In the second half of this interview, I ask a different question. I ask each partner for three things in the marriage that really trouble each of them: "What feels like a weakness in your relationship and why is it painful?" Again, each person does his or her own thinking. Again, I take notes. Again, I summarize with a statement like, "It seems that there are some things in the relationship that are causing you great pain and that these are areas that need some work." This elusively simple framework for an unstructured interview has proven to be extremely valuable for couples. The reminiscing about good things allows them to remember why they coupled and provides a positive frame for future work. Individual recounting of the weaknesses frames work to be done in constructive terms.

By the end of this interview I have grasped a good bit about the dynamics in a relatively short time. In addition to recording the content of the interview, I also watch carefully for the dynamics. Are they happy or angry? Do they agree? Do they find it hard to discuss any strength? Do they get misty eyed as they think of what they love about one another? My goal is to get to the heart of the marriage as quickly and directly as possible without sending the couple home so upset that they are unable to function.

Assessment

In keeping with evidence-based practice, I recommend that group leaders use assessment procedures that are supported by empirical findings. Best-practice assessment will include measures of behaviors, cognitions, and affective experiences in the relationship context, as well as an examination of individual difficulties (Snyder, Heyman, & Haynes, 2005). This assessment should include communication behaviors that are known to be associated with marital satisfaction and durability. It is important to determine both the strengths and the areas of needed growth in the relationship. The therapist wishing to institute assessment as part of a group therapy program has a wide variety of instruments available. In selecting these and administering them to the clients, the therapist should follow a few procedural rules.

Keep It Simple

At an early phase, when the motivation to participate in a group is still somewhat shaky, it is not wise to push the clients to take a large test battery. This would in all likelihood increase resistance and turn people off when they most need encouragement. Naturally, by being brief in the test battery that is presented, one incurs some loss in the solidity of the data. An MMPI-2 is likely to produce more powerful results than an SCL-90-R, but it might also increase the resistance. I often offer standardized assessments at no charge at the beginning of a group in order to firm up diagnostic concerns and collect pregroup data. Couples are very appreciative of this opportunity to understand more about themselves and the patterns in their group, and I am appreciative of their willingness to provide us with pregroup data. Although the process is time intense, computerized analysis aids in keeping time investment at a minimum for the clinicians.

Keep in Mind the Value of Face Validity

For a new group member to be confronted by a test that makes no sense or seems to have no relation to the tasks at hand is a very discouraging and antagonizing experience. Seeing that the instrument given relates directly to couples issues and to one's personal unhappiness motivates the client to fill out the form and to bring it in and share the results with others.

Give Focused and Timely Feedback

Another strategy to enhance people's motivation is to give the testing feedback early on. The scoring should be done expeditiously and an oral report given to the couple as soon as possible. The feedback session can be used to bring the couple's goals for the treatment into sharper focus so as to reduce resistance and denial and to enhance the partners' optimism that their efforts toward reaching the goal are worthwhile and have a reasonable chance to be successful.

Judith's feedback to Trevor and Holly focused on perceived imbalance in Trevor's functioning. Holly and Trevor requested a psychological assessment for Trevor just before Holly accepted his marriage proposal. Although Trevor showed brilliance in his problem-solving ability and possessed a deep sense of wisdom and humor, Holly had noticed unevenness in his functioning. Trevor agreed that at times he was unable to think straight and would cave in from

25

anxiety. Neither understood this phenomenon and both were pleased when psychological assessment indicated no severe emotional disorder. Instead, Judith assured them that Trevor needed to become fluent in intimate conversation, with both himself and another person, in order to achieve higher levels of integration and balance in functioning day to day. Judith suggested cognitive psychotherapy and communication skills as a place to start gaining balance.

Choose Therapeutically Consistent Tools

Assessment is a device that yields more formal information than an unstructured clinical interview. It is useful where there are diagnostic concerns, as well as offers couples written feedback about their own dynamics and the dynamics between them. In deciding whether or not to do formal assessment, the clinician might ask two questions. The first question is "What am I testing for?" In other words, it is never legitimate to assess merely for the sake of assessment. Reports need to be geared toward addressing questions asked of the assessment process. The second question a clinician might ask is "Is this a good financial investment of time and energy in this couple's treatment?" The added value in the formal assessment process needs to offset great investments of professional time and funds.

In addition to the formal assessment, of course, the process of ongoing observation and assessment continues in parallel with the life of the group. Some of the most important information for understanding the dynamics of couples' relationships comes from direct observation of their behaviors in the group context (Heyman, 2001). Group members may fail to disclose certain aspects of their relationships on self-report measures or, just as often, may not even be aware of them. The therapists' conceptualization of each couple's dynamics continues to evolve with the addition of new observational data. The combination of more formal written measures and ongoing interpersonal observation provides a multilevel approach to the assessment of couples' dynamics.

Pre- and Postgroup Assessment Procedures

After the initial consult, I may do more formal assessment if I need more detailed diagnostic information. Another point at which more formal assessment is completed is at the point of joining a couples group. The assessment data provide a foundation for solid pregroup treatment planning based on empirically validated measures. Scoring is done by computer and hand and is processed into a brief verbal or written report by a psychologist trained in this work.

At the Coché Center, a number of assessment measures are used with regularity. The partners complete three measures designed to provide the therapists with additional diagnostic information: the Dyadic Adjustment Scale (DAS; Spanier, 1976), the Marital Satisfaction Inventory (Snyder, 1981), and the Symptom Checklist-90-Revised (SCL-90-R; Derogatis, 1994). The DAS may be purchased from Multi-Health Systems, Inc. (www.mhs.com), the Marital Satisfaction Inventory can be purchased from Western Psychological Services (www.wpspublish.com), and the SCL-90-R is available from Pearson Assessments (www.pearsonassessments.com). The remainder of this chapter will discuss the three measures that I use as well as provide a rationale for pregroup diagnostic assessment.

Dyadic Adjustment Scale

The DAS is very widely used in couples assessment and has impressive psychometric properties (Spanier & Thompson, 1982). It comprises four subscales: dyadic satisfaction, consensus, cohesion, and affectional expression. Scale items include ratings of agreement on important life areas (e.g., religious matters), extent of positive and negative interactions (e.g., "Do you confide in your mate?"; "How often do you and your partner quarrel?"), degree of relationship satisfaction, and degree of commitment to the relationship. It typically requires less than 10 minutes to complete and may be hand scored.

Scores on the DAS can provide an indication of the health of a couple's relationship; however, it is also useful for showing discrepancies between the partners' experiences of the relationship. For example, it can be very informative if one member reports high dyadic satisfaction and the other reports low satisfaction; this scenario would suggest that the status quo may be working for one member of the relationship. Alternatively, it might suggest a greater capacity for denial in the partner with the "rosier" report.

The Marital Satisfaction Inventory

The MSI (Snyder, 1981) is a 150-item self-report measure used widely to assess the nature and extent of conflict in a marriage or relationship. The

MSI addresses 11 dimensions of interactions in a couple, including "affective communication," "problem-solving communication," "disagreement about finances," and "sexual dissatisfaction." It also generates a measure of "global distress." Additional scales indicate the extent to which a respondent's answers are internally consistent and the degree to which he or she may have attempted to present himself or herself in an overly positive light. The MSI is scored separately for each partner, but scores are plotted on a single profile, allowing for direct assessment of each partner's primary concerns and any discrepancies in the way each member of the couple views the relationship.

The Symptom Checklist (SCL-90-R)
The SCL-90-R, which was developed by Leonard Derogatis (1994), is a list of 90 symptoms, ranging from headaches to crying spells. The client rates each symptom according to the degree to which it has been troublesome in the last 2 weeks. Each symptom is either absent (rated 0) or present to a severity ranging from 1 to 4. The test is then scored by computer and produces standard scores on nine clinical categories and three summation categories.

The SCL-90-R typically takes only about 12–15 minutes to complete. Participants have few quarrels with it. Because it asks for the presence of symptoms, it has face validity and clients are reassured to know that I want to know each individual's level of distress. This knowledge reduces the client's inevitable anxiety that he or she might get "lost" to the therapist in a sea of couples.

At some time before or after the second session, one of the therapists meets with each couple and gives the partners feedback on their SCL-90-R profile. Most couples appreciate the time and effort taken, even if the outcome presents either disturbing material or little that is new. If denial or a plea for help (which may appear as an exaggeration of the distress) is evident, these issues can be brought up in the feedback session and suggestions can be made for handling them therapeutically. Usually, couples are also interested in having this discussion of the assessment data continued in the group because they find that the experience focuses their attention on their work for the future.

Couples appreciate the formality and thoroughness of the assessment process. They especially appreciate that otherwise expensive testing is included in the initial package of the couples group at no extra charge. The reason the charge is removed is that, in order to function at top clinical capacity, I prefer to have empirically based assessments, although they may not be clinically necessary. For this reason, I provide the mechanism for thorough diagnosis and dynamic considerations by providing instruments, reports and feedback at no extra charge.

Why Do Assessments?

Assessment Provides Additional Diagnostic Input

Careful diagnosis before inviting a couple to join the group is important in preventing later calamities (Snyder et al., 2005; Spitz, 1979). A couple may present itself quite differently on paper than it did in the initial pregroup interview or even in its couples therapy sessions before the group. Having the assessment data is analogous to receiving an outside consultation from a trusted clinician. One may discover unforeseen trouble spots or hidden strengths. At the very least, one receives a confirmation of one's prior impressions and can share these impressions with the clients.

The Assessment Provides a View of the Defensive Structure

The assessment data, especially the SCL-90-R, can provide glimpses not only of the depth of despair but also of the degree of denial.

Holly wanted to marry Trevor, but was worried about a very rocky interpersonal history. Trevor had had one difficulty after another in relationships, and Holly wanted a lifelong marriage. Holly had spent time in group and individual psychotherapy during her college years, and she knew that she was in danger of caretaking of a husband less resourceful than she was. Prior to their engagement, Holly asked Trevor to work with me in an individual assessment to establish solid working parameters for his therapy. Additionally, the couple engaged in a couples assessment as part of their couples group work. These assessments elucidated dynamics and made treatment planning feasible. They provided me with information that Trevor was able to change once he was introduced to therapeutic intervention. Data indicated that Trevor had adopted a kind of a chameleon-like way of adapting to his environment. The unfortunate side effect of this coping mechanism was that he appeared disingenuous at times and engaged Holly's mistrust in his word. Assessment did not indicate a level of sociopathy for Trevor that prevented solid coupling. To the contrary, data indicated that Trevor would be relieved to give up coping mechanisms that had ruined earlier intimate options. In this way, the assessment allowed a marriage to occur that is successful at this writing.

Assessments Assist in Goal Setting

The Initial Group Goal Sheet (Appendix A-i) given out at the beginning of each group pushes the couple to think of the problem in very specific terms and in ways that conceptualize it as solvable and systemic. Members are encouraged to think about the reciprocity involved in those marital processes that cause them unhappiness rather than blaming each other. They often derive hope and encouragement from getting away from the blame pattern. Thus, early in the development of the group, the Initial Group Goal Sheet or Assessment Form enhances the motivation to stop denying and go to work on the issues.

Assessment Lays the Foundation for Treatment Evaluation

If at any point later on in the group the therapists or the clients want to know how far a couple has come, I can refer to the initial Assessment Form. I can then ask the couple how they see these issues now. This is done more or less routinely in the termination phase of the group when the couple has to decide whether or not to sign up for another group contract period. When appropriate, I can also give the partners another SCL-90-R to see how they are feeling at a later time. This provides data on how much the couple has progressed and how much more therapy is indicated. Here, too, surprises are possible and it may be advisable to have written input.

2

Structuring an Efficient Treatment Package

It's been a deepening experience to see each member emerge as an individual. It's like nothing that I've ever experienced before.

—A mental health professional in a group

COUPLES GROUP OVERVIEW

Once a couple is prepared to join a group—as well as to participate in individual, couples, or family therapy once every 3 weeks or more throughout the life of the group—the couple has agreed to a structure that will enable changes to happen within each member, between partners, and for the group as a whole. The agreement to become part of this group of couples is a bit like beginning regular, rhythmic, aerobic exercise as part of a weight-loss program. Although countless diets are on the market, nothing assures success more than a combined and regular approach to physical exercise as part of an approach to healthy living. Similarly, couples benefit from a carefully integrated package of therapeutic modalities.

I have developed a slow, steady approach to change that approaches the task from many levels and involves multiple therapy experiences (J. M. Coché & Satterfield, 1993). Each experience is designed to maximize the invitation to constructive change and to minimize travel time, inconvenience to the client, and cost. In this chapter, I present an overview of the steps in designing an efficient treatment package. In later chapters, I look at some of the ingredients in closer detail.

From talking with colleagues and from my knowledge of the literature, I came to the conclusion that the "usual" group meets weekly for 1½ hours and is "open ended"—meaning that new members enter the group as others leave it and "make room" for the newcomer (Kluge, 1974). Though this appears to be the most common group psychotherapy model, it is neither the only nor the most efficient model.

I initially chose a group structure of twice monthly sessions of 2½ hours each, framed in an 11-month closed-ended experience. Couples began to come to the group from a distance as word spread about the model. Babies became part of the group as needed. Then, couples asked for a weekend model that necessitated 1 day a month to be together. Initially, I was hesitant, concerned that the infrequency would hinder ongoing change. However, experience showed that the intensity of the experience was magnified by the 6-hour time period, which flew by quickly for all in the room. The intensity of the couples and their issues, the group structure, and the leadership coalesce to create a sense of drama that is a bit like sitting in a Broadway theater. However, there is major difference: As a group member or leader, the drama is your drama and you are in this drama every minute of the 6-hour meeting (Figure 2.1).

To illustrate the power of the drama, I recollect that in one meeting I did visual imagery about emotional mistreatment early in life. I then invited each member to use the other group members to enact the drama each member had remembered during the imagery. Even I was shocked as one painful early experience after another poured into the center of the room as members used a combination of family sculpting and psychodrama to work through what they had remembered during the imagery. Five couples and I were riveted. Bathroom breaks became secondary to the work at hand. The group asked that lunch be later so that the dramas could continue to unfold. Each member was there for each other member in ways that were poignant and healing for all involved. In this way the drama of the imagery acted as a powerful cohesive agent.

Figure 2.1 Couples group psychotherapy takes place in center city Philadelphia in comfortable and professional surroundings, 2008. (Photo courtesy of Dr. Judith Coché.)

A Complete Closed-Group Experience

The couples who sign up for the group agree to stay with it for the full 11-month duration. They will have one 6-hour day session on one weekend each month, providing a total of 11 meetings of 6 hours, or 66 hours. In each meeting, 45 minutes are spent eating a simply prepared, healthy lunch that is part of the monthly fee. Lunch was added when the format switched from the earlier model of meeting twice monthly for 150 minutes. The low-key lunch requires that the members move into a social level of interaction with one another. Thus, members are trained how to move from therapy to friendly discussion, and they are instructed to bring any digression from this policy into the group. Members understand the centrality of this policy and honor it very carefully.

Margaret is a skillful craftsperson, an interest she shares with Holly. Holly has been contemplating switching from corporate America to an entrepreneurial, craft-centered vocation, and she has used group energies to think through some of her future decisions. Margaret and Holly understand that they may share craft patterns over lunch, but will only discuss Margaret's lack of self-confidence as part of the group work itself. In this way, Margaret and Holly are able to keep needed boundaries in both settings. Training group members to move between settings can be accomplished as part of member training.

Closed-ended groups have a better chance to experience group developmental stages together. All group members have to conquer the typical anxiety felt in a group in its beginning stage; together they go through the growth phases of dependence and counterdependence toward the leaders; they struggle with their issues of interdependence, intimacy, and honesty as a unit and, finally, they all face the termination of the group. All these stages provide opportunities for personal growth and learning. Working through these stages together is a bit like going through the stages of life; I think it creates a more intense group experience than can be obtained in a comparable open-ended group.

Developing all group phases together generates an opportunity to feel communality with others not merely on the basis of outside characteristics (such as similarity in age or marital problem) but also on the basis of shared here-and-now experiences. Members go through a group crisis together, solve problems together, and feel similar feelings at the same time. The shared joy, fear, sadness, loathing, and laughter create a kind of universality that is in many ways superior to the level of universality one experiences upon finding that others are also having problems with depression or substance abuse (Rutan & Stone, 1984).

In his listing of the "curative factors" of group psychotherapy, Yalom (1975) describes the factor of "universality" in some detail. It is the kind of comfort felt by group members upon finding that other members are struggling with similar problems. It often helps the client to feel less alone, which encourages the client to greater self-disclosure and subsequent therapeutic benefit.

Having closed groups may seem inconvenient to prospective couples but most understand the power of a group that remains together over time. Some want to start in a group right away. Others may believe that the problem that prompted them to seek marital therapy is less serious by the time the group is ready to start. As a result, a certain degree of loss occurs because the couple's timing is "off." Yet, once a couple is convinced of the potential value of the group by the therapist or by former group members who praised it, they are usually willing to wait until the beginning of the next group round and become group participants then.

Monthly 6-Hour Sessions

Psychotherapy is a consumer service. Our couples lead busy lives and must deal with business trips, babysitters, fatigue at a day's end, and other problems that make traditional weekly appointments difficult to keep. Many couples drive quite a distance to work with us. The model of less frequent but longer sessions was originally created merely for my consumers' convenience. I knew that many couples who lead full lives find it much more manageable to commit to one weekend day per month. The monthly meeting feels more like a time-out together than a chore.

The new baby kept Holly and Trevor so busy that time for the couple disappeared into extra work time for Trevor to support the new family once Holly stopped her lucrative corporate career. Unfortunately, the baby and career shifts were accompanied by reduced sex, reduced intimacy, and reduced desire to be with one another. Bed looked more inviting than informal talk after long days with careers and infants. Although the baby got packed to go to the group with them, the long drive encouraged him to sleep much of the trip, enabling Trevor and Holly to use the drive to and from their group as part of their monthly day for the marriage. The "pepper" of a 6-hour therapy group challenged their complacency and provided a forum for tough discussions. The drive home again provided a shoulder time from treatment to life as usual. Holly and Trevor came to rely on their monthly days together for needed catch-up in their adult lives.

When I instituted the new weekend monthly 6-hour pattern a few years ago, two unforeseen psychological advantages emerged serendipitously:

- The sessions seemed even greater in intensity than in earlier twice-monthly groups. In the 6 hours available, couples found it impossible to hide behind issues of convenience as well as of fear. They were able to delve into matters in much greater depth than they did in earlier, shorter, twice monthly sessions.
- The time span between sessions gave couples more opportunity to work on matters on their own. They could, and did, try out new behaviors, perform therapeutic homework assignments, and try to work out disagreements. They also worked as individuals and couples between group sessions, as they had agreed to when they joined the group. Many individual couples' sessions opened with a genuine sense of accomplishment of homework completed between the monthly group meetings, as if to say, "Look at what I did without you." As far as I am concerned, this was so much the better.

The Rhythm of the 6-Hour Day

On a 6-hour day with no structured exercises planned, the intensity of the work is palpable. Each couple gets more than 1 hour to work in depth with members who know the marriage very well and care very deeply about improving it. The group functions as a hall of mirrors, a cheerleading section, and the nicest kind of nudge. All aspects push the couple forward so that it is almost impossible for a couple to remain unchanged in the face of this warm and friendly nudge toward the goal stated by each couple.

Spencer had the ability to use his intellect to protect himself from emotional discomfort. His recent bride, Robyn, joined with the group in wishing that Spencer might challenge himself in his career more than he had been able to do. Afraid of criticism, Spencer expended 150% effort on small tasks in his job, rather than strategizing how to move into management in the corporation in which he worked. Michael, another group member, recognized the brilliance in the way Spencer thought and spoke, and he encouraged the younger man to challenge himself more in his corporate career. Michael had done this with success in his own life. When Spencer declined, Michael and other group members asked Spencer to explore his early years to see if he could remove blocks that had become second nature to him. With the help of the group over time, Spencer asserted himself in his company and requested both advancement and a transfer to a branch that held more interest. The intensity of the unstructured group work acted as a catalyst to move him through blockage from family of origin material into a new present and future for himself, his new bride, and, eventually, for their first child together.

Brief Group Breaks

In a 6-hour period it is not possible to go without breaks. They can be as brief as 7 minutes, so that members can use the bathroom, get a cold drink, or feed a parking meter. A second form of break occurs during the lunchtime that is part of the 6-hour period of time. A brief 7-minute break midway through the morning gives everyone the opportunity to stretch, walk around, use the bathroom, and get something to drink. Couples also like to take this opportunity to share informal news with each other (restaurant reviews, cooking recipes, news of outings, vacations, or promotions). More significant news bulletins about the welfare of the couple are reserved for the group session. The lunch break functions like an intermission in a two-act drama. Members are respectful of the break and look forward to sitting down to work again as the "second act" of the day begins.

Destination Locations for Group Work

As part of my commitment to making the work memorable, in the early years, I began taking the group participants out of their usual environment and conducted the workshop in a resort location. I traveled with them to Bermuda; Cape May, New Jersey; Ocracoke, North Carolina; and Lyme, Connecticut. Then I purchased a farm in Maryland and I brought them there for a day of work in the countryside. When I chose to relocate from the farm to the beach, couples expressed pleasure in getting to the beach office during the summer. Larger trips fell away and were replaced by monthly meetings in my bay-front offices during the summer season. Despite the need to fight traffic and pay for gasoline, couples heralded the chance to get out of the city environment and work in a resort setting. This setting proved to be perfect for special topics, such as how to handle vacations, individual differences in leisure time preferences, and intimacy and the role of romance in marriage.

STRUCTURED AND UNSTRUCTURED WAYS OF WORKING

A number of clinical intervention strategies are easily integrated into couples group psychotherapy. In the unstructured portions of the group, psychodynamic work is mixed with behavioral goal setting and group dynamics-based, here-and-now work. In the more structured sections of the group, verbal and nonverbal exercises are created specifically designed around the dynamics of the group at that point in time. A discussion of these interventions follows.

Unstructured Couples Group Psychotherapy

In this part of each group, the floor is open to anyone. Couples plan ahead and raise their issues without delay. They bring up whatever pressing problem has arisen or they give a follow-up report on something that had been worked on in previous sessions. Some couples save a hot topic for the safety of the group.

Holly was so angry with Trevor that she thought she might have to divorce him. She loved him deeply and their new son made the dream of the family she had always wanted into a life-changing reality. But he was so forgetful and sloppy that she could not tell if he was being "passive aggressive." As she said, he left chores undone day after day. Each time she would speak sternly to him, in that voice that induced his guilt as soon as he heard it, he would literally try to remove himself from her in the small condo that functioned as their family home. Holly had tried all the strategies she knew to make it easier for Trevor to change. But, try as Trevor might, he simply could not be honest with Holly. Holly relied on the group to help confront Trevor with the dishonesty that threatened to dissolve her marriage. Trevor did not see his behavior as dishonest, but rather as clever. However, with help from the group, he was able to see how bad his behavior looked to other members. Holly felt certain that it was the ability to speak up in group that made the difference.

Usually a natural flow develops. One couple may open up with a problem that is currently "hot" and the others chime in. They may offer observations on the dynamics, may give feedback to another member, or may relate their own experiences. As a specific couple's problem is dealt with, another couple may raise an issue in their marriage, or a particular couple's problem may expand into a more general group discussion of the underlying issue. The result is a pattern of seemingly easy give and take, punctuated by visible clinical power.

Because the group members genuinely enjoy and care about each other, a high level of interest in one another's problems soon develops and the discussion is quite animated. When work is not entirely in the here and now, one couple is generally the focus of the group's attention at any time. Focus shifts from couple to couple as members chime in about their own situation or give their internal reaction to the topic at hand. Most group members become involved in the discussion and contribute their observations and personal experiences at frequent intervals during the group, so all are involved in therapy for the duration of the group. The therapists simultaneously focus attention on the couple in the foreground and on the group as a whole, thereby generating a wide range of intervention options (see Chapter 9) and a high level of involvement of all group members.

Typical Problems in Unstructured Group Work

The biggest risk for the welfare of the group in this unstructured work is getting bogged down in the particular issues of one couple and thereby losing the enthusiasm of the rest of the group. This problem, when it arises, usually emerges from one of two sources: the monopolizing couple or the silently struggling couple.

The monopolizing couple. At times, a couple with an entrenched marital problem takes up a great deal of group time. The same problem emerges in ever new forms without resolution of the underlying issue.

Antonia and Patrick were clearly in great pain and Antonia was skillful at commanding attention for her needs in the group. Month after month it seemed that more group energy was devoted to Antonia's concerns than to the concerns of others. Group members were passive in allowing Antonia to dominate, in part because she was so genuinely angry and unhappy. The group would try to involve Patrick, who sat quietly at first as his wife complained bitterly about his passivity at home. Finally, I decided to work with Antonia until the energy in the group shifted to include direct confrontation by other members. The intervention was difficult but yielded eventual success; Antonia's anger moved from targeting her husband to targeting me. Antonia and I were able to discuss the dynamic, and the interchange enabled a shift in her behavior that heralded large personal change.

The silently struggling couple. Groups can get bogged down and lose enthusiasm when a particular couple is struggling with an issue, but not bringing it up in the group. The reason may be shyness, shame, or the presence of other couples who simply happen to be more vociferous in bringing up issues.

In 2003, Diane was openly unhappy with her new husband, Dwight. Her tone was sharp, although she thought she was being gentle. Dwight tapped his foot nervously, tried to take written notes, repeated what was said in a flat tone, and attempted to deflect the intensity of Diane's jabs at him. Group members pointed out Dwight's behavior, but the group and Dwight were reticent to take on Diane's tone of voice for many months. Finally, the co-lead, Dr. Julian Slowinski, and I helped Dwight bring his anger into the group. Despite his intent to deny his unhappiness with his "perfect" wife, he admitted that he got angry with her, withdrew, and had little interest in intimacy or sex when she was angry with him. This breakthrough was the first time in Dwight's life that he had been calmly assertive about his anger toward a woman he deeply loved. It allowed Dwight to learn to speak up more directly within the group and in his marriage.

Although the group and the therapists knew something was "fishy" in the way Dwight was recounting his reaction to his wife, we were unable to cut through the layers of protection. When, in an outside session, Dwight began to address the issue of anger, the therapist encouraged Dwight to bring this issue into the group.

40

> *In this way a "forbidden" topic was given time to be handled. Once the topic was then taken into the group, there was a sense of relief in the group as a whole.*

One way to guard against this risk of monopolizing a session or avoiding needed topics is for the couple to schedule individual, couple, or family sessions at least once every 3–4 weeks. Such out-of-group therapeutic contacts are part of the pregroup contract and are an integral aspect of the treatment package. Monthly records address when sessions outside the group take place. When a couple "forgets" to schedule, this also becomes a topic for group discussion. The group is aware that one couple avoiding work can slow down an entire group.

Structured Couples Group Psychotherapy

Structured group work can involve many areas of specialization and is dealt with in more detail in Chapters 7 and 11. Among the special areas on which clinicians can concentrate are writing exercises, guided imagery, dramatic activities, psychodrama, movement exercises, and sensual massage. A written, structured intervention, described next, functions to move a couple quickly into previously unavailable dialogue.

Dr. Julian Slowinski and I developed exercises on sexuality and intimacy appropriate for use by my couples (J. M. Coché, 2002b). One of these exercises involves sexual scripts—the lens through which we view our sexuality. Sexual scripts evolve through a combination of genetics, early experiences, and cultural expectations. Many couples are unaware of the power of the sexual script in their day-to-day lives. In order to introduce couples to this concept in a safe manner, a two-page written exercise invites individual reflection on sexual history, followed by leader-led group interaction. In an exercise called "Who wrote your sexual script?" Dr. Slowinski and I pose four statements:

- Here is one message that I was given about sex that influenced my sexual script.
- Here is a second message that I was given about sex that influenced my sexual script.
- Our couple's sexual script reads this way.
- Here is one way that I hope to improve my sexual script during the coming year.

Integrating Structured and Unstructured Group Work

Earlier in the history of my work with couples group, I would split a session and design a structured exercise during the 5-minute break in response to a common theme or prevailing emotion in the group. The exercise might have focused on anger, fear of intimacy, sadness, affection, death, addictions, or other topics. (See Chapter 7 for information on designing, choosing, and conducting useful exercises within a day-long meeting.)

These days, structured exercises are interspersed in days of deep and unstructured work in the here and now. The change in the structure of the group reflects requests by the couples to allow the flow of a longer period of time in order to deepen whatever group work is going on. Although couples like the structured exercises and request that they continue, they prefer a longer period of time devoted to the work around each exercise. Recently, I have designed structured days where exercises form blocks of 3 or 4 hours. Couples enjoy the information conveyed in the exercise, but want to deepen their understanding of the theme through work around concepts of self, family of origin, and emotional trauma.

MIDYEAR EVALUATION AND TERMINATION

At about the halfway mark of the contract, the group refreshes their memories about the goals that the couples had set for themselves in their assessment forms in the early phase of the group. This helps couples to get a sense of how much closer they have come to reaching their goals and also to find out which couples are having trouble. Most of the time this review phase turns out to be an encouraging one. It infuses the group with new energies, creates a renewed sense of direction, and gives the group a sense that time is moving on. It is a way of pointing out that work to be done had best be gotten on with and that spring is frequently a time of quick progress.

As the contract draws to an end, couples have to deal with the inevitability of the "death" of their group. It is usually necessary for the therapists to hammer away at this reality. Most group members do not like to be reminded of death. They would rather continue working on the "hot" issues and enjoy the intimacy and cohesiveness that has been achieved, unencumbered by thoughts of leaving each other. Nevertheless, a constructive coping with the group's ending helps members deal with other termination issues in their lives and proves to be a valuable learning experience. As a member said some years ago, "Every year Judith tells us that the group is about to end and every year I ignore it."

With the realization that the group is about to end, the leaders program time for the couples to review their progress in terms of the goals that they had set for themselves in the fall. At this point, some couples choose to recontract for another year, while others will come to a completion of their group participation. A team consisting of the couple in question, the leaders, and the other group members provides feedback to the couple about the progress they have made. In this manner, the couples community has an impact on treatment decisions for its couples. Clinical wisdom guides the decision about whether a couple will return.

For many couples, there is tremendous pride in seeing how far they have come in the opinions of their peers. Couples revisit the annoying habits and vicious cycles that brought them into the group in the first place and derive a sense of mastery from the successful resolution of past troublesome problems. The credit is rightfully theirs. They did the work. Frequently, the original conflict is still there in one form or another, but solutions have been worked out with which both partners can live. These couples, in my opinion, are ready to "graduate"—an expression quite commonly used among the group participants. Graduation implies that the couple has entered the realm of difficulty that most marriages encounter each month. Marriage is hard, and couples must work out tough concerns together. Graduation does not imply perfection. It implies the capacity to disagree respectfully and remain loving to one another.

Other couples may decide that, despite the progress that has been made, they still need to learn more and change more. This does not mean that they feel bad because they do not graduate. Usually, they are encouraged by the progress they have made and it is precisely because of this encouragement that they want to deepen their learning through another year. Even though these couples will begin another round a little while later, their group as they know it terminates in July. Thus, they have to say farewell just as much as the others.

The final session is frequently a celebration of love and partnership. Couples applaud the graduates and say farewell to one another in a way that often turns out to be humorous, poignant, and very meaningful. Couples sometimes bring in food and sparkling cider to commemorate the progress made over the year. I frequently design a final structured exercise to enable people to say good-bye in an authentic way. An exercise like "the group gift" gives everyone an opportunity to participate in one last round of giving feedback to each other, to the leaders, and to the group as a whole.

The Group Gift

Sometimes at the end of a couples group I give everyone pencil and paper and 10 minutes to write their response to the following: Imagine that this group has given you a great gift this year. The gift can be anything—it can be a real object or it can be something abstract, like a fantasy; it can be for yourself, your partner, any other member, either or both leaders, or the group as a whole. As you reflect on your 11 months with us, what treasure are you taking home with you from this group?

The answers in 2006 were quite thought provoking. The group had spent 55 hours together over a period of 11 months. Some of their responses included:

- This group saved my marriage, and I feel like I've started down a path.
- My self-image was all screwed up. The feedback I used to get from others (in my family) was ludicrous compared to the feedback I got from this group. I got the gift of validation from others.
- I got a chance to have a much better relationship with my wife and children that can actually change my future.
- The hope that my life is getting better.
- I have less anxiety. That is a huge gift. I am more centered.
- I got a better understanding that sex is really an important and healthy part of an adult life and that it is okay.

GRADUATING FROM, RETURNING TO, OR LEAVING THE GROUP

Because the advanced couples group operates on a closed model of group design, all couples start at the beginning of the contract period and end the contract period together. There is almost no instance of dropping out. I attribute the high rate of cohesiveness to group dynamics-based leadership, which builds cohesiveness in the early part of the group. Further, clearly specified therapy contracts (see Appendix A) and handling of group practicalities allow the group to become the safe harbor for emotional interchanges that create interpersonal transformations in people's lives. People do not want to leave the group early and most come back for a second year with the group. The average length of stay for most couples is 2 years, 22 months, 132 hours of clinical time together. In this space of time, marital transformations happen routinely. As Scott Rutan told me during training for national leadership at the American Group Psychotherapy Association some years ago, "The first half of the group is about saying hello; the second half of a group is about saying goodbye."

A more formal ending process begins 2 months before the group ends. At this point, progress reports (Appendix A-ii) are distributed electronically and in paper and members are invited to address their progress over the year to date. These written progress reports become the topic of conversation as one couple after another describes changes sought and accomplished by each member of the couple and the couple as a unit. This is a time when frustrations are expressed and a time when pride of accomplishment is evident. Following each person's reporting on his or her evaluation of his or her work, each member asks for feedback from the other members of the group and the leaders. Typically, specific questions are addressed as all members begin the poignant process of deciding whether returning to the group for another year is clinically indicated.

Despite the depth of affection and loyalty that members have developed for one another, I state clearly that the only reason to return for another group is to continue work that needs to be done. It happens often that a couple, wishing to run from the final piece of work that needs to be done in the marriage, assesses that they no longer need to be in the group, but are informed by other members that it is evident that the marriage work needs refinement and the patina of another year of membership. One rule of thumb that I espouse is that *if you think it is time for you to leave, and all of the members agree that you ought to come back, I encourage you to attend to the feedback of the other members. They may be seeing something about your marriage that you do not see.*

Graduation

People leave the group in two ways. For most couples, there is a badge of courage and distinction when group members and leaders agree that the couple is ready to "graduate" from the group. This means that the work has been accomplished and that the couple is solid enough to proceed on their own. Often a couple who is graduating will do monthly check-ups to ensure that the depth of change accomplished continues after the membership is over. At other times, couples graduate and absorb all of the work of their marriage by themselves. Both models work, depending on the couples and their needs.

Margaret and Michael spent 2 years in couples group psychotherapy. In the first year, Michael reported that he had learned more than he thought possible and could not imagine what more he could learn in another year; however, he wanted to find out. At the end of the second year, Michael and Margaret were ready to graduate from a group that had taught them to parent skillfully as a team, to spend more leisure time together, and actively to treasure the deeply loving marriage that was central to their lives.

As this book was going to press, Michael e-mailed: "Judith, hope all is well with you and the group. I wanted to tell you that I appreciate all your help and the group. Please tell everyone I said hello and wished them well. The effort is well worth it. As Albert Schweitzer said, 'One who gains strength by overcoming obstacles possesses the only strength which can over-come adversity.'"

A second way that couples leave the group is to do a self-prescribed exit at the end of the contract period. Less than 40% of the time couples decide that it is time to leave regardless of what other members say. Sometimes this is because one member is highly resistant to further change and refuses to return. At other times, the couple wants a chance to try things on their own, stating that they will be back if they feel that they need to return. Actual experience, however, demonstrates that couples rarely return to a couples group after they leave the group prematurely. Antonia and Patrick were an exception.

As a couple with young babies in 1987, Antonia and Patrick spent 2 years in the couples group learning how to create an effective marital working team. Issues of anger and depression did not get sufficiently resolved before they left, and they said that they would come back if necessary. Fifteen years passed before they returned, but when their babies were in late adolescence they came back into the couples group to pick up work on a marriage that had developed a deep level of contempt, depression, isolation, and boredom. They looked like a couple headed toward divorce, but they did not want to divorce. The couple was able to begin depth work quickly upon reentrance to the group. They spent 3 years in the group, working through interpersonal anguish, and emerged loving one another deeply, feeling like soul mates for the first time in their marriage, and looking forward to sex together. In the second round of their group attendance, they earned the admiration of all other members by graduating. Their skill and tenacity in working with deep fissures between them created a celebratory atmosphere as this couple found their way to one another. Most couples in their situation would have ended the marriage. Each of them, their children, and the other couples in their group share a deep sense of satisfaction at the level of marital work they have achieved.

Combining Experienced Group Members With New Members

Clinical experience and common sense indicate that it is hard to bring one new couple into a group with experienced members. A group comprising two couples returning for another year and two couples new to group couples psychotherapy forms a frequent pattern. Although, at first, returning couples feel impatient at having to "show the ropes" to new couples, the induction into deep group work goes relatively quickly as experienced members drive the work. Much like big brothers and big sisters, experienced couples act as models to initiate new couples into the power of the couples group experience.

In 2007, three of the couples highlighted in this book returned for a second year together. Antonia and Patrick, Spencer and Robyn, and Holly and Trevor requested that the group remain closed to new members and I agreed. This trio of couples also requested that there be no formal exercises when they returned so that all the work could be in the here and now. They wanted the power of the group to be maximized. Within a short period of time, a tremendous amount of change happened for each of the couples in the returning group. Knowing one another well, trusting one another, and structuring their group for maximal change created an emotional ecosystem in which it was impossible for any of the members to remain the same.

SINGLE LEADERSHIP AND CO-LEADERSHIP

Since 1991, due to the death of Dr. Erich Coché, the co-lead who helped me develop the original model of couples group therapy, my couples groups have been led with various constellations of leadership. It is my conclusion that the most critical factor in effective co-leadership in couples group psychotherapy has less to do with clinical experience and gender and more to do with an ability to think in terms of interpersonal systems and to reach out compassionately to the needs that couples bring.

Two models of co-leadership are frequent: a senior–senior co-lead and a senior–junior co-lead. I have done both. Two senior clinicians co-leading a couples group can relax into the experience, each depending on the expertise of the other to catch errors. The experience is delightful for both leaders. The senior–junior co-lead model is a superb training model for developing clinicians. Much like an apprentice in the studio of a master, the junior co-lead is able to learn the language of group leadership while the group is actively engaged in its own work. At the Coché Center, psychiatric residents and PhD psychology interns co-lead in the groups with me as part of their advanced training. They report that the experience provides them the opportunity to learn interpersonal systems therapy from the vantage point of the leader inside the group.

Co-leadership provides a technical advantage and a therapeutic gain. Because there are two leaders, it is possible for the group to continue working even if one of the leaders has to be absent for professional or health reasons, vacations, out-of-town meetings, and so forth. Further, on a therapeutic level, the leaders provide a valuable complement to each other. If one of them overlooks or exaggerates the importance of a particular issue at hand, the other can provide a balance, bring in an additional point of view, and prevent potential iatrogenic problems.

Rutan and Stone (1984) list a variety of advantages of co-leadership but also stress its drawbacks, citing a number of authors who point out that the complexities of the relationship between the co-leaders may detract from the power of the group. Nevertheless, co-therapy is quite common as a leadership modality and the advantages outweigh the drawbacks for many group therapists. A small number of empirical studies have compared the effectiveness of marital therapy by single therapists versus co-led therapy and found no significant difference in outcome or somewhat better outcomes associated with co-leaders (Hendrix, Fournier, & Briggs, 2001; LoPiccolo, Heiman, Hogan, & Roberts, 1985; Mehlman, Baucom, & Anderson, 1983).

It is a further advantage to the group if the leaders are of different genders (Kluge, 1974). Members of heterosexual couples have the opportunity to project their own feelings toward the opposite sex onto one of the leaders and work them out in the transference (Cividini & Klain, 1973; Cooper, 1976).

Just as it seems necessary for a leader in a heterosexual couples group to understand both heterosexuality and coupling, I feel certain that it is necessary for one member of a co-leadership team to be gay or lesbian in a gay or lesbian couples therapy group. For this reason, I have not yet begun to work with this population, but look forward to the work.

In working with one another, it is essential that the co-leaders have a positive working relationship. They may have different therapeutic styles, but they still have to agree on their basic therapeutic theoretical frame. Considerable differences in the theory of what is helpful to people in a group could severely undermine the efficacy of the therapy (Hellwig & Memmott, 1974). Therapists have to give each other room to unfold and to develop their best therapeutic abilities without fear of criticism or of being undermined by the other during the session. It must be possible for them to disagree respectfully with each other as differences occur, but there has to be an underlying belief in and even admiration for each other's abilities and competencies. Thus, when differences of opinion arise during the course of the group session, group members have an opportunity to observe successful conflict resolution and perhaps even learn from the modeling that is presented by the leaders.

Whatever the relationship of the two therapists is outside the group (colleagues, supervisor–supervisee, marriage partners, family members, or good friends), it is crucial that that relationship be kept viable throughout the duration of the group. Difficulties are likely to arise, as they do in most human relationships, at some time or another, but an inability to resolve such difficulties within a reasonable amount of time is destructive to the group. Groups have a great interest in the relationship of the therapists to each other and some form of group fantasy usually exists as to the nature of their relationship. Signs of co-leader disharmony would be viewed by group members with great concern, especially because, in most couples groups, several members are products of disturbed marriages. On the other hand, a functional co-leadership can provide a reparative interpersonal relationship model for the group members.

As part of an advanced elective offered by the department of psychiatry where I teach, Dr. Juliette Galbraith, then chief outpatient resident in psychiatry, chose to undertake training in couples group therapy. After 2 years of individual group therapy training, she entered into the position of junior co-lead, with me as the senior co-lead for the couples group. A good bit of careful planning and thorough teaming was necessary before this co-leadership team felt confident of the wisdom of this partnership because Dr. Galbraith is my daughter. Carefully crafting my co-leadership proved both rewarding and fascinating. As the group unfolded, members expressed appreciation for the ability to watch a mother and daughter team co-lead together. They noted a difference between the clinical styles of the two leaders and commented that they worked together well, providing a model of a functional intergenerational relationship. One group member openly stated that she loved to watch Dr. Galbraith be assertive with her own mother.

It is also very important that the therapists have a common therapeutic posture regarding their own degree of self-disclosure. Any discrepancy in the levels of self-disclosure that emerges between the two therapists will give rise to some rather uncomfortable group dynamics. The group will come to see the more self-disclosing therapist as more open, loving, and accessible, but also probably as the weaker one, as some of the research on therapist self-disclosure has shown (see E. Coché & Dies, 1981, for a discussion of this issue). In order to prevent such typecasting, it is wiser for the therapists to have a common position on the level of therapist self-disclosure that is acceptable to them.

Couples group therapy lends itself to co-leads who are married to one another and to couples who co-lead practices. It can be great fun to co-lead with a marital partner: One is in constant relationship with the partner both privately and in the clinical setting of the group. The situation in which the two co-leaders are married to one other is a variant of other co-leadership situations (Low & Low, 1975). Everything that has been said previously about the need for respect and admiration for the other's special therapeutic talents is particularly applicable to the co-leader team married to each other. Self-disclosure becomes an even more poignant issue with this type of co-leader team in that the group will naturally want to know as much as possible about how this couple has solved certain marital issues when they came up in their marriage. There is likely to be an even stronger push from the group to get the leaders to open up about themselves than there is already in any therapy group.

The rule of thumb regarding self-disclosure that I have adopted for the groups is that the group receives no more self-disclosure than its members might discern through personal observation and general public knowledge. In the group session, the group can see how co-leads interact with each other in a professional context and can see the manner in which we talk with each other, agree and disagree, and joke around with each other. It is valuable to limit self-disclosure in order to minimize member dependency upon the leader and to contain unnecessary levels of fantasizing about the leader's personal life.

OUT-OF-GROUP PSYCHOTHERAPY WORK

Working with a therapist in individual, couple, or family sessions at least once every 3 weeks is a necessary part of the treatment package. Some group therapy practitioners disagree with this guideline and believe that such a procedure drains energies from the group. In my experience, the larger concern is that a couple's problem "falls through the cracks." Moreover, as spelled out by Whisman and Uebelacker (1999), a greater percentage of couples may benefit from group psychotherapy when individual therapy is integrated into the treatment. Although at one time there was considerable concern that individual therapy might lead to the deterioration of the couple's relationship, a review of studies in this area did not find support for this hypothesis (Hunsley & Lee, 1995).

There is some flexibility regarding who provides the out-of-group sessions. It is often one of the group therapists, but it can also be an outside therapist. If one of the group leaders also sees a couple outside the group, this couple is likely to believe that it has a special relationship to this therapist and may feel superior to the other couples. It is important for the group leader to be aware of such transference issues and deal with them as needed (Ormont, 1981). Sometimes decisions are required that seem to pit one clinical guideline against another. It can be very difficult for members of one group also to be members of a second group. At the same time, the benefit of individual group membership can be augmented through additional membership in a couples group. Leaders need to think through practice and ethical guidelines carefully in reaching clinical decisions. Explicit agreement needs to be reached among all members involved in tricky clinical decisions.

In 2005 and 2006, Margaret and Antonia were members of a small women's group during the time that they were also members of the couples group; this allowed a strong bond to form between them. Members of both groups were aware of the dynamics at hand. In this small women's group, Antonia worked on issues of career competence, while Margaret was improving a badly damaged sense of self. I was able to ensure that material about other members from the women's group was not brought into the couples group because I lead both groups. Likewise, material about other couples was not brought into the women's group. The policies state that material remains in the room and is not shared outside the group. In this way, the bond between the two women enabled them to benefit from their membership in both groups without violating necessary confidentiality boundaries.

Furthermore, rules regarding the use of group material in individual sessions and the use of individual session material in the group must be clearly spelled out between the therapist and the clients. I ask that all agree that anyone—client or therapist—can bring material into the group if appropriate. I assume that everyone will use good judgment as to what kind of material to leave out of the group. Furthermore, I agree with Pittman (1989) that sexual affairs need to be discussed within marital treatment, regardless of whether this treatment is in a group or a couples session.

A different set of issues arises when an outside therapist sees a couple. A particular transference issue that can arise in this case is "splitting": picturing one person as all good and another as all bad (Cooper, 1976; Wells, 1985). In a maneuver not unfamiliar to most therapists, a couple (or an individual) may come to see one therapist (e.g., the group leader) as the "good parent" and the other as the "bad" one. The group leaders must avoid getting hooked into this by becoming defensive or by agreeing to criticisms of the outside therapist. The problem can then be dealt with therapeutically and can benefit the couple considerably.

Splitting also occurs within the group by setting off one leader as good and the other as bad, but this is more obvious and easier to deal with as long as the leaders are a unified team that has its own issues of competition well in control. If they do not, however, they can easily fall into the trap, consciously or unconsciously support the splitting, and battle with it. The situation is quite analogous to children playing one parent against the other, and interpretations of this nature are appropriate and helpful. Finally, working with an outside therapist requires coordination and integration. It is of utmost importance that the outside therapist and the group leaders maintain communication. They have to inform each other of important events in each setting and agree on the major therapeutic goals and the main pathways to achieve them. Here, too, it is crucial that they support and respect each other in their work.

WHAT MAKES COUPLES GROUP PSYCHOTHERAPY EFFECTIVE?

The treatment package presented here has a variety of ingredients that contribute to a constructive psychotherapy experience. These ingredients include an overview of marital strengths and weaknesses, goal setting, progress reports, work in the here and now, structured exercises, and group dynamics work as an ongoing modality. Many of the ingredients could be varied to fit the needs of a different setting. However, even if it varies, it is the complete package that helps the couples to work through their issues in the most useful manner.

The two most important ingredients are the couples work and the group work. Both presume that individual psychotherapy has been done in the past or will be integrated into the work at hand. The presence of the partner allows the other people in the group to see the couple in action and to give firsthand observations on the way in which the partners "wind each other up" to have an argument, set traps for each other, and avoid intimacy. In addition, all the curative factors of a group come into play. Ever since Yalom's (1975) first efforts to formalize the ways in which groups are therapeutic, more and more has been understood about these ways and how they occur at different stages of the group.

I find that in the early stages of the therapy group, *universality* plays an important role in getting couples going and that, in the middle phases, *learning from each other* appears to be the crucial ingredient. The final phase includes evaluating therapeutic gains made during the group, saying good-bye to group members who are leaving, and deciding whether to work in the group during the next contract period. Furthermore, due to its particular composition of members, each group develops its own style of working. Thus, although *insight* may be crucial in some groups, *experiential learning, altruism,* and *receiving feedback* may be much more important in others.

Moreover, the group represents a microcosm of a marital community in which couples show their interactive style. The necessity for individuals in the couple to relate to a variety of people creates opportunities to see themselves more clearly—for example, whether a husband in the group shows condescending behavior only toward his spouse, toward all women, or toward all people.

3

Establishing and Maintaining Workable Group Policies

My husband can carry his own truckload. I'm not going to be his U-Haul-It anymore.

—A woman claiming herself

THE WISDOM OF HAVING GROUP POLICIES

Consistent and clearly spelled out group policies are part of intelligent group psychotherapy preparation. The literature (J. M. Coché & Coché, 1986; Mayerson, 1984; Nichols, 1976) demonstrates that well-prepared group participants have a better concept of what they are supposed to do. They also have a higher expectation that their group will be successful. Well-prepared groups, as was discussed in Chapter 1, build cohesiveness more speedily and have lower rates of absences and dropouts. One of the most significant aspects of group preparation is clarity about the group rules.

Group policies provide an outer frame within which the group process can unfold and flourish. If all participants, leaders, and members have the same conceptual framework with respect to the boundaries within which everyone operates, an atmosphere of safety develops. Inside these boundaries, the group can pursue its task of improving marriages rather than using group time for interminable debates over group rules.

Some group theorists believe that such group debates aimed at creating the group's work rules build cohesion and are therapeutic. Such debates can aid in setting the expectation that the group is responsible for its own processes and should not depend on the leaders to tell the members what to do. Although that is a valuable procedure in groups of professionals organized for the purpose of studying their own group process (as in sensitivity training or group process education groups), I believe that such a procedure is inefficient for therapy groups. In therapy, clients are not focused on the intricacies of group processes. Instead, they are coming for help with their personal or marital problems and are relying on the leaders to create a group structure in which successful therapy can take place. Giving every participant a clear idea of what is expected helps the group to get underway without undue delay. It does not eliminate the need for discussions of the rules, but it does prevent the rules from being too much in focus.

The policies for the couples groups are a modification of policies that operate for all psychotherapy groups at the Coché Center. General policies were developed over the last 20 years and are in keeping with group norms advocated by other authors and clinicians in the group psychotherapy field (Rutan, Stone, & Shay, 2007). These procedures work especially well in moving a group quickly to a cohesive working state and are applicable for all intensive group psychotherapy for adults.

The policies proposed here are derived from three sources: clinical experience, the group psychotherapy literature, and client feedback. Many of the rules I use in the conduct of the couples groups have been debated at some length in the literature on group psychotherapy. In instances where there was no agreement on the best course of action, I was able to rely on my own clinical experience and that of my mentors and colleagues. The following vignette presents an instance of learning from experience.

A number of years ago my groups had no specific rules regarding out-of-session contacts or "socializing." The literature in this regard was quite contradictory at that time. Although some authors were advocating that the group meet without their leaders on some occasions, maybe even regularly in so-called "alternate sessions" (Kutash & Wolf, 1983), other authors warned that this could create certain group dynamics over which the leader had very little or no influence and that could be harmful to the group (Wolf, 1983).

> *At that time, a woman in one of my noncouple groups was having a party at her house to which she invited some but not all group members. The leader was not informed that group members had been invited. There was an expressed expectation that the invited guests would not tell the rest of the group. This alone set up a very uncomfortable situation, with part of the group containing a secret from the rest.*
>
> *Even worse, some group members got into a fight at the party, which they could not discuss in the group. Then word leaked out anyway. The feelings of rejection, isolation, guilt, and rage engendered by the event and its aftermath greatly reduced the therapeutic efficacy of that group. The incident taught us that out-of-group contacts can be very destructive to group work and that groups work better if the members know the limits of acceptable contacts between members from the start.*

Many of the policies may appear self-evident. One might even ask why I would bother to spell them out. The answer is that many of these policies were formulated after I learned from experience that a given policy was not self-evident to everybody who joined my groups. That is understandable when one considers how anxious and vulnerable members of a new therapy group are. I have found that a verbal review of the way in which the group works and written contracts around confidentiality, fees, and other group necessities provide clarity for members at a time of high anxiety.

The Tradition of Group Policies and Written Contracts

When I began to work with groups, psychodynamic principles of group interaction often influenced leaders to let policies be developed by the group itself. The thinking was that this was "grist for the mill." Even before research began to confirm that preparation for group therapy is valuable for members, I began to outline simple policies for my groups. These were distributed before the first group meeting and reviewed in depth during the first group. Some years later I added a written group therapy contract for members, attendance sheets, and other informational records. Far from cutting down on the power of the group, these policies and attestations serve to enhance the power of the group for the members. Policies are examined each year to update them as needed, but they have remained remarkably constant for the most part. Members find it professional and reassuring to have policies on which they can count. These are provided in Appendix A-iii.

Dwight had a history of underachievement combined with parental standards that demanded top-flight behavior. Additionally, medication to reduce anxiety had become part of his daily life. To offset these difficulties, Dwight had learned to try to control his anxiety by overattending to details. Group members requested that he not take notes during the group and he reluctantly agreed. He understood intellectually that taking notes supported his tendency to intellectualize, but he was clearly uncomfortable with remaining emotionally present. When he was invited to join the group, Dwight felt reassured by the written material provided concerning group policies, contracts, and Web sites about group psychotherapy. As part of his treatment, I encouraged him to remind me when details were out of line with his standards of perfection. By incorporating his need for structure and by framing his high standards as helpful and part of his group membership, treatment goals were more easily met. Dwight began to relax in the group, and note-taking moved from an ongoing interference to an occasional sentence scribbled onto an index card. Incorporating Dwight's anxiety into a therapeutically viable group role, Dwight became an expert in the written details of the group. He then went on to help his wife deal with her anxiety by providing her with his expertise in the details of their lives.

THE CONTENT OF THE GROUP POLICIES

The following section presents the thinking behind group policies included in Appendix A-iii. Although some of these rules are the same for all groups, others are specific to couples groups. Many are responses to important ethical concerns; others are more mundane technical matters.

The Advantage of Written Contracts

Written confidentiality forms have long been considered a best-practice procedure. The reasons are obvious: Going over the confidentiality agreement within the group draws needed attention to the importance of confidentiality, and signing a written contract makes it clear that one will be held to it.

It was harder to decide to require signatures for the therapy contract itself because all therapists understand that trust and integrity cannot be legislated. About 6 years ago, I began to circulate the terms of a therapy contract (Appendix-iv) that provided specific requirements. These requirements include payment, attendance, auxiliary treatment, and a spirit of honesty within the group. Our experience has been excellent; members appreciate knowing that there is an expectation for accountability within the group.

Out-of-Group Contacts

As the preceding example showed, interactions among group members between sessions can be quite destructive. As long as a group is in existence, it is in the members' best interest if their contact outside the group be kept to a minimum. Naturally, people will walk from the office to the parking garage together, or they may have a chat on the sidewalk before going home from a group session. I strongly advise, however, that they keep their conversation light and not discuss matters concerning other group members. Should discussions arise, their content is to be brought back to the group. For example, invitations to one another's houses are not permitted as long as both parties involved are still participating in the group. There is still quite a debate in the literature about the advisability of the "no socializing" rule (Flapan & Fenchel, 1983; Rutan, Alonso & Molin, 1984).

Commitment to a Closed-Group Experience

All of my couples groups are closed ended; this means that all couples begin their group year together and stay together for 11 months. At that time, a couple may "graduate," sign up for another 11-month period, or choose to pursue other treatment options.

Couples have to make a firm commitment to stay in the group for the full 11-month duration. On rare occasions it may be unavoidable that a couple must leave (e.g., because a partner is being transferred to another city and the family is relocating); however, dropping out for any less pressing reason constitutes a serious breach of the contract and can cause harm to the integrity of the group. All couples understand this mutual dependence on each other and are therefore loyal to their group and consistent in their attendance. Once couples are convinced of the considerable psychological and therapeutic benefits of closed membership, they are usually willing to make the time commitment and stick to it.

Once the baby was born, it was hard for Holly and Trevor to trek the 5 hours it took to get from their home to the group location with the baby in tow. But they would arrive on time, unpack the colorful baby gear that had made the trip with them, and prepare for a day of alternating baby care inside the group. Stylish toys and bottles of pumped breast milk allowed them to alternate the 6 hours of child care during group time. They preferred the complexities of onsite baby care to a babysitter. Other members were delighted to include the tiniest group member, who gurgled her way into their hearts. Dr. Galbraith and I had to discipline ourselves not to hold this beautiful baby while we were leading a group. During breaks and lunch, members visited not only with Holly and Trevor, but also with their new daughter.

Dealing With Partner Absences

Occasionally, it is unavoidable for a group member to miss a session. At these times, I expect the partner of the absent member to attend. I have found that the sessions in which only one member of a couple is present are often very fruitful for the attending partner, especially if that partner feels stifled in his or her participation by the spouse.

Antonia found it so easy to ask the group for help that, for the first 2 years of their participation, Patrick often faded into the background. Patrick's voice was gentle and tentative, while Antonia's voice could be assertive and persistent. When she was away on business travel, Patrick would come to the group by himself. The men in the group felt great affection for Patrick. They acted as self-appointed cheerleaders for him to "speak up" so that the group could get to know him too. Patrick initially found this easier to do during Antonia's absences. When Antonia was absent, Patrick seemed freer to bring his concerns to the group, whether they were seemingly trivial or life changing. Members were extremely supportive of his development in the group. As he became more comfortable with his voice in the group, members encouraged and helped him to transition into using this voice with Antonia present. This process allowed him to speak more directly and openly with Antonia outside the group as well, and it eventually allowed the couple to tackle difficult problems on a more equal footing.

Dealing With Confidentiality

Confidentiality is the most important policy in any therapy. A group cannot function unless members trust other group members to keep their personal self-disclosures confidential (Davis & Meara, 1982). Group participants are told that they are not to divulge the names or information about the lives of other group members to anyone. They may talk about their own struggles and changes in therapy with others but not about the changes in other group members' lives.

New group participants are informed about this rule before they join the group and again during the first session. Within the first 30 minutes of a new group, they sign a confidentiality agreement and discuss the rule as it is written in the policies. When they do this, it becomes very clear that confidentiality is the cornerstone of good group therapy.

Dealing With Financial Obligation

Members pay the monthly fee for all sessions of a month at the time of the first group session of that month. They receive an electronic invoice of their account at the end of the week during which payment is rendered. This invoice serves insurance and record-keeping purposes. Sessions are to be paid for regardless of absence. Members are aware of this rule at the time they agree to join the group.

If a couple falls behind in payment, it is a therapeutic issue to be dealt with in their couples session or in the group. If there is a genuine hardship situation, special arrangements can be made. However, couples are told to ask for special arrangements *before* they fall behind, rather than after the fact.

During their membership in the group, Holly and Trevor transitioned from earning hundreds of thousands of dollars a year as a couple, to a period of lack of fully salaried employment for both of them. Holly had given birth to her baby and was delighting in a self-chosen period of motherhood. She had no desire to go back to her high-paying professional career. Trevor had undertaken a career move caused by physical relocation instigated by Holly. He found himself unable to get the level of work that had previously earned him high wages. Although the couple agreed on values that embraced minimal spending, financial concerns dominated their lives. They inadvertently accumulated debt without the cash flow needed to reduce it. They came to the leaders of the group and honestly stated their dilemma. They filled out scholarship forms, similar to those used in obtaining a scholarship from graduate school, and received financial subsidization from the practice for as long as their lives required. At the same time, however, they worked clinically with the conflict between them about the advisability of Holly going back to work. They also worked together to resolve on-the-job difficulties that Trevor was having concerning assertiveness. Trevor began earning more, and Holly was able to stay home for a while longer.

Concurrent Adjunctive Psychotherapy Work

In order for the group to be maximally effective, couples need individual, couples, or family sessions between their group sessions. Most couples feel the need for additional therapeutic work aside from the group and schedule their sessions without reminders from the leaders. Occasionally, however, a couple resists the therapy and delays scheduling meetings between group sessions. By the time the resistance becomes obvious to the group, it is already quite late and important therapeutic momentum may have been lost. Clinical experience has shown us that the couples who get least from the group were often those who "slipped through the cracks" and did not schedule their own couples sessions. I now pass around an attendance sheet that includes room for the date of the sessions outside the group.

Trevor and Holly changed markedly during their group work. Near the end of their 2-year attendance, they found it realistically difficult to attend sessions between group meetings. They lived quite far away from the offices, and a baby and long career hours minimized time to travel for sessions. Because the couple was doing very well and because funds were minimal, I worked out a way to do brief check-ins by phone. The phone time was not intended to be depth psychotherapy, but rather as a time to do problem solving and support. Because the couple had already surpassed their goals for work in therapy, this format worked well, but did not offer opportunity for substantial work.

Change is maximized by enabling members to reflect on their in-group experience both inside and outside the group. A couple may choose to discuss its individual or couples session in the group and often does. Usually, when an individual or couple wants to use a session outside the group to discuss group business, the therapist listens to the issue and encourages the persons to raise the issue in the next group meeting.

I often tell clients that the group is like popcorn popping and that so much is going on in a short period of time that work outside the group enables the members to process the learning and to individualize it to their lives as individuals and as part of a couple. The treatment package is thus conceptualized as a tailor-made combination of modalities that suits the needs of each couple at each stage of their psychotherapy.

Diane and Dwight handled their therapeutic needs through a combination of modalities with more than one therapist. Diane combined an individual group, which helped her deal with her anxiety in an ongoing way, with her couples group experience. Dwight entered individual therapy with a male colleague of mine, who engaged in multimodal therapy with him around issues of sexual performance and assertiveness. Both Diane and Dwight used medication as another helpful treatment component, creating a powerful mixture that was both efficient and economical. They were able to receive a winning combination of depth psychotherapy, medication, interpersonal psychotherapy, and cognitive work. The group became a constant in their relationship, allowing other therapy modalities to augment the foundation of the work in the group.

PROCEDURES TO IMPART GROUP POLICIES

Group policies are so important that it is advisable to communicate them to new clients several times and in different ways. The screening interview, which often invites the couple to the group, is the first time the procedures are mentioned. Shortly after they accept the invitation and before the membership is finalized, couples get paper and electronic copies of group therapy policies. Further, the first group meeting begins with a review of the policies while all couples are present. Questions are answered. Disagreements are discussed. Confidentiality agreements and group therapy contracts are reviewed and signed in the group so that all members are present when they agree to keep the contract. The policies go into effect by the middle of the first meeting. An in-depth discussion about how to work with group therapy policies follows.

What follows is a brief, verbatim explanation of group policies extracted from the 1990 videotape, *Techniques in Couples Group Therapy:*

> Welcome to the couples group. I ask that you respect the policies and pro-cedures of the group. I ask that you maintain the strictest confidentiality about your names and your lives outside of this room. I ask that you not socialize with one another for the duration of your membership in this group … I ask that all of the energy remain in the group. I also expect that you will work with your own therapist outside of the group, on the average of once every 3 weeks. That way, the learnings in the group will be intensified … I expect that people will be absent because of illness, an emergency, or some sort of family business or travel. I ask that you tell the group before you will be absent because the group misses its absent members … The group is actually a group for individuals who are in partnership with one another. You will benefit each time you come. I ask that you be forthright and honest as much as you possibly can in this group. That's the way you will get the most from it. And although that's a little bit frightening at first, the best way to overcome the fear is to simply take the plunge.

Discussing the Group Policies Before the First Session

Group psychotherapy preparation starts in the screening session in which the idea of joining a therapy group is first broached. In order to convey a sense of safety to the prospective group member, a couple is informed about issues like confidentiality and the commitment for the group's duration. In this discussion, it is very important to convey these policies not as dictates from above, but instead as parts of a larger framework that has been developed over years and has been found to be advantageous to people in groups. The goal is to obtain agreement from the participants and cooperation in functioning within these boundaries, not only because they respect the therapist who relays these guidelines, but also because the new members believe that these regulations are in the couple's best interest and are the building blocks of a group treatment approach designed to maximize therapeutic efficacy.

Open discussion ensues to handle members who try to lessen therapeutic involvement by attending group only. When needed, leaders explain that a member who attempts to do work only in the group slows down the group for the other members because that member is relying on the group to carry his entire therapy. Explained in this manner, the rationale for additional psychotherapy sessions becomes clear to those in the group and cooperation is easier to ensure.

Recapitulation in the First Session

The first session begins with a recapitulation of the policies. A good deal of time is spent on this quite purposefully. One of the therapists reviews the rules (as set down on the policies sheet) one by one. The tone is declarative and low key. It does not sound like a reading of the Ten Commandments and it is not meant to be a selling job. It would be a mistake and would set the wrong tone for the group if the leader were long winded or authoritarian in this presentation. If that were to happen, the group would be in danger of becoming much too dependent on a leader who is perceived as extremely powerful; it would set people up for passivity (and therefore boring group meetings) or for a rather dramatic—though not necessarily therapeutic—phase of counterdependence a few sessions later (Bion, 1960).

Instead, the task of policy discussion is one of explanation, aimed at fostering discussion and, ultimately, at obtaining agreement based on understanding. Just as I discussed the way in which the group works as part of the screening process, I also want the whole group to hear and accept the wisdom of these guidelines.

Furthermore, while the policies are being reviewed, members understand this as an invitation to discuss what is being presented. In this process, it also becomes clear that although most of the policies will not be changed simply because a group member prefers it, policies are certainly open to discussion. People understand that the leaders are interested in the feelings engendered by certain rules and respect these reactions, even though there are some definite limits to the power that a group has in trying to "overrule" the leaders.

It is very important to avoid misunderstandings in this regard early on. A group that later finds that it has a good deal less power than it was originally led to believe it had will become quite frustrated. The frustration can lead to a resigned passivity or a very angry counterdependence. Therefore, the leaders need to be clear as to the limits of flexibility inherent in the group's policies. Occasionally, special circumstances surround a group. For example, in 2006, the couples contracted to invite an award-winning documentary journalist to be an ongoing observer in their group. Although complete anonymity was a necessary part of the contract, considerable detail needed to be reviewed to establish the viability of giving a journalist entrée into a confidential, closed experience.

Antonia and Patrick, Spencer and Robyn, and Trevor and Holly were all stimulated by the predicted benefits from having an observer in the group. They talked about her observational skills, her ability to write their story well, and the advantage of being able to read about themselves in print. Margaret, Michael, Dwight, and Diane were neither anxious nor enthused about a potential observer. All members wanted to clarify details of the role the observer would play in their group before making a final decision. Anxiety centered on how the guarantee of anonymity in any written material would be achieved. For example, the couples with children wanted to ensure that their children would not be able to recognize themselves in a book. In order to avoid misunderstanding and to empower the nascent group to make final decisions at their level of comfort, a 10-way phone call was scheduled on the office conference line. Each member prepared questions for me and the journalist and discussion ensued for over an hour. Carefully drafted legal contracts and releases of information created the foundation for the level of trust, which was enhanced through ongoing discussions of the role of the observer. In this way, group policies were varied to enhance the clinical power of the therapeutic experience for the members.

THE KEEPER OF THE STRUCTURE

When I was working in a co-leader team, I designed a complementary overlapping structure of roles for the leaders (Coché & Coché, 1990). I have found it advantageous to have one of the leaders designated as the "keeper of the structure." This person is the one who pays particular attention to the boundaries of the group. He or she sees to it that the group starts and ends on time, that people pay their fees when they are supposed to, and that other structural policies are kept as agreed.

This kind of task assignment between the leaders is not meant as a rigid role division, but instead as a difference in cognitive emphasis and attention. It also helps to avoid slip-ups—for example, when people break group rules such as paying on time and nobody notices. Most of the time, the group itself will see to it that its rules are maintained. People who arrive late more than once are usually told by other group members how disruptive it is. Having a keeper of the structure, however, provides the safeguard that someone will enforce group rules when the group does not do so on its own.

The keeper of the structure is useful for both training purposes and general clinical effectiveness. I developed the concept as part of the training program in group psychotherapy, and I use it in my teaching for psychiatric residents and clinical psychology interns. When it is used in a senior–junior co-therapy team, as is the case in a training program, the junior leader naturally functions as the keeper of the structure.

In a senior–senior therapist combination, as often occurs when I co-lead the couples groups, I still recommend that one co-leader be the keeper of the structure, but that the roles be richly interwoven beyond this job. In this way, the structural elements are handled without much fuss, but things are also not allowed to slip because neither leader has felt fully responsible. In this way, the group is free to function without undue energy expenditure on mundane matters.

Setting up the group structure by careful planning and execution of structural details creates a foundation for clinical work that is both safe and predictable. This foundation ensures fairness for members and leaders, creating an interpersonal contract for all present that encourages the likelihood of a solid relationship over time. In this way, much as a marriage contract both binds and frees partners to relax, a group therapy contract maximizes the likelihood that members and leaders can rely on the contract that they signed.

Section II

Psychotherapy With Couples in Groups

A group never changes the subject.

—J. Scott Rutan, PhD

4

Treatment Skills With Intimate Partners

For the first year after I met [my wife], I made love continuously. I mean, occasionally I got up to eat, but that was about it.

—A nostalgic husband

INTRODUCTION

How in the world do I help partners remember why they married when it seems years since they knew? How do I help heal the narcissistic injuries that cripple sensuality and create contempt? A couples group is only as effective as the couples involved and the clinical work accomplished (Figure 4.1). Clinical work is done with each couple in and outside the group. Clinical work precedes their entering the group and lasts beyond the last group meeting. Early work prepares couples to enter the group. Once couples leave the group to try their newly won skills, they still need ongoing clinical support to prevent relapse. This chapter reviews key concepts in working with couples both in and out of a group setting.

Couples work is a vast clinical body of thinking, practice, and research. Much of the pioneering work is found in the literature from family therapy (Keeney & Silverstein, 1986; Satir, 1967; Whitaker & Bumberry, 1988; Whitaker & Keith, 1981). Other work targets clinicians interested in the

71

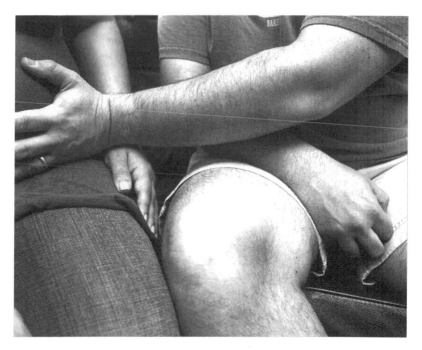

Figure 4.1   Trevor and Holly get acquainted with their unborn child. (Photograph by Nicholas Nixon. Copyright 2007. Used by permission of the photographer.)

marital unit (Bader & Pearson, 1988; Dicks, 1967, Fisher, 1994, 2004; Gottman, 1999; Gurman, 1985; Johnson & Greenberg, 1994; Markman, Stanley, & Bloomberg, 1994; Mitchell, 2002; Perel, 2006; Prager, 1995; Stanley, 2005; Stosny, 2005). Still other work comes out of the field of individual psychotherapy but can be integrated, with some variation, into ongoing work with couples (Bugental, 1981, 1984; Wexler & Rice, 1974; Rogers, 1957; Seligman, 2002; Truax & Carkhuff, 1967; Young & Klosko, 1994).

When I train colleagues, they tell me they need hands-on knowledge of clinical techniques, so I am providing them. In addition, I provide the philosophical foundations underlying the couples and couples group therapy and, to some extent, the group therapy that I do. In this chapter, I discuss my rationale for the therapeutic choices I have made for the couples with whom I work.

I begin with a short discussion of the principles of circular thinking and isomorphism in couples theory and then discuss the existential foundations of my work. After presenting some key concepts, I describe the intergenerational focus in the couples therapy. I discuss my existential and strategic-based view of the dialectic of human change and conclude by explaining briefly why and how I teach couples to think as systemically as family therapists. By the time someone graduates from a couples group, he or she often thinks more systemically about his or her life than some clinicians I have met who are trained in a model of psychotherapy that is individual in nature.

INDUCING CIRCULAR THINKING

Each year I teach the second-year psychiatry residents how to induce circular reasoning, and each year someone thanks me. Inducing circular-reasoning thinking is one of the simplest and most useful skills in a couples' therapist's repertoire (Selvini-Palazzoli, Boscolo, Cecchin, & Prata, 1980). It can be taught to a couple, a family, or a beginning family therapist. I learned it from Olga Silverstein in 1986, when I studied with her at Ackerman Family Institute.

It is useful to think of causality in human experience as circular, rather than linear. What is meant by this is the following: Instead of the usual thinking underlying most scientific thought and much of behavioral psychology—that A causes B, which causes C, and so on—it is useful to think in terms of a reactive process that involves A, B, and C. A has an impact on B, which is also influenced by C; B adjusts to A in a way that modifies (strengthens or lessens) the signals given out by A. B's "response" is the result of a series of quick and often minute exchanges between the participants in which each has the capacity to impact the reality substantially. The causality for the event that then occurs is interpersonal, systemic, and dependent on the views that A, B, and C have in relation to each other and to the reactive pattern among them.

Applying this paradigm to my work with couples means that I also teach them that all reality in psychotherapy is *relative* (not absolute) to the parties who view it and *interpersonal* in nature because it is dependent on the persons involved. Therefore, it follows that a view of reality that is relative and interpersonal can be shifted by the parties involved, and that any person in the system has the capacity to affect the reality greatly and therefore the behavior and thinking of anyone else in the system.

Moreover, I believe that couples need information about new ways to construct reality and that some couples are able to grasp the concepts presented previously if they are presented in a concrete and interesting manner. Therefore, as early as the initial consultation, I begin to educate couples about how to ask new questions about old problems. I begin to show them how the problem shifts from an impossible, earth-shattering dilemma to something more manageable once the view of the problem moves from a linear to a circular one. Further, I believe that until members of a couple are able to move to this circular view of relationships, a couple is severely hampered in its capacity to solve marital dilemmas on its own.

Trevor's high intelligence allowed him to manipulate concepts easily; however, he had never been exposed to training in systemic, interpersonal thinking. He was accustomed to training in linear causality, in which A causes B and B causes C. Early in the group he would ask questions like, "Why does it matter what Holly thinks about it? It's a good idea." I briefly explained that interpersonal reality is always relative and that causality is multifaceted. I trained him and the other members, as part of the group experience, to consider the impact of their behavior on their partners. I asked them to imagine what it would feel like to be their partners, and they were able to respond. Trevor was relieved to replace his black and white thinking with a way of viewing his marriage that allowed him to be closer to his wife much of the time.

Isomorphism in Treatment Modalities

Elsewhere, the principle of isomorphism is discussed as it applies to work within the group. The principle, which states that processes that operate at one level of functioning are simultaneously operating at other levels as well, is a useful way to understand the rationale behind the combination of in-group and out-of-group treatment that I use and recommend. Benefits at every level directly influence the other units: the individual, the couple, and the group.

Finally, working as a couple is a gift to the next generations. Again, by the principle of isomorphism, work done in one generation benefits other generations in a family. Thus, the integration of the couples work with group and individual work builds a psychotherapy momentum for the group and each of its members that is hard to duplicate when any single modality is utilized without the others.

74

AN EXISTENTIAL FOUNDATION FOR
THE PROCESS OF CHANGE

I offer clients an existential foundation within which to view the process of behavioral and interpersonal change. Through clinical interventions and my use of self, I teach and model a number of concepts basic to a way of being in the world, as well as to ways in which I believe people in couples and in families can experience constructive and lasting personal and interpersonal change.

Often, I rely on contributions from existential philosophy (Kaufmann, 1975; Nietzsche, 1960; Sartre, 1948b) and from philosopher–theologians (Buber, 1958; Tillich, 1952) as conceptual underpinnings to the work at hand. Within the professional mental health literature, I rely most heavily on the thinking of Whitaker (1989), Whitaker and Bumberry (1988), and Whitaker and Keith (1981), Bugental (1981, 1984), Watzlawick (1978, 1983, 1984), and Watzlawick, Weakland, and Fisch (1974), although each has been modified to work within my fast-paced, somewhat more cognitive, highly systemic model.

I have, on many occasions, assigned sophisticated clients some readings to do at home: David Schnarch's *Passionate Marriage* (1998), Helen Fisher's *Anatomy of Love* (1994), John Gottman's *The Seven Principles for Making Marriage Work* (1999), Victoria Collins's *Couples and Money* (1998), Milsten & Slowinski's *The Sexual Male* (1999), Steven Stosny's *You Don't Have to Take It Anymore* (2005), Shirley Glass's *Not "Just Friends"* (2004), and Patricia Evans's *The Verbally Abusive Relationship* (2003). These more recent works have not replaced earlier suggestions, including Napier and Whitaker's *The Family Crucible* (1978), Buber's *I and Thou* (1958), Fromm's *The Art of Loving* (1956), and Tillich's *The Courage to Be* (1952). Clients often report that the reading is worth the time and effort even though it is more demanding than the popular psychology they are used to finding on their own.

Existential psychotherapy is an extremely varied field with many, very individualistic thinkers. Yet there are some common unifying principles. I will discuss here three of the conceptual underpinnings especially important in my work with couples:

- Clients seek to be more of a person in an intimate context.
- Adult intimacy involves taking responsibility for the self.
- Clients need to exercise life choices.

Clients Seek to Be More of a Person in an Intimate Context

I agree with Whitaker and Keith (1981) that the goals of psychotherapy are to establish a sense of belonging, to provide the freedom for persons to individuate, and to increase personal and systemic creativity. Fundamentally, people enter psychotherapy to learn to be more of a person than they have been able to figure out from their life experience to date. Another way of saying this is that, although everyone seems to desire more intimacy than he or she has been able to achieve, the obstacles that he or she constructs maintain stability within the personality structure. Being more of a person means to free up new levels of energy and creativity by overcoming some of the obstacles constructed by oneself and by one's family. This, in turn, creates a sense of greater personal freedom without necessitating the same unsuccessful behaviors. Meaning is increased and the person or couple need no longer return to the earlier and frustrating modus operandi.

Adult Intimacy Involves Taking Responsibility for One's Actions

Intimacy is at its best for adults when each partner is able to take responsibility for his or her thoughts, feelings, and behavior in relation to the other person. Therefore, adult intimacy is best achieved when partners are skillful and careful in their communication with one another. This translates into learning to respect personal boundaries in being close to someone else, regardless of one's background.

This way of viewing intimacy also translates into the necessity for each person to learn how he or she feels, to learn how to communicate feelings, to learn to listen to the thoughts and feelings of another person, and to negotiate conflict in a respectful manner. These are skills that I teach couples.

Living Life Fully and Responsibly Entails Making Life Choices

No matter what happens in life, each person is faced with continual choices. On a large scale, big life choices belong to the person, barring unforeseen natural disasters and illness beyond one's control. People have to decide whether or when to divorce or separate, when or whether to have and raise children, and how to feed and care for their bodies and intellects.

I am not saying that people are to blame for the choices they make, but rather that it is part of living life fully for people to own their choices as a way of enjoying their pleasures and learning from their mistakes. Choices are often made on the basis of hidden existential conflicts echoed in the legacy inherited by children growing up in a family that was in a painful situation in the world. During childhood and adolescence, the powerful force of the family of origin, with all its beliefs, traditions, and adaptive styles handed down through generations, exerts its pull and shapes the person's beliefs about the ways in which decisions are to be made. Because I have these assumptions, I often magnify the existential theme for a couple who seem to be struggling with a common, everyday problem. To their surprise, drawing attention to the larger existential issue often opens new ways to "unstick" the everyday dilemma.

As an executive who traveled over an hour to and from work each day, Michael legitimately found himself unenthusiastic about helping with child care for his three teenage children. When the children were younger, Michael had slowly withdrawn from an active part in their parenting. Although he tried to help Margaret by getting angry with the children when they disobeyed her, his well-meaning attempt backfired. His children became first isolated, and then alienated, from him. He felt like a visitor in his own home. The level of conflict between Margaret and Michael rose as Margaret became increasingly overwhelmed in handling the children by herself. Interventions at the level of asserting the fairness of mutual parenting failed to impress Michael, who had become accustomed to being peripheral. However, when I began to discuss the existential significance of modeling effective coupling and parenting for the future lives of the children, Michael's intellect became engaged. Abashedly, he said that it had never occurred to him that he had responsibility for the way his children viewed marriage. He quickly began to grasp the power of presenting a united team for the children in a way that was both gentle and engaged. He and Margaret began family meetings in which issues were openly discussed. The family saw quick and deep progress once they conceptualized change at the existential level of significance that it deserved.

AN INTERGENERATIONAL FRAME FOR COUPLES WORK

The preceding few paragraphs already point to the second conceptual frame for my work with couples, which is intergenerational in nature. This conceptual frame has two important clinical consequences:

- Those who understand family history are not doomed to repeat it.
- Current couple's conflicts always relate to issues from each partner's family.

Those Who Understand Family History Are Not Doomed to Repeat It

An old adage says that those who do not study history are condemned to repeat it, but I have seen individuals and couples spontaneously correct dysfunctional interactional patterns. Nevertheless, when couples work with us, they are continually working with issues in their families of origin. No blame is placed on the family by the therapists, although many adults go through a period of intense anger and blaming as they realize that some of the problems they now experience were created before they knew any better. It is part of my work to assist each member of a couple in understanding the legacy received by the family in relation to values, ethics, communication styles, and gender role issues.

After individuals better understand their legacy—through direct discussion with family members, through bringing photos into therapy sessions, and through rethinking old assumptions—I enable the couple to make new and, I hope, more effective choices in the areas they want to change (Stone, 1988). These changes have an impact not only on their marriage and their own generation, but also on their children's generation and, at times, on the parental generation.

Current Couple Conflicts Always Relate to Issues From Each Partner's Family

Recent empirical research has confirmed what clinicians have long believed—that patterns of conflict in couples reflect patterns from families of origin. For example, Whitton et al. (2008) found that adolescents who experienced more hostility in their families of origin were more likely 17 years later to show hostility during marital conflict resolution. Despite its cynicism, I occasionally paraphrase a quip by Carl Whitaker and tell couples that there is no such thing as marriage. There are only emissaries from two families of origin, fighting for control of the next generation. After laughing at the ridiculous nature of this situation, couples often are able to put a conflict into a reality frame that enables them to problem solve in a new way.

Dwight had the benefit of understanding the dynamics of his nuclear family. They had been high achieving and could be unintentionally harsh in their opinions of him as a child. As a result, he sometimes found himself inadvertently critical of himself and of his wife. Diane found his criticism painful and anxiety generating, and she asked him to be more supportive and less worried about details. The couple found that, when they could discuss instances in which his tone and words felt critical to her could connect this dynamic to the family in which he grew up, it was easier for Dwight to contain his criticism and easier for Diane to withstand his cutting words.

RESISTANCE AS AN ALLY IN THERAPEUTIC CHANGE

From work done with Olga Silverstein at the Ackerman Family Therapy Institute, as well as from related readings in strategic family therapy, I have come to value the concept of dialectic between stability and change (Keeney & Ross, 1985). I believe that therapists need to introduce new elements into the change process gradually, testing to see if the couple is ready for increased change. Therapists also need to realize that couples will naturally work to maintain stability and balance by remaining unchanged. Resistance is not an enemy in psychotherapy, but rather a natural occurrence in the process of change for individuals, families, couples, and groups.

I see resistance as a friend to therapy, rather than a foe, because it represents the couple's need to remain stable and predictable. I believe that a solid therapeutic alliance between therapist and clients redirects resistance rather than doing battle with it. Resistance in therapy has a number of phases (J. M. Coché, 1990) and an awareness of the process of working with resistance enables the therapist to have a cognitive set toward

79

it, which allows a tracking of the phase of the resistance and thereby a control over moving the process along. After the initial consult, one can see three phases:

- **Joining and reframing.** The task here is to enable the couple to feel a connection with the therapist at the same time that the therapist sets limits on the boundaries of their experience together. Whitaker calls this phase the battle for structure (Neill & Kniskern, 1982).
- **Enabling people to feel deeply their fear of not changing.** People change when nothing else is left to do. The skill at this stage is basically to offer support and listening skills while the couple worry that they may be so stuck that couples therapy—and even couples group therapy—will not help.
- **Turning the corner.** After enabling people to connect intimately with their fear of not changing and to join others who are able to listen to them and to echo the themes they discuss, a freeing-up usually happens in relation to the issue that has proved frustrating. It is as if a therapeutic corner is turned. But, as one corner is turned, the resistance dance begins again because the next therapeutic corner is, indeed, just around the corner.

REQUIRING COMMUNICATION SKILLS TRAINING AS A PRECURSOR TO COUPLES GROUP PSYCHOTHERAPY

Communication skills preserve marriages and lead to more satisfying relationships. It is impossible to avoid communicating with a partner (i.e., there is never no communication in a marriage). For this reason, effective communication has been the subject of considerable research. Strong evidence indicates that good communication is associated with good relationships (e.g., Litzinger & Gordon, 2005; Sevier, Eldridge, Jones, Doss, & Christensen, 2008).

John Gottman and colleagues have conducted much of the work in this area (e.g., Gottman, 1993; Gottman & Krokoff, 1989). They used a wide range of laboratory techniques to observe couples' interactions; based on patterns that they observed, they were able to make remarkably accurate predictions about which couples would stay together and which would not. Important principles emerging from this work include the following five points:

1. Stable relationships require about five positive communications for every negative communication. This ratio can be achieved in different ways—for example, a lot of total affective communication ("volatile" couples) or little total affective communication ("avoidant" couples). However, positive communication must predominate (Gottman, 1993).

Trevor would have done anything to make his marriage perfect. He loved Holly tremendously and felt like a really lucky guy to have married her. As a man who respected numbers, Trevor found it illuminating to know that he needed to work toward five positive interactions for every negative interaction. That goal was something he could shoot for. He later reported that his averages were going in the right direction, and Holly happily agreed.

---

2. The expression of anger is not necessarily bad for a relationship. Anger tends to be expressed when a couple is experiencing strife, but over the course of the relationship, the direct and honest expression of anger has a relationship-preserving effect (Gottman & Krokoff, 1989). More harmful than anger appear to be Gottman's "Four Horsemen of the Apocalypse": criticism, defensiveness, contempt, and "stonewalling" (Gottman, Coan, Carrère, & Swanson, 1998). Additional research by other groups (e.g., Kim, Capaldi, & Crosby, 2007) has confirmed that anger expression per se is not damaging to a relationship. As later research demonstrated, the absence of affect in general predicts eventual divorce (Gottman & Levenson, 2002).

3. Active listening, which was thought to be an important couples communication skill, was not found to characterize successful couples conflict communication. As Gottman and colleagues conclude, expecting couples to practice active listening (e.g., reflecting emotion, paraphrasing) may set an expectation of a skill level that a couple in conflict may find hard to reach (Gottman et al., 1998). There has been a vigorous debate about this conclusion by Gottman and colleagues, especially by Stanley and colleagues (e.g., Stanley, Bradbury, & Markman, 2000); they argue that training in active listening skills is indeed helpful for couples, citing as evidence their psychoeducation program that includes an active listening component (Markman, Renick, Floyd, Stanley, & Clements, 1993; Schilling,

Baucom, Burnett, Allen, & Ragland, 2003; see also a meta-analysis by Butler & Wampler, 1999). However, their program includes other elements; currently, there is insufficient evidence to state definitively whether training in active listening per se promotes relationship health (Halford, Markman, Kline, & Stanley, 2003; McArthur & Russell, 2003).

Many clinicians continue to teach active listening skills, and couples at the Coché Center find this training very beneficial. Although heightened conflict makes empathic listening difficult, the skill can be learned and taught quickly to couples as a common language. The language of intimacy is the language of feelings. I train couples to find ways to return to a nervous system at rest before they attempt to listen to the position of the other. The ability to empathize with another person and compassionately absorb his or her point of view in no way indicates agreement with that person's position. I teach our couples to listen with their hearts to their partners' viewpoints before they indicate agreement or disagreement with the view expressed. Marital partners are able to listen to the meaning behind the words of the partner, whether or not they agree with the position at hand.

In this sense, I teach couples to express respectful attention to the feelings of their partner. I have found that couples are able to be quite self-disciplined in their ability to understand a position with which they disagree. Further, once the partner's position is understood, an honest and heartfelt discussion can allow a couple to reach agreement in areas that were previously conflictual. Respectful listening and expressing feelings from the heart go a long way toward increasing intimacy. I agree with Gottman (1994) that it is impossible to discuss and listen to feelings from the partner until both are calm. Deep breathing, self-soothing, and mindfulness exercises can be helpful to return to a calm state that enables respectful, intimate communication.

4. Patterns of withdrawal during conflict are predictive of poor relationship quality and divorce (Caughlin & Huston, 2002; Stanley, Markman, & Whitton, 2002). The tendency to withdraw may be especially problematic when one partner demands interaction and the other seeks to escape (Heavey, Christensen, & Malamuth, 1995). Although withdrawal is more common among male than female partners (e.g., Christensen, Eldridge, Catta-Preta, Lim, & Santagata, 2006), a substantial proportion of females also reports exhibiting this behavior (Stanley et al., 2002), and female withdrawal also is associated with worse relationship outcomes

(Roberts, 2000). Therefore, greater engagement between the couple during discussion of conflicts may lead to enhanced relationship satisfaction and endurance.

5. Men who reject the influence of their wives are more likely to see their relationships deteriorate (Gottman et al., 1998). Escalating negative communication often seems to be an attempt by men to "push back" at their wives' requests, suggestions, or demands. Couples were more likely to divorce when men (but not women) refused to accept influence from their partners.

The preceding five principles have been integrated into many approaches to couples therapy both in and outside a group, and they can be useful in all intimate relationships.

Colleagues have expressed great interest in integrating psychoeducational skills with clinical treatment. It is necessary for couples to be very clear that psychoeducation can be exceptionally valuable, but is not the same as psychotherapy. Many behavioral scientists have developed research-based programs offering communication skills workbooks, Web sites, and DVDs in user-friendly formats. A description of communication skills is covered briefly in Appendix C. Readers will find many supplements and can choose among a number of excellent resources.

Another field useful in the work of couples involves collaborative as opposed to competitive conflict resolution. First, research indicates that collaborative conflict resolution correlates with greater relationship satisfaction (Greeff & De Bruyne, 2000). Second, couples can be taught that it is all right to express anger and that, in fact, anger is not always a negative emotion. On the contrary, its expression can point to areas of the relationship that need to change. In this regard, men can be counseled on the importance of a willingness to accept influence from their wives because their most important relationship may depend on this willingness.

Third, although it is not clear that some of the elements of active listening (e.g., paraphrasing the partner's position) are required for successful conflict resolution, couples may benefit from seeking a style of conflict resolution that includes nonverbal signs of comprehension and respect (e.g., head nodding or allowing the partner to finish speaking before responding). Finally, couples can be educated about the withdraw and demand dynamic and its effects on the relationship. Both partners can work toward greater engagement by resisting urges to flee from or to "chase away" one's partner.

Margaret would get very quiet when she was angry. She was so quiet that Michael did not know that she was unhappy with him. She would withdraw into her thoughts and worry. Once she knew that he really cared about how she felt and wanted to know about her emotional reactions to him, she found it a little easier to be more verbal about her unhappiness. The couple has learned to take time to talk when both are calm, and it has really helped.

The preceding points demonstrate that the level of complexity in couples work ranges from basic psychoeducational skill building to complex handling of sexual dysfunction and attachment abuse. Paradoxically, years spent in individual therapy by one partner have calcified the reality frame at the level of "it's all his or her problem." Getting couples unstuck often means teaching adults to know what they feel, how to listen actively to someone else, and how to communicate clearly. Part of my assessment procedure is an assessment of these factors.

The following steps are useful in increasing the fluency in couples communication:

- Teach partners to recognize what they feel.
- Teach couples to listen actively to the partner.
- Teach partners to communicate clearly and carefully.
- Teach couples to negotiate differences respectfully.

These steps in increasing the fluency of couples in communicating with one another are adapted from schools of humanistic psychotherapy (Wexler & Rice, 1974; Rogers, 1957; Truax & Carkhuff, 1967) and from Satir's (1967, 1988) work in couples communication.

The first two steps comprise a kind of basic language course in feelings and empathy. I train people to learn how to deal with what they feel by teaching a four-step model to identify the feeling physiologically, to label it with words, to consider the alternatives in acting on the feeling, and, finally, to handle the feeling in a preplanned manner. I may even hand out a "crib sheet" of about 300 words that name feelings in the English language. Although the sheet began as a spoof on humanistic psychotherapy, I have found that some very task-oriented clients find the assistance very helpful and have been known to carry the sheet with them for those situations in which the word describing the feeling escapes the partner who wishes to communicate more effectively with the spouse.

Using the *Communication Workbook* (J. M. Coché, 2004), I teach people to know and describe how they feel and I teach them empathy skills. These skills draw on earlier work by Carl Rogers and Virginia Satir, among others. Couples tell us that this very basic human skill allows them to feel understood by their partner, sometimes for the first time. Although the skill is easy to teach and simple to learn, it is very hard to use when there is conflict. Hence, the couples group becomes a way to deal with the specific concerns of each couple to enable them to achieve the level of mutual understanding that creates intimacy.

Once the other three skills have been developed, couples have a foundation on which they can negotiate, with mutual respect, differences along the many dimensions that adults disagree about in an intimate relationship. Here I borrow more from the business community in teaching negotiating skills and I create exercises that fit the group as needed.

These four basic steps cut across the usual areas of trouble (sex, money, children, etc.) and provide process tools by which couples can build stronger relationships within themselves and between themselves and other group members. This kind of skill building increases the likelihood that, after therapy is completed, the marriage will be one in which change is maintained in the desired direction because the tools to maintain the change have been internalized.

As an executive, Michael was accustomed to problem solving quickly and effectively. Margaret was appreciative of Michael's ability to cut through verbiage in helping her discipline the children. She was less appreciative when Michael applied executive problem-solving skills before even listening to what was troubling her. It felt to Margaret like Michael was solving a problem that he did not really understand. She needed to know that her words could hit the air and that Michael would help her by absorbing what she was trying to say. But every time Margaret spoke with Michael about this, he would problem solve her concern and thereby seemingly dismiss it. When Michael learned that he had to come to a 6-hour course on communication skills, he condescendingly mentioned that this had been part of his executive training at work, implying that he did not really need any training at all. I affirmed the necessity of learning the language of coupling at the same time as one's partner did. I explained that, even though these skills had been covered in a different setting, it was necessary for Margaret and

85

*Michael to integrate the skills into their marriage in a very personal man-
ner. This position made sense to Michael, and the couple learned the skills
with the other couples. Unlike many couples who do not practice the skills
once they are learned, Margaret and Michael pulled out their workbooks and
practiced the intimacy loop and the business of coupling with one another.
With no extra therapy, they became adept at getting through areas that had
been previously problematic for them. Not only did Margaret feel heard,
but Michael and Margaret together also became formidable problem solvers
once they were able truly to listen to one another. Often they did not agree,
and the differences between them contributed to creative problem solving in
family issues.*

GENDER ISSUES IN COUPLES DEVELOPMENT

Much of the clinical work in couples and group psychotherapy is founded
on concepts based in general systems theory as applied to adult male and
female development. The field of adult development as a source of theory
and research has played a central role in thinking about members of my
couples as individuals and in partnership with one another. These related
fields of adult male development and adult female development have
yielded clinically valuable findings for conceptualizing and treating my
couples. A great deal of the work in these fields has been concerned with
gender differences in developmental phases within adulthood for men
and for women.

Levinson, Darrow, Klein, Levinson, and McKee (1978) and Vaillant
(1977) added to my understanding of the centrality of career identity
for adult males; Gilligan (1982) and Miller (1976) began to alert us to the
value of further exploration of women's ways of knowing, feeling, and
experiencing what life brings. Work by Judith Coché on female therapists as clients (1984) and on the impact of roles on family development
(1980) indicated the centrality of these concepts in an earlier clinical
formulation.

Current thinking and writing continues to explore gender issues
in couples and group work with ongoing enthusiasm. These ongoing
shifts in my knowledge base as a social scientist were soon reflected
in clinical guidelines in gender-sensitive family therapy (J. M. Coché,
1984; McGoldrick, Anderson, & Walsh, 1989; Walters, Carter, Papp, &
Silverstein, 1988). Other theorists have contributed to my understanding

of the role of gender specifically in the couples group setting (Feld & Urman-Klein, 1993). The result of this remarkable deluge in extending my reality frame to encompass contemporary views of role and gender in marriage has been incorporated into my work with relief and enthusiasm.

Over the last 15 years of the couples groups, dramatic shifts in gender roles have become part of most couples' experiences. A body of work on emotional abuse in marriage (P. Evans, 2003) has created an imperative for respectful communications between the genders. Huge shifts in the percentage of women who work and who achieve high job status and career remuneration have made it more normal for the female member of the couple to be the higher earner.

Early in the marriage, Antonia was able to earn more than Patrick. When the first baby was born, it was natural for Patrick to stay home while Antonia continued in a high-paying job. In the tiny community in which they lived, this arrangement was highly unusual. It was hard for Antonia and Patrick to talk about the discomfort they felt about the woman earning more than the man. As the second child moved into latency, Antonia wanted to stay home more. Patrick had received advanced training and was appointed to a position of high responsibility. For some period of time, the role reversal diminished as Patrick became the high earner. In more recent years, both Patrick and Antonia have been experiencing high job success. Although Patrick continues to earn more, the high career status afforded to Antonia allows the couple to think of themselves as equal partners.

To summarize, any therapist's couples' work is a rich and dynamic tapestry, woven from philosophical beliefs and values, personal and professional experience with couples therapy, previous training in therapy, and the wish to give couples practical skills within a highly abstract philosophical framework. Within this model, the philosophical framework presented here is based on concepts integrated by us from the fields of existential and strategic family therapy, as well as psychodynamic and humanistic ideas.

5

Building Cohesiveness in Couples and Groups

As much as I hate to come here, I really do look forward to it.

—A woman changing

INTRODUCTION

Intimacy between members is the hallmark of a cohesive unit. A group in which members can share important aspects of their personal lives has to be cohesive in order to make such sharing possible. As the group members become more open in their honest disclosure of deeply felt emotions or details of their private lives, their group becomes increasingly cohesive. The mutual reinforcement of sharing and cohesiveness is one of the distinguishing properties of a well-functioning group.

The same is true for couples. The cohesive marital unit is one in which partners openly share intimate notions, thoughts, feelings, and memories. As more of this sharing occurs, partners feel close and strongly bonded to each other. Where there are secrets and a refusal to let the other participate in one's inner thoughts and feelings, there are always distance and isolation between the partners. Given that the same circularity between cohesiveness and honesty can be observed in couples as in groups, we shall discuss the issue of cohesiveness in the group simultaneously with that in a couple.

Cohesiveness can be described as the degree to which the group is attractive to its members (Sherif & Sherif, 1969). Phrased differently, cohesiveness is the degree of the desire of the members to be in the group. Thus, cohesiveness is measurable by the expressions of the group members regarding how much they enjoy the group and are glad to be in it. Conversely, a group in which members complain a great deal is not likely to be very cohesive. A less obvious yet still useful yardstick is the eagerness with which people come to group. Are they on time or early? Are they willing to go through particular hardships like bad weather, car trouble, and so forth in order to attend? Finally, the sentiment of not wanting to leave group (especially in the later sessions) can give an indication of cohesiveness.

In this way, cohesiveness, which is sometimes seen as some mysterious force that holds the group together, becomes much less mysterious. The presence of this force is noticeable in a group and the leader is well advised to stay tuned to its manifestations and to any indications of its absence.

WHY IS COHESIVENESS IMPORTANT IN GROUPS?

Cohesiveness is crucial to effective group functioning (Nobler, 1986). Research in group dynamics and group psychotherapy has shown that cohesive groups are more effective in reaching their stated goals (e.g., Budman et al., 1989; Joyce, Piper, & Ogrodniczuk, 2007; Marmarosh, Holtz, & Schottenbauer, 2005; for a meta-analysis see C. R. Evans & Dion, 1991). Cohesive groups foster not only more openness but also more altruism and helping behaviors. In turn, the increase in altruism and openness enhances cohesiveness.

Group psychotherapy outcome ultimately depends on these factors. If clients are to benefit from their group or couples therapy experience, it has to be one in which members explore their thoughts, feelings, and beliefs in some depth. People will do this only if they feel a sufficient degree of safety and if they choose to attend and remain present in the group.

SIX BUILDING BLOCKS OF COHESIVE GROUPS

In order to enhance and safeguard the cohesiveness of a group, the leader can employ a number of strategies, which will be described later in this chapter. Before discussing these strategies, however, it is worthwhile to examine a number of group properties that are typical of a cohesive group and will emerge if leader and group members cooperate in bringing these properties to life. Although the leader has a great deal to do with the generation of these building blocks of cohesiveness, ultimately, the group must participate in the task and must curtail covert or unconscious efforts to block cohesiveness. This is harder than it sounds.

It also is important to note that group member behaviors that facilitate cohesiveness may vary across the developmental stage of the group (Budman, Soldz, Demby, Davis, & Merry, 1993). Behaviors that foster cohesion in later stages, such as intense emotional expression, may not promote cohesion in early stages of the group before group members feel comfortable with one another. Conversely, behaviors that foster cohesion in early stages when members are just getting acquainted, such as presenting "issues about their lives *outside* the group" (Budman et al., 1993, p. 211), are not associated with cohesion in later group stages.

The following are the six major building blocks of cohesive groups:

- the safe harbor of the group;
- acceptance;
- assumption that the power to change is within the couple or the group;
- modeling of honesty;
- universality; and
- humor.

The Safe Harbor of the Group

In order to risk self-disclosure, group members have to feel reasonably safe. They have to have some sense that the other members, and especially their spouses, will not attack them for what they disclose and will not use the information against them.

Sex was hard for Dwight to talk about because it was hard for Dwight to perform to his unrealistically high standard of achievement. He referred to "climbing the mountain of orgasm" as a way of indicating his anxiety around achievement. For months, he balked at Diane's overtures to discuss this very important topic in a group setting. The presence of Dr. Julian Slowinski, a male sex therapist, as the co-lead of the group at that time, enabled Dwight to feel a greater sense of safety. Julian and I decided to break the group into two gender-based minigroups in order to give each gender the opportunity to speak freely. For 1 hour, I led the women in a frank discussion of frustrations with themselves or their partners in their sexual lives. Julian met with the men in a different room and invited them to speak frankly about their sexual concerns. Dwight was relieved to find that he was in good company and that others were also sensitive to implied criticism from their wives around sexual performance. The safety of a male subgroup enabled Dwight to find a safe harbor for the toughest problem in his marriage. He was able to bring his concerns back to the group as a whole from that point on.

One strategy that contributes to the members' feeling that the group is a safe harbor is the clear explication of the group policies at the beginning of the group experience. The rules regarding confidentiality especially help the members to know that their contributions will be handled with care. In this atmosphere, the leader will be able to encourage risk taking and self-disclosure. Greater self-disclosure has been shown to lead to greater group cohesion (Kirshner, Dies, & Brown, 1978) and to be perceived by observers as indicating greater group cohesion (Stokes, Fuehrer, & Childs, 1983). The sharing of actual here-and-now emotions—for example, the anxiety felt by most participants in the first session—will help members to understand that such sharing not only is safe but also contributes to a discovery of a shared emotion and thus to greater cohesiveness. Empirical research has demonstrated the effectiveness of here-and-now (vs. "there-and-then") disclosure at promoting group cohesion (Slavin, 1993).

The building blocks of cohesiveness are crucial to the welfare and therapeutic power of a group. Becoming a safe harbor for emotion, feeling acceptance for the members, tracing the power to change to the group itself, modeling honesty, identifying universal themes of human lives, and good humor combine to create an elixir for interpersonal and internal personal change that increases human life satisfaction.

Acceptance

Related to the concept of self-disclosure is the concept of acceptance. People in the group need to feel confident that their group members accept them. This does not mean that the other people in the group have to accept or approve of everything the member says unconditionally. On the contrary, members can be and often are quite annoyed, irritated, or perturbed about a certain behavior that is being described or shown in the group. Hopefully, however, there is still a basic acceptance of that person as a group member.

The thought should come across that the group still wants this person in its midst even though he or she may show some very antagonistic or even socially unacceptable behaviors in and outside the group. In this way, the acceptance of the group members for one another models the acceptance that marriage partners feel despite the inevitable antagonisms that develop when partners cohabitate. Partners often contemplate divorce or some way to get the personal freedom they need within a marriage. I am unsure to whom to credit this one liner, but at some point someone in a group said to me: "I never think about divorcing my partner ... I may contemplate murder on occasion, but never divorce." In this way, members of a group accept and welcome each other, despite or because of who they are.

The main strategy for the group leaders is to prevent criticism from becoming a dominant tone in the group. Leaders can help members to learn to distinguish between constructive feedback and taking potshots. Although criticism of people's actions may at times be desirable and necessary, it should not permeate the group to the point that people become afraid of self-disclosure or interaction with others. Sometimes, this requires giving people instruction in such a way that the feedback does not come across as a moral condemnation.

Because Dwight was anxious, he often seemed excessively involved with details in the group. It made members nervous when he pulled out an index card and took notes on snippets of interchange that seemed valuable to him. Members were not sure what he was writing, and their body language was often critical as first the pencil and then the card appeared. "What are you doing?" was asked in a tone of voice that felt like an attack on Dwight's capacity for critical judgment. Rather than allowing Dwight to become defensive, Julian often intervened by commenting that the notes might not feel comfortable to others. Dwight would stop taking notes, and the ease of other members was restored.

Assumption That the Power to Change Is
Within the Couple or the Group

People come into couples therapy because they are in pain and want to change. Naturally, there is a concomitant resistance to making changes. It is the task of the therapist to facilitate those forces within each person that are pushing toward constructive change. In doing so, the therapist has to avoid the fantasy that he or she can actively change a person. The same goes for the group. The impetus to make changes and strive toward greater intimacy and honesty is already present in the group, though the group is also laced with fear. If the leader can deal with this resistance to change in a creative manner, the group can make changes that will have their parallel in the members' personal lives and marriages.

At one point, I designed an exercise to work with sexual scripting in the family of origin of the members. I led the visual imagery correctly and was astonished to find that the group dealt with family-of-origin issues that did not explicitly relate to the task of considering early family messages for sexual scripting. As I contemplated my work, I realized that I had enthusiastically placed my own schedule for change on a group that needed to work historically in general ways before it would work on sexual history in a group setting. The power to change was clearly in the group and my leadership needed to adjust to their timing.

Most importantly, there are ways in which the leaders communicate either the belief that the power to change lies in the group or the opposite fantasy of omnipotence—that is, the belief that the leaders can produce the change. If the group is convinced that it has the power to change with merely some assistance from the leader, a more cohesive and actively working group will result.

Modeling Honesty

In order for the group to be cohesive, leaders must be honest with each other and with the group. Any kind of falsehood will be sensed and reacted to negatively by the group. If the leaders communicate to the group that it has the power to change its rules in a democratic fashion, but then block all the changes that the group wants to make, an atmosphere of resentment and mistrust will arise quickly. Likewise, the group will be very distrustful of co-leaders who interact with one another in an unreal, phony way.

Clearly, the matter of honesty between the leaders is as important in a couples group as it is in a couple. Pittman (1989) writes about the model of honesty as the foundation in a marriage. We agree that honesty is especially necessary when it is painful to the couple.

Universality

Groups work better together if participants know that others in the group are going through experiences similar to theirs. Knowing that one is not alone in facing a difficult marital problem helps the couple feel at home in the group. The group support enables couples to work hard at finding a solution to their problems, frequently with the help of those in the group who are struggling with similar issues. The universality in a couples group begins with problems in a marriage; all couples have them. All couples have to deal at some time with certain marital issues that we call "the universals of marriage" (J. M. Coché, 2004).

The other kind of universality, which also greatly contributes to cohesiveness, is the common struggle with a current group problem. Whether this is anxiety at the beginning of the group or discomfort at the point of a group crisis, the knowledge that others in the group are troubled by the same problem and are equally intent to work it through helps the members feel more committed to the group.

Humor

Just as much as a group needs sadness and tears of honest confrontation of difficult problems, it also needs the comic relief from humor and laughter (Bloch, Browning, & McGrath, 1983). Frequently, a couple is helped by a hilarious parody of their incessant repetitive fights more than by repetitive confrontation of the same absurd interaction. However, it is important to watch out that the parody and humor, even though biting, are not disrespectful and do not give a couple the impression that their problem is not being taken seriously. "Accidents" in this direction happen. A couple that has a mirror held up to it in a comical way occasionally takes offense initially. However, if the group can simultaneously communicate its caring for this couple, the bite will be effective and the humor can have its therapeutic effect. Such an experience frequently turns out to be a strong cohesiveness builder.

Humor is also a central ingredient in many of the structured experiences. A good number of these can be successfully conducted only if the group members maintain a sense of humor about them. If they do, they experience a very positive and enjoyable way to learn something important. At times during the life of the group, Trevor's sarcasm would bounce off Spencer's understated wry humor to produce peals of laughter from all involved. This elixir permitted tough confrontation during other parts of the life of the group and allowed all to benefit.

LEADERSHIP SKILLS THAT ENHANCE COHESIVENESS

A frequent concern of the professionals attending our workshops centers around the skills involved in building cohesiveness. It seems hard to build cohesiveness in a group of couples because the couple is so powerful. Actually, it is easy as long as leaders have expertise in both family therapy and group therapy. Here, the skills of the leaders can be doubly useful: While they concentrate on building a cohesive working group, they create a therapeutic community that simultaneously models the qualities of a successfully intimate and cohesive marriage.

Some important group leadership skills that enhance cohesiveness include:

- communicating the leaders' belief in the group;
- prepositioning;
- employing structured exercises;
- enabling group celebrations and teaming;
- distributing leaders' attention among all couples; and
- encouraging constructive self-disclosure.

Leaders Communicate Their Belief in the Group

Leaders demonstrate their belief in the group in a variety of ways. If they go out of their way for the group, make sure that the group begins and ends on time, manage to get to the group despite weather and other calamities, and help members to overcome their difficulties in getting to the group, they are sending a message: This group is important to us. If, conversely, they cancel for reasons that sound unimportant, come late, or appear disinterested, group members will follow their lead and develop a careless attitude about the group. Even as early as in the preparation for the group, the leaders can sound convincing and enthusiastic, or perfunctory. This early impression can swing members' attitudes and make the group seem appealing or unappealing.

"Prepositioning"—A Leadership Skill

For years, we have informally referred to the connecting of people in the group as "prepositioning" because prepositions function to connect one part of a thought with another in a sentence. The group leaders formulate connecting terms (like the prepositions in grammatical structures) that demonstrate to the members how their issues are related to those of others in the group. Similarities and differences, transferences, subgroupings, and hierarchical relationships can all be highlighted to help members feel the invisible lines between themselves and others in the group.

For this, some groups need no help from their leaders; it comes naturally to them and they virtually sparkle with frequent expressions such as, "That's exactly what we do, too!" Other groups need lots of help to see the connections. Here the leaders' knowledge of the couples in the group comes into play and formulating the prepositions turns into an art form. Prepositioning can take the form of merely pointing out similarities in the problems with which two or more couples may be struggling, or it can rely on more sophisticated strategies such as helping people see the complementarity in their mutual struggles. In the latter case, a person may be struggling with an issue represented by a group member who responds in kind.

Spencer has worked in sales at a wholesale department store for over 10 years. Anxious about achievement, Spencer prefers to "play it safe" and enjoy his free time. His first wife divorced him in part because she considered his underachievement to place a burden on her for increased earnings. Patrick also did not earn for his level of ability—in this case, due to an undiagnosed learning disability that he confused with general intellectual dullness. Robyn and Antonia, married to these two bright and underachieving men, sought treatment initially in part to find ways to help their family finances reflect the capacity for earning that their husbands were not achieving when they entered treatment. Patrick had diagnosed his learning disability and had discovered that he could succeed in highly technical mechanical operations. Hence, by the time Spencer met Patrick, treatment had helped Patrick achieve high earnings as well as management training. Likewise, Michael had advanced solidly into executive management within his not-for-profit corporation and was invested in helping Spencer advance to the level of his ability. This theme of male underachievement ran throughout the group, surfacing as any of the members repeatedly invited Spencer to work on his "job thing." Once this connection was established, leaders needed do no more to ensure that Spencer work on his issues. Wife Robyn was joined by other members in raising the issue in the group, forcing Spencer to address it head on month after month. Both Spencer and Robyn were relieved to find that this group work enabled Spencer to move ahead within his chosen career.

Employing Structured Exercises

We find that structured exercises that promote cohesiveness can be of special value early in the life of a group. This can be done in a variety of ways. Research in group relations (e.g., Sherif & Sherif, 1969) has shown that the cohesiveness of a group can be enhanced by purposeful common activities. We have found that sharing, fun, and deep emotional experiences have the most power.

Promote sharing. In the beginning stages of a couples group, exercises that encourage people to share data about themselves in a somewhat formalized way speed up the process of getting to know the other people in the group. Going-around activities are the most natural way to do so and everyone in the group takes a turn to respond to instructions such as, "Introduce yourself" or "Tell us what it is you want to get out of this group. How can the group help you?"

Another sharing exercise comes about quite naturally. In the second group session, we ask couples to share with the group what they wrote in response to specific questions on their group goals. With the friendly eyes of other couples across the room, members find it easier to move on to the more painful questions such as, "What are the major issues in the marriage now?" Giving each person a chance to present his or her view of the marriage encourages self-disclosure, helps members to get to know each other, and avoids monopolization by the more verbal members.

Promote fun. Having a common enjoyable learning experience greatly enhances a group's sense of cohesiveness. Conducting an enjoyable exercise merely for the fun of it is a risky venture. People may enjoy the exercise at first (thus, it will increase cohesiveness), but they may soon believe that they are wasting their time and that the group is not addressing serious issues. On the other hand, planning a group exercise that packages some significant learning in a delightful shell not only deepens the learning but also creates a common group memory, which the group will occasionally remember as a part of its history.

Common moving experiences. As the group matures, members will share more and more profound feelings. Love, hate, pain, and dread are openly discussed; narratives of painful experiences punctuate a session. Frequently, the telling of experiences is not planned at all; however, when it happens, it is a sign of the trust, maturity, and cohesiveness of the group.

During the course of one group's life, Holly became pregnant, miscarried, became pregnant again, and gave birth to a baby girl, Kat. Due to logistics and finances, Kat attended the group for most of her first year of life. The group loved Kat. Dr. Galbraith and I loved to hold Kat during group breaks. Antonia and Diane bounced her on their knee during the group, to relieve Holly and Trevor from baby care. Robyn was moved to see Holly become successfully pregnant because she had suffered a traumatic miscarriage in an earlier marriage. This common moving experience bonded Holly and Robyn, enabling Robyn to do depth work in the group on her loss of an unborn child. A year later, when Robyn became pregnant, the joy for both couples was palpable in the group. Both leaders and members were moved by the experience as two healthy babies became part of the group history. At the final meeting of this group, two baby girls joined their parents in an unforgettable 6-hour experience.

Enabling Group Celebrations

Many groups will spontaneously celebrate birthdays, anniversaries, births, etc. Sometimes, people will bring in food and in that way let the celebrant know that the group cares about the special occasion and wants to share in the joy. Celebrations should, however, not be forced. I encourage the festivity if it is initiated by the group and is kept in a frame that does not detract from the therapeutic goal of the group.

Leaders Distribute Attention Among All Couples

A group in which people feel that one person, couple, or segment of the group is getting too much attention will soon become disgruntled about this situation. Whether this arises from the activities of a monopolizer or because the leaders (perhaps unconsciously) favor some participants over others, it is a phenomenon that definitely undermines cohesiveness.

At times, some unevenness arises because a couple is in a kind of permanent crisis and appears to need a lot of attention, perhaps to keep from separating or divorcing. At these times, the leaders need to be particularly watchful. At first, the group is likely to rally around this couple, thereby rewarding its crisis-laden style of interacting, and the group rally builds cohesiveness. After a few sessions, however, the group will become dissatisfied and the members' desire to be there will drop sharply (see Chapter 6 for more on this topic). At that point, the leaders need to make special efforts to bring the whole group together and to reengage the rest without disregarding the couple in crisis. Sometimes, a frank discussion about this situation is the best strategy.

Encouraging Constructive Self-Disclosure

Research in the field of patient self-disclosure has shown that a positive tone of self-disclosure is more therapeutically effective than public self-criticism, especially if this torture is prolonged (E. Coché, Polikoff, & Cooper, 1980). It is sometimes desirable to conduct exercises that give group members the opportunity to shine or even brag. It is certainly valuable and builds cohesiveness to focus occasionally on people's competence and to give others in the group a chance to get to know the sparkling sides of a couple as well as the less attractive ones.

Focusing on the positive in people's self-disclosures does not mean that one avoids confrontation. Where it is indicated, the leaders will still need to hold up a mirror to the group members regarding their behavior inside and outside the group—or encourage the group to do so. That, after all, is one of the jobs of good group leaders. I am merely advising against the repetitive and therapeutically useless public self-flagellations to which depressives are especially prone. I want to encourage some enthusiastic exercises, especially early on in a group's life.

THE REWARDS OF COHESIVENESS

Groups that are cohesive are a pleasure to lead. Usually, they are earnest and hardworking, yet still able to have fun and an occasional good laugh. Members have a sense of purpose and feel that they are participating in something that is valuable and helpful to them. Thus, they are eager to be there and get down to work.

This thought was expressed most eloquently by one of our members who, in the last session of his group year, was participating in a termination exercise in which we asked the group participants to think of farewell gifts for the other members (persons, couples, and the group as a whole). To express his affection for the group and his sense of the importance it had for him, he responded, "I'm giving this group my gift of perfect attendance."

101

6

Making the Most of the Stages of Group Development

It might be better for me to come back and regret it than not to come back and regret it.

—Client in a group (June, 1988)

INTRODUCTION

Groups have developmental stages very much like the stages of human development. A group has to go through certain processes, which repeat themselves as a group progresses from its first meeting to a working stage of development (Bennis & Shephard, 1956; Bion, 1960; Thelen, 1954). Stages are, to some degree, predictable. Frequently, they have marker events by which one can tell that a group has reached a stage or is moving from one stage to the next. Stages imply a certain developmental task that the group has to master.

Often the atmosphere in the group will convey to the leaders that the group is struggling with such a task. Understanding these tasks and working with them maximizes the effects of the group. Thus, if a group is dealing with issues of joining and acceptance, the leader is ill advised to focus on mutuality and intimacy in the group; those issues belong to later stages. Instead, it is advantageous to help the group clarify the current stage task and guide the group in its search for stage-appropriate solutions to its issues.

From our clinical work and our knowledge of the literature, we believe that a number of repetitive patterns can best be understood as developmental stages (Feld, 2003; Kirschenbaum & Glinder, 1972). Our way of organizing them is, at this point, still tentative and awaiting experimental verification. However, we believe that the stage sequence as described here provides a useful way of looking at group development and can help in understanding group phenomena that would otherwise be quite puzzling. This sequential course assumes that the group is closed ended and lasts an adequate number of sessions; thus, it will not be accurate for a short-term couples group or for an open-ended one.

Throughout the life of a group, a dialectical dance occurs between the forces of therapeutic progress and those of stability or resistance. No one yields old patterns gladly, be they ever so painful. Therefore, resistance is a major issue for the duration of the year. Interestingly enough, however, resistance takes on different forms in the different developmental stages. In the following discussion, we will take a look at these forms of resistance as we discuss the stages one by one.

STAGES IN GROUP DEVELOPMENT

The five major stages in the development of the group are

- joining;
- beginning working phase;
- group crisis or dissatisfaction;
- intensive working phase; and
- termination.

Joining

The first phase of the beginning couples group we call the *joining stage.* In the first few sessions, people in the group show much concern with acceptance and fear of not being accepted. A great deal of the anxiety experienced by people in the first session is reflective of a fear of being rejected. Some of the surprising behaviors shown by some group members in the first session can be explained as new members' attempts to cope with this anxiety as best they can. Of course, because people under stress tend to overutilize their preferred defense mechanism, the talkative person chats more and the shy person even less in the first session and people may, in fact, end up showing themselves from their least favorable side in the session. In other words, a member frequently demonstrates the areas in the self that need work through the member's introduction of self in the group.

The first stage is also marked by much social politeness and propriety, something we have termed "social lubrication." Couples behave in the way they have learned when they get together with other couples: They are more polite, more social. Because of this, the beginning of a couples group tends to be somewhat slower than that of a noncouples group. Another reason for the slower start is that individuals who come to the group with their partners are often somewhat more reluctant to self-disclose than they would be if they were there without their spouses. The following reasons seem to contribute to this phenomenon:

- People may be afraid to report on certain problems in front of their partners. Many couples appear to have a silent agreement in the marriage along the lines of "we don't wash our dirty laundry in public." Even if the public is their group, shame about vulnerable issues prevents self-disclosure at first.
- Each couple has certain taboo topics that the partners are not able to discuss, even when they are alone with each other. Partners often are unaware of these taboo subjects as problems worth mentioning.
- No couple wants to believe that it has the worst marriage in the group. Consequently, couples are rather tentative at first and, when asked to tell the group the problems that brought them to the group, they often minimize the problem, leave out important aspects, or deny large chunks of the trouble. Obviously, especially in the early stage of the group, loyalty to the partner takes priority over loyalty to the group.

Although this is still likely to be true over time, a group member will become better able to adhere to a group norm of openness even when honesty feels disloyal to the partner. Therefore, a group needs to do some work on this issue early on. Self-disclosure needs to become a group norm that is understood as beneficial to the marriage, so that even if it *feels* like disloyalty to the partner, group members can offer acceptance and under-standing. Leaders need to distinguish for the group that group loyalty does not supersede couple loyalty, but rather that the couple benefits from a group norm of self-disclosure.

Although Dwight understood the need for honesty as part of this therapy, shame and fear of internal humiliation prevented him from being honest early in the group about sexual performance concerns. He preferred to work with these concerns outside the group. Diane, widowed after a highly joyful sexual marriage, needed the group precisely because she needed to discuss sexual concerns with others she could trust. Diane knew that Dwight could benefit from the experiences of Spencer and Trevor as they moved into second marriages, and she wanted her marriage to progress as quickly as possible. To achieve this, I introduced a general group discussion about how to talk about what is hard to talk about. Although Dwight did not enter into this discussion actively, his marriage benefited as other group members helped move the norms of the group to the high level of self-disclosure that became the norm.

Resistance in the early stage often takes on the quality of "even if you do not agree with me, stay by my side in group" or "if you love me, you will agree with me in group." The group at this point is rarely sophisticated enough to deal with this kind of collusion by couples. Therefore, the leaders have to spearhead the movement to confront it.

Another phenomenon of the first group phase is that of dependency on the leaders (Bennis & Shephard, 1956; Bion, 1960; Thelen, 1954). Groups at this juncture have to establish their basic interactional norms. Frequently, they are not sure which of the norms they are permitted to set for themselves and which are simply prescribed by the leaders. Thus, they will look to the leaders for guidance to a considerable degree. Our response to these dependency issues is often to discuss the phenomenon out loud; thus, the group is able to understand that its dependency needs will have to be met by spouses and other members rather than by the leaders.

The first phase is also characterized by ambivalence over being in the group. It is not unusual for a new group member to have joined merely because the spouse insisted—perhaps even with a veiled threat that signing up is the last chance for the marriage. Naturally, a person joining the group under these circumstances is there under duress and may participate only perfunctorily or put up active resistance. A variation of this phenomenon occurs when one or both partners in a couple have the belief that only one of them has a problem.

Spencer and Robyn agreed when they joined that the group would prevent dysfunctional patterns from earlier marriages from taking hold in their new marriage. Honeymooners, they were blissfully happy about life together, but recognized that deep fissures could occur if dangerous interpersonal habits were not corrected. Ambivalent about interrupting the bliss of their new marriage, they began each group by stating their ambivalence about having to examine dysfunction during this happy time in their lives. The open discussion of their ambivalence allowed them to move into their concerns with full group support. Eventually, the deepest of concerns was addressed in the group, and their goal of preventing bad habits was achieved.

The hesitancy over becoming a fully committed member is also related to the previously mentioned anxiety over acceptance. New members of any group are worried about being accepted by others. This phenomenon exacerbates the problems described earlier: Members become reluctant to self-disclose ("if I let them know this about me they might not like me"); they feel leader dependency, and they actively deny that they have a problem. After all, "if there is nothing wrong with me, there is less self-esteem to lose and if the group rejects me it will not be much of a loss."

In order to move on to the next level and get some meaningful work done, the group has to find workable solutions to three issues: self-disclosure, dependency, and membership. In terms of self-disclosure, members must agree that it is in each couple's best interest to talk freely about painful and embarrassing personal and marital issues. In terms of dependency, members have to learn that the leader is not there to provide answers; rather, solutions to the pain that brought the couple to the group have to emerge from the members themselves (Bion, 1960). Finally, in terms of membership, a commitment to the group by all members is necessary. Partners who entered the couples group believing that they joined only because their spouse had a problem have to be introduced to a more systemic view of their pain. Couples must begin to understand the interactional problems of the marriage in systems terms in order to improve communication skills effectively, as discussed in Chapter 4.

Beginning Working Phase (and Prelude to Crisis)

We call this the *beginning working phase* because members have found a preliminary solution to the tasks of stage one and have settled in to work on marital problems. Frequently, it is the impatience of those group members who are already fluent in the language of family systems work through earlier therapy that moves the group to this stage. These members settle the self-disclosure issue simply by "taking the plunge" and modeling openness for the others, which catalyzes the group.

Margaret had done extensive work on finding her voice within the marriage and the family she treasured. A member of a women's therapy group, Margaret used this women's group to gain support and insight into how to speak up to her mother-in-law. Margaret worked in a business that her mother-in-law owned, and Margaret hoped to inherit the business one day. The women's group helped her to be kind and gentle but firm in establishing boundaries with the mother-in-law, who was accustomed to being in charge of all business decisions. Margaret was already more assertive at the time she and Michael joined the couples group, but found it excruciating to tell Michael how angry she was that he did not support her in speaking up to his mother. Margaret felt no support from her husband in negotiating the difficult interpersonal terrain between the generations. As the group moved into an active working phase, Dr. Slowinski and I helped Margaret engage the support of other group members in working with Michael on the issues preventing him from speaking up to his mother. Michael moved from discounting the value of Margaret's concerns to working with his need to deny the problems between him and his mother.

One of the hallmarks of this stage is what might be called "moving from couple identity to personal identity." Members, who at first were seen by the others in the group merely as partners in a couple, begin to emerge as individuals with their own styles and problems. Although this is very useful in the process of getting to know each other, the leaders have to be watchful that group members do not take sides in the marriage by seeing one partner in the couple as the source of the problem. The systemic view I present as the therapist is essential to countering this form of marital scapegoating.

Resistance to group movement at this stage is often a symbolic expression of projected dissatisfactions of a couple with each other. The complaint of a couple about the group always contains a grain of truth, but this blame process is reflective of the unhappiness in the couple and often of its tendency to project blame in the marriage. For example, in one group where I wanted the group to work with attitudes toward sexuality, the group remained determined to work with anger. The members were not ready to expose sensitive issues about sexuality and expressed anger toward me by dwelling on anger for the entire group meeting. When it was ready much later in the group contract, the group moved easily into frank discussions involving explicit sexual concerns.

Much of each group meeting is unstructured. At the start of a group contract period, one couple after another introduces itself by asking the group for help with a recent marital crisis. Others join in by sharing their opinions and feelings on the matter, by giving advice, or by reporting on their handling of similar problems. Because it is still early in the group, a good deal of information is shared in this phase (family constellations, children, family of origin, parents, and jobs). These data are significant and necessary for the group in order to understand the particular life situation of a couple. For the leaders, this level of sharing can feel less meaningful than the kind of work that goes on in the later phases.

Furthermore, in some groups, a particular couple may repeatedly open the session with an account of yet another quarrel, reflecting merely a variation on a theme; however, because of the early developmental phase in the group, the group has not yet developed skills to deal with members who monopolize. Likewise, the partners are not yet able to work out the underlying conflict in a more definitive manner. Here, leader intervention can be critical in preventing monopolizing and scapegoating.

Antonia often came to the group with topics for discussion prepared. While other members gathered their wits at the beginning of a session, she frequently maximized the group opportunity by stating clearly that she needed to work with Patrick on one topic or another. Patrick would quietly agree that this was a good idea; consequently, Antonia often galloped into a discussion of the most painful parts of her marriage before other members had decided what they wanted to work on. Although other members were angry about what felt like monopolization, they frequently allowed the work to continue. After all,

Antonia was utilizing the group correctly by planning her topics before the start of the group. Further, her enthusiasm to get work done enabled them to be helpful while minimizing their own need to get work done. To counteract the high probability of scapegoating, I often moved the group to the level of discussing how they felt about the amount of time and energy the group spent on Patrick and Antonia. The other couples agreed that the work was important and needed to be done, and they acknowledged that they sometimes hid behind Antonia's take-charge stance. Although they were reticent to share their anger with Antonia directly in the early stages of the group, scapegoating was avoided. Much later in the life of this group, Antonia and Patrick were able to resolve many of the issues that plagued the highly troubled marriage, and group members could rejoice in progress made by slogging through early meetings to help Antonia and Patrick progress in so many areas of their mvarriage.

Thus, although the group is working from the first minutes of its existence, in the earlier phases much of its interaction sounds tentative, superficial, and perhaps repetitive to leaders used to cohesive groups. To the new members, the group feels like a working group; however, the more experienced members and leaders know how much more a group is capable of. Thus, the experienced members are often the first to become dissatisfied and restless. Even if no couple returning for the second year expresses dissatisfaction, one or two people or couples are always eager and able to work at greater depth. They become displeased with what is going on in the beginning group.

Most of the time the disgruntlement is directed at the group and is expressed, with apologies and embarrassment, as a vague impatience with the group's seeming politeness, superficiality, and repetitiveness. At other times, the dissatisfaction is directed at a specific member or couple in a typical scapegoating maneuver. Leaders need to take care to avoid scapegoating by teaching the group about whole-group processes.

Finally, the dissatisfaction may be directed at the leaders (Bennis & Shephard, 1956). Because they are still somewhat dependent, members expect leaders to take responsibility for the group and to push the group to work at a greater depth by preventing the superficial rehashing of marital spats. In a typically counterdependent move, the group turns on the leaders and the stage is set for a crisis. This kind of stage-dependent crisis occurs also in individual (noncouple) psychotherapy groups (Agazarian & Peters, 1981; Rutan & Stone, 1984).

It is necessary to evaluate the degree to which the group is justified in blaming the leaders for the lack of depth at this point. As discussed earlier, some degree of superficiality is unavoidable. The group, after all, is still in an early phase and the level of self-disclosure necessary for successful group work is still very difficult to reach and maintain. However, the therapists have considerable power in determining the measure of superficiality they allow. If complaints are made about the way in which the group is run, listening to the feedback before automatically diagnosing the problem as purely developmental is always wise.

Crisis, Expression of Dissatisfaction

At the end of the second stage, the group goes into a crisis. What begins at first in stage two as dissatisfaction, scapegoating, or counterdependence often turns into a real battle in this phase. The onset is usually sudden: One couple may come into a session and threaten the group with dropping out if the "bullshitting" does not stop, or a person may suddenly lose his or her temper and noisily attack the leaders or another member. Then the battle is joined.

The fight is usually a struggle for more depth and intimacy. Members require deeper levels of self-disclosure to work on painful and embedded marital problems rather than remain at the level of superficial fights. Yet, with each important group movement, a countermovement will take place. Some members will resist by whatever means they can devise. They may counterattack the disgruntled attackers. They may joke around. They may pontificate about the dangers of too much openness and stepping into sensitive areas. They may deflect the attention of the group by pushing it into a seemingly important direction, yet one in which the current stage task does not get done.

The countermovement against greater disclosure and intimacy in a group is usually motivated by fear. Although some members in the group are ready and eager to plumb greater depths, others are frightened by this prospect. They are afraid of what they might find if they were to take a harder look at their marriage, so they resist. Often their fear is fueled by a vague belief that the problem of their marriage is so serious that it is insoluble and that the dissolution of the relationship is an inevitable outcome. For the therapist, it is hard to determine how much of this fear is unrealistic. Marital incompatibility or personality dysfunction can also create therapeutic resistance.

111

Ultimately, the resolution of the crisis comes about through a dialectical process in which the people who want to move to greater depths prevail while the fears of the others are still taken into account. At times, the leaders may have to side actively with the forward-moving section of the group by commenting on the phenomenon for the group to hear. Somehow, the group needs to master the task of resolving the crisis lest it remain stuck in an untenable situation in which work gets attempted and dropped. Leader comments can be helpful—for example, "Trevor and Spencer's impatience with Patrick is actually an expression of their need to have the group work at a more intimate level."

Intensive Working Phase

Once the crisis has been overcome and the group has tacitly agreed on a comfortable level of self-disclosure that creates an atmosphere in which therapeutic work can be done, the group enters its second working phase. Early in this phase, the group may still be reacting to the anger of the crisis phase and may exaggerate its dedication to this new determination to work yet harder and more intimately with one another.

One reaction to the potentially exaggerated nature of initial postcrisis work can be the relaxation of a lunch break. As part of the 6-hour meeting period of each monthly couples group, lunch is served and enjoyed together. During this lunch break, couples move from working in the group together to visiting with one another, chatting about social topics, and relaxing a bit. The return from the ease of the lunch relationship to the intensity of the clinical group interaction requires a transition for members. This is eased by dining outside the group meeting room, entering the meeting room after lunch is over, and closing the door. However, joking and storytelling are especially tempting after a pleasant lunch with members who like one another. Antonia and Robyn frequently acted as task leaders, reminding members gently that "it is time to get back to work." This invitation was frequently followed by a process of taking stock of work yet to be accomplished. A leader or a member frequently asked, "Okay. Who still needs to work?" This transitioning aided members in overcoming resistance and getting back to the work of the group.

At this stage, the group is very cohesive: Members express genuine liking and affection for each other; they enjoy coming to the group, and lateness and complaints about how hard it is to get to group are at their lowest. The group is least resistive to serious work and one painful situation after another becomes the work of the group as members produce moving emotional experiences in these sessions.

A most striking phenomenon about this phase of the group is the intertwining of levels of personal, marital, family, and family-of-origin systems in the content of the group's work. Members work on couples issues, but spontaneously involve their families of origin in their explanations and narratives, or they work on a group-as-a-whole matter yet make discoveries on an individual level (through feedback from other group participants). This leads to significant personal and marital change. At this point, the group moves from level to level with ease and couples become adept at applying the learning from others to their own marital dynamics. A group working at this level is more skilled at systems therapy than most therapists trained in an individual treatment model. Leaders can enjoy the fruits of their own and the members' labors.

Having successfully overcome the earlier struggles that, by necessity, were more superficial, the group is now able to tackle the more significant problems of power, mutuality, and intimacy in the marriages as well as in the group. The group has become central in the lives of its members. It is a time of exciting, significant, and permanent personal and couple changes. Partners may find that the unspoken contract with which they entered their marriages is no longer viable. Reconfiguring the marriage contract is fraught with resistance, anger, rage, and, occasionally, underhanded ploys; yet, couples succeed in renegotiating past misunderstandings.

Holly and Trevor had entered their recent marriage with the understanding that Holly would continue to earn over $200,000 annually, while Trevor did his best to establish a successful professional financial management practice. Although Holly had wanted to give up working at the birth of their first baby, it did not seem financially viable. However, when their daughter was born, Holly said that she needed time off from a skyrocketing career that had involved constant travel. Trevor was frightened that he would be unable to support the family in the style to which they had become accustomed. He had trouble being assertive at work and had grown up pleasing his mother despite *the need to be untruthful. He had learned to charm his way through a situation to the degree that it was sometimes hard to know when he was being honest. The confrontation of other group members in helping Trevor be honest with his wife about how well his career was moving forward turned out to be central in helping the couple adjust financial expectations to their newly reduced economic options.*

Termination

At some time soon after the annual workshop, one of the leaders reminds the group that this group will end in 8 weeks. Group members usually react to this announcement with denial. The end is still weeks away and, after all, at least one couple has already announced its intent to recontract for another group year after the summer break. Ergo: "We [the group] don't have to deal with termination." Ergo: "Our group will be the first group not to end."

Despite the denial, the knowledge is there that this group will end. Even though some people may reenlist for the next group, the group as it is now will cease to exist. The members know this. After a while, the denial falls apart and the termination phase has begun.

This phase has two subphases: the pretermination rough spot and the termination itself. The first subphase is marked by some form of regression. Frequently, some of the earlier symptoms return as couples revisit some of their old trouble spots. The group can be heard moaning: "You're not fighting over *that* again are you?" However, the group has come far from its old days of projection.

Even though there is some deterioration and return of old material, the group is not usually blamed. Members now understand the concept of resistance and deal with it with more sensitivity, directness, and humor. However, the return of the old patterns is often quite poignant. It is a couple's way of signaling to the group that the partners are afraid to go on without support from the group—that they are not sure enough of the gains they have made and are ambivalent about ending their group participation. The deterioration, at times, takes the form of acting out. A member of the group may show his or her displeasure and concern over the impending end by breaking some group rule. Usually, only one member of the couple acts out and cannot get the other one to join in; this is quite unlike what would have occurred earlier in the group year when the partner would have felt compelled to participate out of loyalty. Furthermore, the group is likely quickly to become quite impatient with the acting out and stop it.

Holly refused to discuss one topic in the group. To group members, this felt like acting out because they wanted her to be honest about all facets of her life. I knew of the topic from her individual work. Holly was involved in voluntary training and leadership of a business in crafts that involved huge amounts of her time for no financial gain. The crafts enterprise depended on the idealism of the leader to be willing to work for no direct payment, reducing Holly's ability to earn a living. The strong tie between Holly and her buddies felt intrusive to Trevor, who wanted her to get a part-time job to help with finances. Holly refused to bring the topic to the group because she predicted that the group members would encourage her to consider an addictive quality to her voluntary energies. Trevor was very angry that Holly refused to deal with it openly and also that she refused to stop the alliance in favor of a paid position. Holly asked him to agree to keep the topic out of the group and he complied, tying the hands of the leaders and members in assisting the couple in working through the issue. Holly had predicted accurately that the group would become very angry with her behavior and would try to get her to reconsider her priorities, which she was unwilling to do. At termination, the topic remained unresolved.

The second subphase is the termination itself. This is marked by members experiencing sadness and a feeling of loss. During this phase, recontracting becomes a major issue. Couples decide if they want to end their membership or join again for another year. They ask for feedback from the rest of the group and they report to the group on their progress made during the group year. Much of that progress is clearly visible to the group, such as when a partner has stopped being condescending to his or her spouse. However, some of the progress has to do with "back home" behaviors like child-rearing practices or sexual harmony. The group is dependent on couples' self-assessments for such issues.

Often, at this phase, initial assessment goals are reviewed to give members a clearer evaluation of the progress made. Members are sometimes astounded by how "long ago" the problems of last year seem.

There is an atmosphere of sadness about ending the remarkable experience of the group, mixed with the pride and team spirit that come from hard work.

Resistance at this stage usually shows itself in an unwillingness to recontract for another year even though the other group members, the leaders, and perhaps even the spouse believe this is very much indicated. Members may find it quite daunting to resist such concerted forces. However, if the couple has already changed a good deal, the resisting partner may just be too frightened to go even further.

For the leaders, moving a group from beginning to end is the journey of being a parent to a group and helping it through early tender growth to full-blooded maturity and then through saying goodbye to trusted teammates. The fruits of one's labors are very sweet when, at the end of the group, the members, their marriages, and the couples community have grown to a greater level of independent functioning and life satisfaction.

7

Designing Effective Structured Interventions

We'll send you to Couples School after you get engaged. You weren't expecting a normal gift from us, were you?

—A mother to her young adult daughter

INTRODUCTION

In the earlier model of couples group psychotherapy, groups met for 150 minutes, and much of the second half of each session was spent executing a specially designed, structured exercise. At the bathroom break after the unstructured part of the group, the leaders met and designed or chose an activity likely to deepen or refine the learning that had begun in the first portion of the session. If, for example, the group had been discussing the parts of themselves that embarrassed, humiliated, or shamed them, the leaders might have designed an exercise on the impact of poor self-esteem on a marriage and on careers.

More recent formatting of the group has moved to a monthly meeting of 6 hours, in which much of the time is spent in "here and now" work with ongoing issues suggested by the members themselves. Members requested "special times," in which structured exercises and invited guest leaders could be included, rather than taking large portions of work time that felt precious to them. For this reason, structured interventions are planned far ahead, often with guest leaders who have expertise in a particular specialty. However, the combination of solidly working through painful areas for each member with carefully designed structured exercises targeted to deal with group themes continues to be extremely powerful therapy. It confronts issues in the background at the same time that it works actively and intensively with ongoing concerns. In this chapter, I review concepts necessary to assist leaders in designing their own exercises.

BASIC CHOICES OF EXERCISES

How do we choose and design the exercises? They are garnered from our knowledge of group dynamics and family therapy, from our knowledge of the couples in therapy, and from our own existential view of human intimacy in marriage. The exercises are *not* a grab bag of things to spring on a group. As in strategic family therapy, our exercises are formulated by our thinking of the entire group as a system and structuring a clinical intervention likely to "unstick" some members or the group as a whole. Although the earlier edition of this book contained five basic exercise modalities, I have expanded my selection to reflect changes in thinking about couples work in the past two decades. Each of the following categories can perform a specific and useful function for the life and growth of the group and its members:

- writing and drawing exercises;
- leader-led guided imagery;
- directed verbal sharing around leader-selected topics;
- dramatic activities: role playing, family sculpting; and
- film clips, massage, and dance: nonverbal sensuality builders.

Let us look at each briefly. Examples are found in this chapter and in the appendices.

Writing and Drawing Exercises

Writing and drawing tasks enable cognitive exploration of a particular issue and sharing thoughts and feelings with a partner or with the whole group. The method is simple: Each group member or couple takes paper and a writing implement (pencil, crayons, and/or colored pencils) and responds to a question through words or drawings. After sufficient time, couples share their responses with each other.

Typical topics range broadly from "draw a picture of your marriage" to "write your own obituary." In one instance, couples performed a variation on the "meaning of marriage" exercise given in Appendix B-ii. I asked each couple to tape blank paper to the window, grab crayons, and draw a self-portrait of how it felt to be a couple. The discussion was especially rich because of the need to agree on how to draw themselves. On another occasion, a co-lead and I asked each partner to write his or her favorite sexual fantasy in order to have it read aloud to the group. The leaders read the fantasy of each member aloud without saying who had written it. The job of the group was to see if partners could guess the fantasy written by their beloved. The members were 100% accurate in guessing who wrote each fantasy. The writing cemented the thoughts of the group member and enabled high disclosure in sharing sexual material in a group setting.

Writing and drawing exercises are especially useful for less experienced leaders because they can be carefully structured ahead of the group. They are also useful for earlier stages of group development, when members are a bit reticent about deep here-and-now work for long periods of the group session.

Leader-Led Guided Imagery

Group members love guided imagery. It enables depth work in a group in a very gentle manner. In guided imagery, group members are put into a relaxed state through some mild induction or muscle relaxation instructions as described by Lazarus (1971). While in the relaxed state, the group members are given an instruction to visualize a particular scene or encounter (Leuner, 1969; Singer & Pope, 1978). After sufficient time for each participant to become involved in his or her visual adventure, the group members are gently brought back "into the room." Each person is then encouraged to share with the group some of the discoveries made while in the slightly altered state of consciousness, which was somewhat closer to their unconscious processes.

Guided imagery enables members to get in touch with preconscious feelings and beliefs about certain issues in relation to self, spouse, family of origin, children, or others.

Directed Verbal Sharing Around Leader-Selected Topics

In this simple group exercise, a question is posed to the group such as, "How do you feel about your first name?" or "How is your relationship with your spouse similar to, or different from, the one with your parent of the opposite sex?" Each person takes a turn at reflecting on his or her response to the question, and the group discusses the similarities between members and the meaning of the question for their marriages. Directed verbal sharing helps people to get acquainted, builds cohesiveness, and fosters universality.

Directed verbal sharing can be limited or can lead to very deep insights and compassion for all group members. In terms of depth, it can be leader directed, so it can be used at various phases of group life.

Dramatic Activities: Role Playing, Family Sculpting, and Media

In this group of exercises, modifications of psychodrama (Moreno & Moreno, 1959), role playing (Langley & Langley, 1983), and sculpting (Papp, 1976) are included. At times, it is worthwhile for a couple to sculpt a particular family problem (Papp, 1982). At other times, a couple may role-play a particular scene that another couple has described.

Occasionally the therapist may feel that a particular couple's struggle is reminiscent of some well-known couple in literature (e.g., Romeo and Juliet, Antony and Cleopatra, or Ginger Rogers and Fred Astaire) and may ask the group to act it out. Amid all the hilarity that ensues, some profound learning takes place. Dramatic activities function to provide powerful, direct, experiential learning upon which the group can later reflect via group discussion.

Film clips, massage, and dance can provide nonverbal sensuality builders. Familiar media like films and music provide instant contact for many members. Because the member feels immediate identification with the character or the melody, depth of insight can follow relatively easily.

Media segments of various kinds can be instrumental in assisting couples in many ways. Couples are accustomed to watching television and movies together and often live on their computers. A way of working with a film clip follows in the "sex" section of the content of the exercises in this chapter. In addition to themes grasped easily from popular media, more sensual activities, including massage, dance, and nonverbal sensuality builders, are covered more fully in Chapter 11. Dramatic activities are very powerful and are best done during deep working phases of the group's life.

CONTENT OF THE EXERCISES

Many of the exercises deal with life issues that trouble most couples. We call these themes the "universals of marriage" because they truly do affect us all. These are

- sex;
- money;
- in-laws and family of origin;
- children; and
- illness and death.

Sex

In order to stimulate and raise awareness of the value of love play, a huge range of sexual enrichment material is available—for example, from the Sinclair Intimacy Institute (www.bettersex.com) and other educational organizations. Unfortunately, some of our couples find it hard to learn from the voice-over of a sex therapist, although others think this format is very safe. Fortunately, there are educational opportunities for all tastes. The ultimate guide to adult videos (Blue, 2003a) is an overview of various forms of erotic video entertainment that couples enjoy once they give themselves permission. I have compiled a smorgasbord of arousing material for different ages, genders, and predilections.

As a result of my research, I organized five couples to gather one evening in our video room at the Stone Harbor office. Dr. Slowinski and I had chosen a collection of film clips from <u>March of the Penguins</u>, <u>The Full Monty</u>, and <u>Wild Orchid</u>. The five couples had become accustomed to sharing very intimate knowledge with one another verbally as part of their life in the group. However, they gathered in the movie room tittering a bit like early adolescents as they contemplated how near to sit to their partners and whether or not to hold hands. Therapeutic trust was high as they allowed themselves to follow blindly in an evening where they had no idea what was to happen next. They *relaxed as they watched the elegance of penguins as they couple and parent. One couple went home that evening with a new term of affection, calling each other "my little penguin." Energy began to sizzle as men disrobed near the end of* <u>The Full Monty</u>, *with appropriate female giggles from the appreciative wives in the group. The segment on the sexual awakening of a severely disturbed young man in* <u>Wild Orchid</u> *is exceptionally moving: Through reaching out to another person he makes intimate contact for seemingly the first time in his life. As the third film clip ended, Dr. Slowinski and I allowed silence to permeate the group until someone was ready to speak. Little by little, couples spoke about how much they had enjoyed the evening and how relevant the segment of the penguins was to their lives as couples. More than one couple vowed that they would bring home tasteful adult DVDs in the future. Antonia was clearly uncomfortable with the film evening, but managed to remain in the room at all times. The group was able to absorb her awkwardness and still reported how much they enjoyed the evening. It would never have occurred to them to watch sensually arousing material with their group, but they felt closer to everyone as a result of the experience. Watching the films with other couples and discussing their reactions modeled greater freedom than many had been able to accomplish.*

Many couples enjoy reading erotic material as part of love play. Couples often share with one another choices in books, articles, and poetry. Unlike books on sexual technique, erotic reading material aims to engage fantasy. For example, Violet Blue (2003b) has edited erotica for couples and women (Web site: www.tinynibbles.com). Her work can be found on a Web site that many of our couples enjoy: www.goodvibrations.com.

Working With Finances and Security

In the last decade, conflict around financial management has replaced sexuality as the hardest thing with which our couples must deal. Difficulties include practical concerns about how to understand and manage finances; however, they are most poignant when they involve dysfunctional ways of thinking about money that inadvertently create emotional disasters in the lives of couples. In a recent workshop, Scott Budge, PhD (2008), discussed the quickly growing field of behavioral finance and encouraged mental health colleagues to include routine interviews concerning the ways in which their clients think about finances and security.

For our couples, financial troubles range from inability to balance a checkbook to deep futility about financial power battles, helplessness, and denial. My experience is that couples find it easier to discuss sexual disinterest in a group than to discuss their shame about credit card debt and overdue taxes. Typically, when one member of a couple begins to express concern about money, a derisive element enters his or her voice. The contempt that we know to be frequent among deeply troubled couples (Gottman, 1994) can be clearly heard.

Trevor and Holly had trouble making ends meet after they relocated to a city new to both of them. Accustomed to comfortable affluence, they chose housing that quickly became a financial burden in their new life situation. Trevor tried to encourage Holly to trade their monthly expenses for more modest living accommodations. Naturally optimistic, Holly expressed hope that the current difficulties were temporary and that they could withstand the pressure. As month after month passed, Trevor's concern began to have an edge of criticism and futility.

With the help of Dennis Allen, CPA, CFP, I designed an approach to helping couples tackle the assumptions and emotions around handling finances (*The Couples Money School Primer,* Coché, 2002a). The basic communication skills can be applied to discussions around money, which often represent discussions about life security. Earlier trauma can appear in adulthood around themes of financial security and anxiety about financial stability.

We have designed a series of exercises that our couples find most helpful in getting underneath seeming bickering about who spends what. For example, we ask couples to consider the nature of their financial personalities and teach them to dialogue with one another from a position of respectful individual differences. We ask them about the meaning of money for them and help them to understand the difference between bringing home a salary and retaining money for their future. We help them to manage spending before it manages them. For the most part, couples express tremendous relief when they learn of ways to work with the meaning of money as part of couples' life. Many of our couples learn to plan for the future and to budget in the fall for the year to come.

123

One of the most interesting exercises conducted in groups with an interest in work around the details of finances in coupling is called "My Necessity Is Your Luxury." I designed this exercise based on my marital experience that two husbands, who were different from one another, also differed from me in what each of us considered a necessity for our welfare. Generalizing to patterns I saw in other couples, I began to understand that an expensive suit may be a necessity for an upwardly mobile young attorney, just as a weekly manicure may feel necessary for someone in the fashion industry. By allowing couples to place their expenditures within their value systems, I found that members of a couple could be respectful with one another about items that they had previously ridiculed. Teaching them interpersonal problem-solving and negotiating skills was a further step in helping them tackle the business of coupling.

Patrick is one of two people I have ever met who are able to dismantle a boat entirely and put it back together again without a manual. Since childhood, Patrick's great love has been purchasing, repairing, entertaining, and babying his boats. At one point, there may have been five boats—four more than Antonia found optimal. For Antonia, not only is a boat a luxury, but it also represents a kind of expenditure that was not part of her development. Patrick is economical about his boat expenditures because of his extraordinary skill: Repairs that might cost thousands of dollars can be neatly handled through an eBay purchase and a few hours of time. In addition, during part of their marriage, Patrick would invite Antonia to join him for a Saturday boat trip, offering her lunch at a nearby restaurant; he felt rejected when Antonia expressed her preference for reading a good book or working on a course on her computer. Although Antonia supported Patrick's interest in his boat world, the level of expenditure of time and money seemed so wasteful to her that her resentment would come through. In an attempt to hold on to the world that he needed to enter in his spare time, Patrick would sputter a bit, look frightened, and try to explain: "I really, really like the boats." With the help of the group, Patrick and Antonia came to be able to discuss and agree on the level of time and financial expenditure that the marriage would bear. At the time of this printing, Antonia is looking forward to riding with her husband on one of their current fleet of three boats. They now picnic together and sometimes stay overnight.

The preceding examples are merely a few of the myriad subjects for discussion between members of a couple who are able to work together financially.

In-Laws and Family of Origin

One of the most important tasks facing each couple is to form a marital unit that has its own solidarity and independence without alienating the respective families of origin of each partner. Simplistic or drastic solutions (e.g., cutting off ties) cause considerable grief in the future of the couple. Continued dependence on parents or siblings robs the couple of its own identity. There is little choice but to individuate. Bringing this conflict into the open, where couples can try to process it, can be freeing for many group members.

Dealing with the aging parents of either partner is a subcategory in the in-laws group of issues. The parents' dependence on the younger couple creates new challenges that may overwhelm the strength of the couple. The death of a parent and the emotional turmoil created by this event strain the marriage further.

Exercises that can assist with these themes include a family genogram that traces how anger was handled in family of origin, how female authority was managed by men in a three-generation family, patterns of divorce and remarriage in a clan, or tracing addictions through three generations.

Children

In the "good old days," couples married and had babies, but this is no longer the case. The decision of whether or not to have children and, if so, at what point in the development of the marriage represents a major hurdle for many couples. Once the choice has been made and children are there, differing expectations of who is responsible for what produce marital dilemmas. As the children get older, issues of triangulation and playing parents against each other become new tests of marital strength.

When one is designing an exercise for couples around children, it is frequently difficult to find something that touches each couple in the group. Most of the time, the group members are at different developmental stages in relation to raising children. Only more broad-based difficulties, such as the amount of time allotted for career versus children versus spouse, touch all couples, with or without children.

One of the most powerful exercises is deceptively simple. Each person in the group ranks the importance of three issues: financial stability, children, and marriage. No ties are allowed and ranking must be done quickly. After each has written down his or her ranking, partners take turns reading out their hierarchies. The discrepancies between two marriage partners are usually quite remarkable and present an excellent stimulus for discussion. It is important in the discussion to clarify that no superiority of one answer over the other is implied in the question; rather, differences in rankings may be giving a couple trouble and are deserving of further attention.

Margaret never intended to put her children before her marriage, but Michael was away at his corporate career so much of each week that the children became the central focus of her life. Michael hoped for some snuggling, some romance, and a bit of fine dining when he finally returned home on the weekends, but Margaret was too angry about the need to take full care of the children to want to spend much time with her husband. When they tried to discuss this alone, the discussion produced further anger. As they engaged in a discussion in the group, it became clear that both wanted the marriage to come first, but in order to put it in its proper place, it would be necessary for Michael to take a more active role as the father of his children. Discussing the priority of the marriage really helped him to understand the way to a better future. Michael began to parent more actively, to support Margaret, and to listen to her parenting concerns. The rebalance that both sought followed as they began to parent together. The anger subsided and the marriage moved into first place.

Illness and Death

At some point, couples also must come to grips with their vulnerability as human beings. The physical illness of one of the partners or coming face to face with death through illness, a serious accident, or even a near miss places a new set of questions and fears before the couple. Many couples come through such a crisis with a renewed appreciation of one another. Others come through it with considerable disappointment and resentment, feeling that the other did not behave in a way for which the sick partner had hoped. If one of the couples in a group is struggling with this issue, an exercise regarding a partner's illness can be very fruitful. For example, the following vignette describes how I integrated the tragic death of my husband into the life of a clinical practice that appreciated and embraced him.

In January 1991, Erich Coché died unexpectedly at age 49 of cancer. Erich and I had used the very communication skills that I now teach to couples, and these skills allowed us to take leave having discussed openly all aspects of his impending death. We had no choice but to accept reality, and accept reality we did. Erich had been part of the practice and part of the couples groups, so I decided it best to use the crisis of his death as a living, practice-wide example of coming through an unavoidable crisis. At a memorial service at the University of Pennsylvania, where we taught, over 500 people came to honor my first husband. Perhaps 100 of these people were clients, who had read of the service in the paper. To help them work through the crisis that had befallen us all, I invited them to contribute letters and written vignettes about Erich. I also published a small newsletter about his accomplishments and allowed grieving to take place openly in the practice. To care for myself at this time of cataclysmic disaster, I developed a team of professionals, colleagues, friends, and family. This armament of honest caring and grieving allowed the practice and me to heal without harming clients. Without the open interchange of this time, I am unsure how I might have been strong enough to be there for others in the very time that I was tender and hurting.

As becomes clear from the preceding examples, the universals of marriage are not seen just as trouble spots and difficulties. They constitute developmental tasks that each couple needs to master at some point in its development. Frequently, couples who seek help do so because they have run into a snag with one or more of these tasks. The solutions they found have backfired and caused palpable emotional pain. Working through these problems in a caring and respectful community of others who are struggling with similar issues often opens completely new vistas for the couple and gives rise to solutions of which neither of the partners and neither of the leaders could have thought by themselves.

THE ANXIETY OF SPONTANEITY

These exercises are somewhat like a chemistry experiment in school. The experiment does not always work; sometimes it falls flat or the point it was supposed to make is not made. Yet, it is important that leaders be willing to take the risk of having an exercise backfire or fizzle out. It is only this kind of risk taking that allows the group to grow, keeps leadership alive, and gives the members courage to try new behaviors. The exercises require a sense of humor on the part of everyone, especially the members. Frequently, an exercise may seem silly or funny at first, and the important message or shock of recognition comes only after everyone has participated in good spirits.

People must become vulnerable enough to each other to create a working bond. The vibrancy of the group will be the reward for doing so. For the therapists, too, a vibrant, hardworking group is the reward for the challenge presented by having to design an activity that responds to the turmoil and learning needs of a particular group with a multitude of couples issues at a specific moment in its development.

Section III

Integrating Theory, Research, and Treatment for Couples in Groups

By the group we are wounded, and by the group we are healed.

—Gary M. Burlingame, PhD, in *The Wall Street Journal* (March 24, 2009)

8

The Intervention Hierarchy
Four Levels

Too often I hear what I fear instead of what she's saying.

—A coupled man

INTRODUCTION

A visitor observing a couples group in action will find the group absorbed in some kind of subject matter. The content of the group's work ranges from the trivial to the most profound and from pregroup social banter to an intense grappling with life-threatening issues. In our couples group, for example, issues on a given evening can range from the quality of the mustard at the gourmet shop where clients buy coffee before the group meets to a member's prognosis after a heart attack.

It is only logical, then, that an observer would wonder how we decide when to intervene, when not to intervene, and how to intervene. Further, an observer would question whether one type of intervention is preferable to another and, if so, how a leader chooses one type of intervention over another. These questions are crucial to the welfare of the group and to the quality of the treatment. The types of interventions available to the leaders of couples group therapy are varied and rich. The issues around therapeutic interventions deserve a great deal of consideration. Many of our interventions depend on our own maps as therapists.

131

The logic behind our interventions is best understood through the metaphor of the "therapist's map." Imagine, for a moment, trying to drive from New York to Kansas without a decent map. You have some notion that Kansas is west of Kentucky. Last time you went to Kansas, you flew, and you have no idea which roads intersect with which highways, how much in tolls and gas is required, or how much time to estimate for travel. All you know is that it is west of Kentucky and it is far. What would you pay for a decent map before starting your journey? Plenty.

A therapist's map, as the term implies, refers to a tool in the mind of the therapist. It is a cognitive written or unwritten organizational framework, understood by the therapist, that includes components necessary for engineering the treatment. In individual therapy, a therapist's map includes a working understanding of the diagnostic essentials and treatment strategies for a client or client system. When the client system is a couple, the therapist's map must also include the structure of the couple's relationship along typical interactive dimensions, along with an understanding of the intergenerational issues for each partner.

When the client system is a couples psychotherapy group, still another dimension is crucial: a group map of the subgroups and dyads and an understanding of the properties of the group as a whole (such as norms, roles, cohesiveness, and leadership patterns) in the various stages of the group's development over time. Naturally, the therapist's map of a couples psychotherapy group is complex and can best be charted through an understanding of couples or family therapy and of group therapy.

Organizing the content of a group's activity efficiently and sensibly has been discussed frequently in the theoretical and research literature in group psychotherapy (Flapan, 1981). Borriello (1979) directs his attention to the leader in proposing an organizational map that highlights three "intervention foci": the personal, the interpersonal, and the group as a whole. Each forms a level for therapeutic intervention. In our opinion, an added dimension is present in couples psychotherapy groups: the dimension of the unit of the couple or dyad.

THE INTERVENTION CHOICES

In order to include the richness and complexity of the couples' dimension in our organizational scheme for couples group psychotherapy, we must expand Borriello's (1979) concept in two ways. The first includes the ability of the leader to intervene at the level of marital interaction itself. This is couples psychotherapy in a group setting. It allows the therapist an additional possible focus: the dynamics between two partners. The second expansion has more sweeping ramifications for the group and for the therapists. We find it useful to consider that the intervention foci choices can be made not only by the leaders, as Borriello suggests, but also by the group members themselves, who can direct their attention spontaneously to these foci in the course of group work. Thus, we refer to these foci as levels of intervention or as levels of interaction.

Let us consider in more detail this proposed four-way classification of group content. According to this scheme, the activity of a group can take place on any one of these four levels at any time, as well as on a combination of more than one level simultaneously:

- At the personal level, group talk is centered on one individual.
- At the couples level, the group focuses on one of the couples.
- At the interpersonal level, interpersonal relationships between two or more members or couples are in focus. If the group's attention is on two people, these are not intimate partners, but rather members of a subgroup, or cross-couple interaction.
- At the group-as-a-whole level, the group works on its own group process.

Personal Level

At this level, group members work intensively with an individual group member. At times this looks like individual therapy in the presence of others, but at other moments this is the intervention of choice in order to make possible the most powerful impact on a person.

Spencer had been an active and central member of the group for quite a while. His comments were sharply defined, thoughtful, emphatic, and extremely helpful to other group members. Yet, over the last few months he had become increasingly unsettled, as though wrestling with something. Invited to deal with what was going on inside, Spencer made an individual appointment between group meetings and confided in his individual therapist that he was worrying about homosexual urges that had not entirely ceased after he married his beloved Robyn. He had been afraid

133

to tell her about his concerns and the anxiety plagued him. He gathered his courage and decided to deal with this in the group where Robyn could also get the support she needed to process the complexities of the situation. The group was ready to help. When they directed their attention to him, it became clear that Spencer was deeply in love with Robyn and attracted to her, but felt guilty because his fantasies included homosexual themes. Through a combination of individual work outside the group and work within the group, Spencer was able to put his fantasies into perspective and enjoy his marriage to Robyn.

Couples Level

A group working in the couples mode may spend time on the dynamics of one particular couple.

Holly and Trevor were considering moving away from Baltimore and return- ing to the northern New Jersey location that Trevor had called home since childhood. The decision was wrought with complexities and needed to be reached quickly. To afford the move, it would be necessary to move in with Trevor's mother, which did not seem ideal to anyone, including Trevor's mother. Rolling up their collective sleeves, the members of the group unani- mously announced that they were ready to get to work to help the decision get made in a way that was both timely and thorough. The move was thought through, undertaken, and successful. The group continued to act as a support team through all phases of the move and adjustment to the new location. This working through served to prevent inevitable complications from overtaking the positive outcome that the move had on the lives of this couple and their daughter.

Interpersonal Level

The activity of the group is often focused on interpersonal relationships between members or couples in the group. Members learn that others are struggling with similar issues and discover that they can be helpful to each other by sharing similar struggles and their attempted solutions. Many of Yalom's (1975) "curative factors," such as universality and altru- ism, can come to full bloom in this mode of working. At times, the mere discovery of similarities is healing; at other times, only a more extensive sharing of experiences can bring about therapeutic change.

All three of the couples in a small couples group were having major conflicts around the level of assertiveness each man was able to show in his marriage. Spencer, Trevor, and Patrick often found it easier to let Robyn, Holly, and Antonia have their way than to say no to their wives. All three couples had entered their marriages with the unstated marital contract that earning a living and making major decisions were the equal responsibility of both partners, and the members of each couple were angry that the power seemed out of balance. The group was quite aware of the similarities among the couples and turned openly to each other for support and working through of the issues at hand. The men joked and chided each other affectionately, which helped each to be more assertive. Going over this theme and using a variety of examples and exercises, the couples were able to find different ways of decision making. As sessions progressed, assertiveness replaced bickering and outright disagreements replaced passive aggressiveness. Men and women learned to ask directly for what they needed and to attempt to work out discrepancies between needs cooperatively.

Group-as-a-Whole Level

Themes are present at the level of the entire group at all times. Directional shifts, group decisions, norm enforcement, or explorations of participants' roles in the group are all group-as-a-whole topics. In order to be successful, the group has to work out problems in its own dynamics. Lewin (1951) provided seminal thinking on the centrality of context. Some of these problems are part of the natural development of groups described elsewhere (MacKenzie & Livesley, 1983; Schein & Bennis, 1965; Thelen, 1954). Themes like developing a mature relationship with the leader, with minimal dependence or counterdependence, fall into this category.

Other problems may not be common to all groups, but rather are unique and stem from the particular constellation of people in the room. For example, a monopolizer can drain group energies, and an acerbic relationship between two members can prevent the group from working independently. Group-as-a-whole work enables the group to progress developmentally from dependence through cohesiveness to

135

interdependence. Without this intervention level, a group is in danger of remaining stuck in an early developmental stage. Although it is possible to gain therapeutic benefits in such a group, the results are likely to be less substantial than in a group that has gained some mastery over its group dynamics and is better able to control its own destiny.

In 2007, at the end of the 11-month contract, two couples were ready to graduate while the three remaining couples still needed and wanted to work within the group for one more year. The three couples requested that the group remain closed to new members, meet monthly, and concentrate solely on here-and-now group work. It specifically requested that no guest co-leaders be invited into the group. Rather, members asked that Drs. Coché and Galbraith be available at each meeting to be the solid co-leads of a process group in depth. As Dr. Galbraith and I reviewed their preferences, we agreed that the format they requested was ideal to accomplish their goal of deep work for one more year. The three-couple group took charge of its own preferences, stated them clearly, and went on to graduate all three couples at the end of the next contract period.

Improving group functioning by working at a group-as-a-whole level is of central importance (Agazarian, 1997; Agazarian & Peters, 1981). Obviously, it is never stated as the therapeutic goal by members entering a couples group. People enter group therapy because they need change at the individual or couple level. They care about the proper functioning of the group and about understanding its mechanisms only insofar as it helps them to gain from the process therapeutically. For most members, working out group process issues is only a means to an end, albeit a very significant one. Yet, successful mastery of a troublesome group problem is nearly always viewed as a significant therapeutic step for the group.

Although we do believe that there is a group atmosphere that is observable and open to influence by the leaders, individual members, or subgroupings, I want to discourage mythologizing the concept. The whole group is a gestalt (i.e., a configuration having more power than the members taken singly; a system greater than the sum of its parts). However, a concept of a "group mind" can encourage vague and mystical interventions. In fact, many directional shifts in a group are not made by the group as a whole, but instead by a few influential members (or even just one), with the rest of the group remaining silently attentive and eventually following suit.

MEMBERS ASSUME LEADERSHIP

Many shifts in the level of group interaction occur not because the therapist chooses the shift but rather because the group so chooses. A couple may raise a topic on the couple's level of interaction by introducing a particular marital conflict. Soon, other members chime in, discussing similar problems in their marriages, and members move the group activity to an interpersonal level. Such shifts may occur several times in the course of any session and feel natural and comfortable to everyone involved. When this occurs spontaneously, the leaders do not need to intervene in this process of shifting levels. The group is doing its work unaided. However, the leaders do need to remain aware of the change of levels and must determine whether this shift might be a sign of group avoidance and of trouble.

Some years ago, a client in a group became very critical of Dr. Julian Slowinski, my co-lead in the group. She accused him of intentions that she found superficial. She especially did not like that he joked around before and after the formal group meeting. She decided his behavior was unprofessional. Dr. Slowinski, a diplomate in family psychology and nationally known sex therapist, listened quietly to her. I asked the group if others shared her concern, and nobody did. At the time, the client was engaged in an emotional affair long distance. The therapists tried to help her connect her criticism to her interest in avoiding dealing with the topic at hand, but she refused to consider this interpretation. However, the open discussion cleared the air.

MIXING LEVELS OF INTERACTION

On some occasions, it may be difficult to detect the level of group interaction. Work on two levels can go on simultaneously. For example, one group member may focus intensively on family-of-origin conflicts while another couple is working out something critical to their marriage by helping the person working on the family-of-origin material. Thus, while the

137

one member is working on an individual level, the two others are working on a couples level.

Patrick began to be quite assertive in the third year of his group membership, in keeping with his goal of speaking up more in his marriage. He spoke up to Antonia, and he encouraged Trevor and Spencer to speak up more to Holly and Robyn. The three men worked individually on this concern while each couple supported the other two in their efforts. The result was a mix of individual work for the men within the context of couples work for all three couples.

This simultaneity of levels is quite rare. More often, leaders can sit back and listen to the group work on one level, then another, then back to the first, on to a third, and so on. It is a bit like sitting at the ballet during a performance of Tchaikovsky's *Nutcracker* at Christmastime. First one gets the gestalt of all the children in the party scene. Then one concentrates only on Fritz, the impish brother who breaks the nutcracker. Then one watches Fritz with Marie, his sister. Finally, one watches only the lovely little girls rocking their dolls in the center of the stage as the adults cluster around them. All levels of activity are, in fact, going on simultaneously, but one level after another becomes the focal point of the drama that unfolds on the stage and captivates the attention of the viewer.

THE FLUIDITY OF A GROUP IN PROGRESS

A shifting of levels is often a useful and natural occurrence in a couples group. It indicates that the group is ready to move to a different subject or is ready to expand the subject at hand. The group may need to include more people to make things more interesting or to work more intensely by focusing on fewer members. However, a shifting of levels can also be a sign of a group in trouble. Sometimes groups spend so much time moving about between these levels of interaction that one gets the feeling of aimless chaos and lack of focus. Frequently, this phenomenon does not even appear as a shift from one level to another. Instead, a group discussion takes place at one level while it becomes clear that the matter should be worked on at a different level. It is reminiscent of the scene in Stephen

Crane's *The Red Badge of Courage* where the soldier has held his battle position valiantly with great fear and turmoil, only to be told later that the real battle was on another hill.

The therapist or a member may observe or decide that the group is misdirecting its energies. For example, a group works ad nauseam at a couples level when a burning group issue is lying dormant. When a therapist or group member becomes aware that avoidance is occurring, it is essential that group energies be refocused.

THREE TYPES OF MISDIRECTED GROUP ENERGIES

Despite all good intentions, groups get confused, anxious, and out of synch. Following are three instances in which this can happen and create larger problems if not checked:

- split ambivalence;
- fighting a couple's problem with someone else's partner; and
- fighting a group problem as an interpersonal problem.

Split Ambivalence

In this marital pattern, an *internal* conflict present in each partner is played out as a *marital* argument. In actuality, each partner is highly ambivalent about the issue in conflict, but each projects one side of the ambivalence onto the other partner, keeping the other side for himself or herself.

Spencer and Robyn had to decide whether to leave the country and return to England, which was Robyn's birthplace. An offer had been made to Spencer that might allow him greater salary and career growth than if he remained in the American division of the corporation that employed him. Spencer loved England and was more enthusiastic about the move than his British wife, who relished the ambience and weather of her life in Philadelphia. For a period of time, the way they divided up the conflict was that Spencer wanted to move and Robyn wanted to stay put on Yankee soil. This way of splitting the ambivalence allowed each a firm position, but kept both bickering with each other. To get to the ambivalence each faced about this enormous decision, I invited them to look at advantages and disadvantages that each felt about moving and

139

staying put. The group helped them to think through which position might be best for them in the long run. At this writing, they are still on American soil and each can see both sides of the decision.

Fighting Out a Couple's Problem With Someone Else's Partner

This happens frequently when a marriage partner is getting internally ready to tackle a problem in the marriage, but as yet lacks the courage to deal with it directly. The member tries it on a person with similar personality traits.

Spencer sometimes sat on his hands when Antonia got angry with Patrick. It seemed that by sitting on his hands he could refrain from intervening in the painful interaction within this couple. Spencer found Antonia's depression reminiscent of Robyn's moodiness. In both couples, the men had trouble speaking up. In both couples, the women got depressed regularly. Because of Spencer's sharp wit and quick mind, he often was able to speak more easily with Antonia than he could speak with his own wife. He would get tongue-tied when he would try to confront Robyn, as if her ebullient nature intimidated him a bit. The group was able to help Spencer and Robyn resolve issues while simultaneously helping Antonia and Patrick. To do that, however, it was necessary to encourage direct discussion between both members of the couples.

Fighting Out a Group-as-a-Whole Problem as an Interpersonal Problem

Here, one individual takes on a particular crusade, seeming to embark on a personal battle with someone in the group. In reality, an acute group issue is being worked on.

Near the end of the second year of a 3-year couples group, Antonia was furious with me. In an openly critical and hostile attack, she directly confronted me on issues that had long been bothering her. In reality, the entire group had been concerned with Antonia's membership and wanted to integrate her better into their small group of three couples. The atmosphere in the group as

Antonia confronted me was electric. I decided to encourage her forthrightness in order to flush the concern to a level of accessibility with which the group could deal. After a long confrontation, the group began to work with the issue of moving forward with greater unity.

It is the task of the leader to be alert and to watch for the shifts in levels. Missing their significance can cost valuable group time and keep the group stuck. Conversely, if a group is stuck for a while, it behooves the leader to search for possible manifestations of the misdirections described here. One might ask oneself, "What is going on here? What could be the real issue?" We suggest looking first for the group as a whole as the seat of the real issue and then looking farther as needed.

THE PRINCIPLE OF ISOMORPHISM

Isomorphism is a concept well known to systems theorists. As we discussed in Chapter 4, it asserts that similar structures and processes occur on several levels in related systems. Accordingly, a troublesome issue can manifest itself—with some variations—on an individual level (within a member of a couple), on a couples level (between members of a couple), and on a group level (for each group member).

Trevor and Holly have had a long-standing struggle over bantering with one another versus deep discussion of serious concerns. Holly has suggested that Trevor do affirmations to help himself get himself organized, but this superficial level of intervention merely applies a band aid to a lifelong pattern of over- and under-responsibility with which Trevor has struggled. Early in the life of the group, Holly customarily took the role of task leader in the marriage, ensuring that tasks got accomplished; Trevor preferred to play a team sport in his spare time. One day in the group they were fighting about whether Trevor had time for his team sport. In the group discussion, it became clear that they were really struggling with a split ambivalence: Both Trevor and Holly wanted to have free time and get needed jobs done, yet neither could choose between the two options.

From the group's rather spirited response, a matching issue on the group level became apparent: In the initial early sessions, the group had been working on a relatively superficial level. They were ready to move on to more serious therapy matters. Trevor and Holly's issue became a model for the group in working out its conflict over fun versus responsibility. It touched people on personal, couple, and group levels.

The principle of isomorphism is nothing mysterious. Understanding it and applying it to a group enables the therapist to think on several levels simultaneously, to respond with more flexibility to the challenges of the group, and to unravel otherwise strange shifts in levels.

Sympathetic Vibrations

From the foregoing discussion it becomes clear that it is to the advantage of the couples group therapist to be attuned to all four levels simultaneously. Most issues raised by a couple or individual resonate on other levels. In the world of music, a piano, when its pedal is depressed, will resonate in the appropriate string when another instrument produces that tone. In a group, other members will be affected by the struggles of an individual. Yet, as in the piano metaphor, members have to be open to the experience and the conflict has to touch a part for which they have a corresponding structure.

Awareness of the various ways in which problems manifest themselves gives the therapist a great deal of latitude in making choices. Assessing the most efficient place for intervention greatly enhances the therapist's effectiveness. In many instances, an intervention can be made on more than one level.

Diane opened the session with a report on her latest difficulty with her husband, Dwight. She had berated him for something, and he got hurt and became angry. He pouted for some time, which increased her anxiety and sense of aloneness.

Because of the particular stage that the group had reached, this issue could at that time be conceptualized on all four levels:

1. *Personal level.* Diane knew all too well her own difficulty. She needed to curtail her need to shape Dwight's behavior through

criticism. She had a long history of trying to change Dwight through what the group considered overly critical evaluations of his behavior. Most of the time she was, in fact, rather successful with it and got Dwight to do what she wanted him to do. However, she was unable to get him to make love to her often enough. Diane rarely connected her behavior to Dwight's lack of sexual appetite, but occasionally, especially in the group, she made a connection between less sex and more nagging. At these times, Diane became aware of the tremendous cost of her style of influence. Dwight, on the other hand, was extremely susceptible to guilt and highly vulnerable to criticism. He was an easy mark for Diane's version of behavior shaping. He had grown up in a highly intellectual Jewish family who shaped behavior through guilt and blame. When he would get angry, he might yell but would more frequently resort to mumbling under his breath and snide comments. In this way, he isolated himself and Diane from his own anger. During these periods, sex would decrease even more than usual.

2. *Couple level.* Both partners were involved in a repetitive, interactive sequence in which the untoward behaviors of one partner fed those of the other. Both were profoundly unhappy with this sequence and suffered considerably, but had no way to give up the pattern. Diane had been critical for many years before she met Dwight. Dwight had handled anger under his breath since his adolescent years. Both were imprisoned by a pattern that was unworkable in the marriage.

3. *Interpersonal level.* Patrick and Antonia, two other members in this group, had a similar issue. However, the mutual reinforcement of their behaviors was more obvious: Antonia used to berate Patrick for all the time he spent playing with his boats. Being lonely in his marriage and afraid to be assertive with his wife, Patrick felt compelled to get out of the house and play to get relief from his loneliness. Antonia resented the many hours he spent away from home because he did not do the chores she thought needed to be done there. She became impatient when he would take his sons out for rides on a Saturday rather than finishing projects at home. Patrick would react to her complaining with considerable guilt and anger. To make matters worse, he would withdraw; part of his motivation to work on his boats was to soothe himself.

143

4. *Group-as-a-whole level.* Expressing one's anger instead of running away was also a general issue in this group, especially with the male members. The members were feeling some anger at one another, but were reluctant to express it. Though there was no actual staying away from the group, members felt a lessening of the desire to work in the group, and the interaction moved more slowly rather than more quickly. The group was at a point of considerable opportunity. If it could work out the anger issue, greater intimacy and self-disclosure would result. However, if the members ran away emotionally, the group would remain stuck in a problem-solving, superficial mode that plagued it. Indirectness was no longer workable as a means of communication between the couples, between group members, or for the group as a whole. Though problem solving has a place in good group work, it was less than this group was capable of.

As this illustration shows, a group leader is faced with a number of options regarding the level at which he or she can choose to intervene. Which level is selected depends on a number of factors. However, choices need to be made with forethought and with an eye on the current status of the group and its members. There is little wisdom in merely doing what feels right or in getting caught up in the confusion of an unfocused group.

THE CHOICE OF INTERVENTION LEVELS: THERAPIST GUIDELINES

Knowledge of and sensitivity to the processes on all four interactive levels can be bewildering and may leave the therapist with the need for some handy rule of thumb that could indicate which level is the most advantageous at a given time. Unfortunately, no such easy rules exist. The decision about intervention levels needs to be made over and over in response to the changing dynamics of the group. A few general guidelines, however, include:

- There is latitude in the choice of levels.
- Shifting levels often resolves issues.
- Work at the level of greatest group pain.
- Consider all levels in each group session.
- The greater the member involvement is, the better.

Let us now consider each guideline in some detail.

Guideline 1: There Is Latitude in the Choice of Levels

Because the choice of intervention level has some latitude, selecting an ineffective level is not a major problem. At worst, it may result in boredom or flight behavior in the group. Usually, it soon becomes apparent to a therapist that a wrong tack has been taken and the members are losing interest. A skillful shifting of levels at that point can usually set things straight. Only a prolonged time span at an ineffective interactive level that fails to involve a sufficient number of members is likely to have detrimental effects.

Guideline 2: Shifting Levels Often Resolves Issues

Despite the latitude in intervention options, a shift in levels often helps in resolving an issue. If an intervention has failed on one level, one may try to attack the problem on a different level.

Antonia was true to form in being verbally domineering in the group in very much the same way in which she dominated her husband, Patrick, at home. I was not very successful trying to effect a change by dealing with this problem at a couples level. After I led the way in one of the groups, however, a few members in the group became annoyed with her verbal style and "took her on." At this interpersonal level, Antonia was finally able to see how costly her behavior was in the long run and that more listening and less talking would be to her and the group's advantage. After discussion in individual therapy, Antonia decided to join the group fully and relate to all the members, rather than just to use the group to do her own work.

Guideline 3: Work at the Level of the Greatest Group Pain in a Cohesive Group

There is some wisdom in working at the level at which the most pain and the most despair can be found. Whether one follows Freud, who insists that *Leidensdruck* (pressure of suffering) must be present in order for treatment to be successful, or Whitaker, who speaks of heightening the level of despair in order to effect change, the message is the same: On the whole, people are most amenable to change when they are in the most discomfort. The reverse of this guideline is also true: Working at a level that misses the pain and despair will feel strange or insulting to the member who is feeling it. It will also miss a valuable opportunity.

However, this guideline has some limitations. The person complaining the loudest is not necessarily the one in the most pain or the one most ready to make changes. Much to the contrary, the noisy complainer may very well enjoy the attention and care from the group but remain settled in his or her self-defeating ways. Often, it takes some astute observation by the leader or a group member to look through this pattern of complaint and no change and stop it.

Guideline 4: Consider All Levels in Each Group Session

Over the course of a group, all levels need to be kept in mind to an adequate extent. Any prolonged neglect of one of the four levels is likely to keep the group from being as successful as it could be. Such neglect could even have a detrimental effect on the group or its members. It is very much like a family. Though the parents may focus their attention temporarily on their marriage or on one of the children, any prolonged neglect of anyone will be very troublesome. Despite the attention to all levels, sessions usually take on a tone of being mostly focused in one particular area. The research study described in Chapter 10 is based on the assumption of such naturally occurring imbalances.

Guideline 5: The Greater the Member Involvement Is, the Better

Most of the time, the more members who are involved, actively or silently, in a discussion, the better it is for the group. A whole-group level of intervention, if done skillfully, can keep everyone in the group emotionally involved and working hard. In contrast, individual work can tempt people to drop out emotionally with internal self-statements such as, "That's not my problem," "This lady is weird. I'm glad I'm not like that," or "Let the leader handle it. I'll relax."

Yet this rule has a limitation too. Sometimes intensive individual work can be inspirational to others. All these guidelines are meant only as general directives. Interpersonal sensitivity, experience in working with couples and groups, and a consistently high level of attention to the many simultaneous processes in the group will guide the leader to make useful intervention choices.

9

Handling Predictable Problems in Ongoing Groups

I think we both have black belts in blame.

—One member of a couple

INTRODUCTION

In order to keep a therapy group vibrant and effective, the therapists must be prepared to handle a variety of problems that arise during the group's development. Many of these are familiar to every group therapist and seem to "come with the territory" of group therapy. Other types of problems, however, are indigenous to *couples* groups. In this chapter, we discuss problems of both kinds and possible solutions.

HANDLING ROUTINE ISSUES AND MINOR MISHAPS

Many emergencies and serious group problems happen because minor difficulties and annoyances are not handled well. Therefore, dealing with the early warnings of impending trouble keeps a group functioning and fluid. The kinds of leadership decisions that later have a profound impact often seem routine. More often, they are composed of many small decisions in a group's life. Catching a mistake before it gets big can prevent later trouble.

In these pages I have frequently mentioned Antonia, who inadvertently sometimes dominated both the group and her husband through subtle and open criticism. The astute reader may be wondering why I did not prevent the problem from occurring. I could find no way to intervene successfully and mistakenly continued to overlook the problem. The warning signs were there: Antonia had begun to detach more angrily from the group through storming out of the session. Her body language continued to be withdrawn and angry as she sat session after session with a pillow on her lap to cover her body. But I overlooked it, and the group paid the price. Had I strategized how to deal with the problem earlier, I might have worked with the group as a whole to educate them about Antonia being in danger of acting out the group's resistance to facing the ending of the group. Had the group dealt with the issue as a unit, Antonia might not have needed to be hostile in the group for as many months. However, in this instance, the combination of her dynamics, the dynamics of the couple, and the group dynamics mixed with my leadership style to produce a chronic group problem. In this way, a chronic but minor difficulty grew to unnecessarily major proportions because it was poorly handled.

I find that routine issues and minor mishaps are well worth attention by the leaders, who can prevent problems from getting worse by problem solving and working with the issue while it is still small. These issues seem to fall naturally into a number of categories:

- physical setting;
- absences;
- lateness; and
- finances.

Physical Setting

Group members deserve a setting that is visually attractive and physically comfortable. Excessive heat or cold, intrusive noise, or uncomfortable seats create distractions that keep a group from maximal functioning and ultimately detract from group cohesiveness. It is helpful to have nearby bathroom facilities and a small kitchen for coffee or water. Some group therapists might disagree with the idea of providing amenities like coffee or tea; our experience has shown us that it serves to create an aura of safety and thus enhances cohesiveness.

Our group rooms were designed to have the atmosphere of a living room. We believe that this ambience helps to get the group going because it gives a message that the group room is a place in which people can safely make disclosures about themselves. It is a kind of "safe harbor" that is part of the larger world, yet psychologically removed from it. It is a room in which people are expected to know themselves and each other very, very well.

Absences

The two kinds of absences are necessary absences and unnecessary absences. Necessary absences are to be expected in a group of highly functioning individuals over an 11-month span of time. Most people are absent very little, but many adults must be out of town on occasion. We expect about two such absences per year for each couple and tell the couples so beforehand. A necessary absence is therefore dealt with as a routine matter. We request that people tell the group if they know in advance they will be out of town for an upcoming session.

When a member is ill, group members often write a get-well card during the session, using the paper, crayons, and stickers we have on hand for such purposes. The attending spouse transmits the card and well-wishes. This adds to the cohesiveness of the group and to the missing member's feeling of belonging. Members tell us that this kind of thoughtfulness means a lot to them.

An unnecessary absence is of more clinical concern and will be discussed later in this chapter under "emergencies." When a member is absent with a superficial excuse—for example, that a weekend golf game is more important than the group—we consider this a group emergency and deal with it accordingly.

Lateness

Lateness in a couples group usually involves a couple because most couples travel to the session together. We also find, paradoxically, that people with a tendency to be late marry people who insist on being on time or even early. Because of this dynamic, the couple that comes late more than once usually raises it as a problem. It is usually the time-conscious partner who is troubled by the tardiness and is likely to have the group's sympathy because punctuality is desired group behavior. Lateness becomes a topic of discussion, sometimes accompanied by the laughter of recognition by members who are also often late in their lives. People who come late may hate to sit around and wait for things to start, and those who need to be on time may have been raised in an environment (family or school) in which lateness was severely punished. The discovery of these causes and the discussion of responsibility and time management in earlier family times often lead to greater appreciation of the partner's discomfort. This frequently eases the lateness problem.

Likewise, latecomers gain a better understanding of their spouses' anxiety and feeling. It also helps the latecomers to hear from the group what went on while the group was waiting. Often, the members of the couple in question have no idea that sitting in the waiting room before the meeting and engaging in pregroup socializing is fun and that, in fact, they are missing something by being late.

More importantly, group members let the late couple know—perhaps even with anger—that their lateness has kept the group from getting started and that it creates a waste of time and money for the people who are present. Most of the time, the late couple had not considered the importance of time management in building an intimate relationship.

Finances

The full monthly fee is due on the first day of that month. If a couple has not paid by the second session of the month, the leader who is the keeper of the structure mentions this at the beginning of the second session. Couples know ahead about this procedure and instances of late payment are rare. When it is necessary to make late payment a group issue, the discussion is not set up as a public flogging, but rather as a therapeutic issue that increases understanding of the motivation for the nonpayment. Because a couple can simply request an extension of payment when needed by discussing the reason with the leader, I am able to distinguish among carelessness, actual financial hardship, and a therapeutic issue.

A couple who falls behind in payment repeatedly probably does so because the handling of money is a clinical issue with that couple. A discussion that gets started due to unpaid fees can often help this couple and others in the group deal with the complexities of couples' financial management in a clinically valuable manner. Once again, the resentment of group members about "wasting time" when discussing carelessness in finances is quickly interpreted as a way in which carelessness engenders hostility in a relationship.

If a couple is unable to pay because of some unforeseen financial disaster, we do make arrangements for extending credit or for a reduction in the fee. However, in keeping with the trust in a good working relationship, these arrangements need to be made when the difficulty occurs, rather than when the couple is already in arrears and a group is annoyed at their nonpayment.

DEALING WITH NATURALLY EMERGING MEMBER ROLES IN THE GROUP

Member roles are naturally emerging group phenomena. In the course of interactions in the group, each member behaves in such ways that the group begins to expect this behavior from the member. The behavior always satisfies certain group needs, such as avoidance of a tough issue or comic relief, so the member's behavior is rewarded by the whole group or by some segment in it. Group roles emerge from the systemic interaction between member and group. In a group, it is likely that if a particular member did not take a role, someone would be "elected" by the group to fulfill a given function.

A group role is the set of behavioral expectations placed upon an individual member to behave in certain predictable ways, which in turn allow the group to deal with this member in accordance with the expectation. A number of excellent descriptions of typical group roles have been presented in the literature (Bogdanoff & Elbaum, 1978). The following discussion focuses on those naturally emerging member roles that we have encountered most frequently as they unfold in couples groups:

- the scapegoat;
- the joker;
- the polite socializer;
- the monopolizer;

- the competitor;
- the would-be co-leader; and
- "I'm just here for my spouse."

The Scapegoat

The scapegoat is usually the recipient of the group's anger at any time in its development. He or she has some kind of abrasive behavior that irritates other members, who either become angry in the group or smolder. The scapegoat provides a convenient target onto which to unload anger that might be more properly directed elsewhere, such as at the leader, the partner, or the whole group. Most of the time, the behavior stops or the group learns to deal with it and goes on to the next developmental stage. Sometimes, however, the scapegoat is in danger of getting stuck in the role and the leader needs to intervene. This can be done by making the process conscious and pointing out what is going on or by reframing (providing the group with a new way of looking at the scapegoating phenomenon). Although the scapegoat can be a member or a couple, it is most frequently one member of a couple.

Dwight had been annoying a number of group members with his anxiously bouncing leg and his penchant for taking notes during sessions. Furthermore, his witty comments often diffused group work. For example, Dwight liked to state that he was doing a good job in the group. He would often point out how much he had learned and how far he had come in the group. This sounded vain, although his intent was not to brag but rather to protect himself. When someone in the course of making a point about his marriage would mention his note taking, he would launch into an apology followed by a defense of the behavior ("I just want to be able to remember what Dr. Coché says"). Instead of allowing the group to pounce on Dwight and make him even more defensive, because his self-esteem was shaky, I provided a reframing by pointing out that Dwight was learning things that were hard. I might have pointed out that Dwight was performing an important group function. He was keeping the group from moving too fast into uncharted waters, a concern shared by some other members. Thus, his seemingly passive aggressive behaviors served to divert the group's attention from the unsettling issues it needed to address.

The Joker

The joker protects the group from anxiety by deflecting it through humor. Although the group needs some comic relief at times in order not to be paralyzed by the anxiety in the room, it is the role of effective leaders to supply this relief, which is very different from the part played by a joker.

The joker's "funny" remarks are not usually timed well. They are often interruptive and not warmly received by the group. They seem out of place or too frequent. Yet much of the time the group rewards the joker's behavior with laughter. It is only when someone in the group has the courage to intervene and to ask the joker to tone things down that the joking diminishes and the group can return to serious work. At times, an intervention from the leaders is needed; when that is the case, it signifies that the joker has too much latent support in the group because the group as a whole is resisting work. At times, a request from the group for the joker to settle down does not suffice and stronger confrontation of the joker is needed. In this case, the joker's behavior is more clearly characterologically determined and less of a temporary group phenomenon. Some therapeutic work on the origins of the behavior is necessary for things to settle down.

The Polite Socializer

This role is more frequently seen in a couples group than in other adult psychotherapy groups. Socializing and making polite conversation with other couples is, after all, part of a couple's social identity. Thus, the polite socializer is usually a well-meaning person who does not yet understand or is afraid to understand that a different type of behavior is expected in group psychotherapy. This person was often raised in a home in which one lived by the motto: "If you do not have anything nice to say in social circles, do not say anything."

We avoid trouble by educating prospective members about the difference between group psychotherapy and social conversation. We also teach the group to make a clear distinction between the conversation that goes on in the waiting room before the session and the ongoing group work in the session. We sometimes liken the hall to a kind of tunnel through which a person passes and becomes transformed into a working group member until passage back to the waiting area. Often, a group still opens a session with a few minutes of social banter. We do not participate in this banter because we do not want to send confusing messages to the members about desirable within-group behavior. After a few minutes of social conversation, one couple usually gets things going with a real issue. If the banter goes on too long, we provide an interpretation of its content or comment that the group is avoiding its task.

The polite socializer is someone who, despite the leaders' educational efforts, still does not understand the difference between group work and chatter. If the group is in a state of anxiety and avoidance, it may well support the socializing. More often, however, group members will become impatient and push the group back to its task, disregarding the polite socializer's chitchat in a more or less polite manner.

The Monopolizer

This is usually an anxious and needy member who takes a large portion of the group's "air time" in a whining but authoritarian manner. Content varies from engaging the therapists in frequent, lengthy debates to presenting a stream of narratives meant to illustrate a point but that keep the attention focused on that member. Psychologically, the monopolizer is a needy child who is unable to share parental attention with other siblings, who needs to dominate the group, and who is resistant to the leaders' efforts. The monopolizer attracts the group's attention in an abrasive and nonconstructive manner and is in danger of becoming a scapegoat if the behavior continues unchecked.

In order to handle the monopolizer, we suggest involving the group in a planned intervention based on the leaders' assessment of the underlying interpersonal dynamic. One needs to be careful, however, that involving the group does not push the monopolizer into a scapegoat role.

The Competitive Member

Competitive behavior can be expressed by interruptions such as, "Oh, that happened to me, too"—a remark upstaging others rather than expressing empathy. Competitiveness can be seen in giving feedback that criticizes another member instead of expressing a feeling. At times, competitiveness arises between the partners in a couple, at other times between group members, and at times it goes from member to leader. Appropriate interventions include labeling the behavior for the group ("John, you sound like you are in competition with Jim") and relating it to family-of-origin issues.

If competitive behavior in the group is frequent, especially between the same two people, it is advisable for the leaders to look at their own dynamics and assess whether they are competing with each other and whether their competitiveness is repeating itself isomorphically in the group.

The Would-Be Co-Leader

This member, frequently a mental health professional needing couples therapy, is able to offer incisive observations and helpful comments to other members. But, as I know, it is hard for therapists to become couples. Other group members usually respond positively at first and express gratitude and admiration for all the expertise and help. After a while, however, it becomes clear that the helpfulness and profound insights act as a shield behind which the member hides and is protected from self-disclosure and the need to work on his or her marital issues. The leader can intervene by making the process conscious to the person in question. Just as frequently, however, another group member will express dissatisfaction at the lack of personal openness of the would-be co-leader and the group begins to apply pressure on the pseudotherapist to be a full group member.

Dwight really wanted to help. His career, executive coaching, developed in spite of difficulty with academic achievement. He was not at all defiant in his role as a client. In fact, he was grateful for help received, but he really wanted others to know how competent he was in his own field of work. After he became less anxious and stopped taking notes to use at home, he relaxed into his membership in the group and made huge transformational changes in his life and his marriage. He was so proud of his own work and the work of the group, that he became a bit zealous on occasions. He would intellectualize in the third person ("It is always wise to have career interviews") rather than speak directly to the member. Although Dwight in no way thought he was more knowledgeable than the co-leaders, he did need and want recognition for the long road traveled to his own change. After some time, the members stopped humoring Dwight and began to give him feedback that it did not help when he pontificated. Dwight took the feedback gracefully and tried to change, though his personality structure indeed predisposed him to intellectual explanations of emotional events. Over the course of a decade of treatment, Dwight began his group membership as a person who hid from his emotion. He emerged as a warm and funny husband.

Pseudoleadership can be effective or ineffective. Effective pseudoleadership goes undetected longer because the member is able to integrate helpful comments and insights into the member role, seems modest, and phrases comments well. In contrast, the ineffective would-be co-leader makes ill-phrased, ill-timed observations that are presented in a showy or pompous manner. After some initial gratitude, the group usually resents and rejects these "interventions" and the member is in danger of losing the respect of the group unless the behavior is modified. Although effective pseudoleadership seems less problematic, in fact, both styles are problematic for the group and its members.

"I'm Just Here for My Spouse"

This occurs in a couple in which one spouse has carried the symptom for the marital unit. At first, denial is collusive as both members agree that one of them is "sick" and in need of help while the other is mentally healthy. They also collude in denying the existence of a marital problem. Although the denial is not pervasive enough to prevent them from signing up for the group, it still impels the spouse to come into the first group session and proclaim to the group: "I'm just here for my spouse. The marriage is fine and so am I." The group is rarely fooled and sees its work cut out for it.

A group will not put up with this for long. After a few sessions, the supposedly healthy spouse is likely to be confronted on a behavior that exacerbates the other spouse's symptoms. If done with sufficient firmness, tact, and concurrent support for the member in question, the confrontation can turn the reluctant fence-sitter into a full-fledged member little by little over the ensuing months.

HANDLING OF CLINICAL EMERGENCIES

The minor mishaps described before happen in most couples groups and can be handled by straightforward interventions. However, emergencies require concentrated effort by and cooperation of the leaders, their staff, and the group. In the following sections, we will describe some common clinical emergencies and possible responses to them.

Resistance by No Show

Why do members fail to appear for a session? Although rare, this behavior usually occurs because a spouse is so angry at the partner and so disgusted with the marriage that he or she believes that the group is worthless because it is not helping the spouse to "shape up." Alternatively, the member may be suspicious that the group is siding with the spouse in the recurrent marital disputes. When this happens, the member may not show up for the group session or be absent with a very lame excuse. The spouse is likely to come in and tell the group of the events leading up to this nonappearance.

A situation like this calls for a very definitive and active intervention from the leaders and from the individual couples therapist. The couple clearly is in a crisis. If no help is given at this point, the couple might be lost to the group, much to the detriment of everyone involved. We suggest that the keeper of the structure place a call to the absent member while the group is meeting and discuss the situation immediately.

A more serious no-show situation is one in which both partners refuse to come to a session, although this has not happened in our experience. In such a case, we would schedule an emergency therapy session with the missing couple before the next group session and discuss the whole matter. We can imagine two kinds of situations that might lead to a rebellious no show of a couple.

- When it is still early in the group's development, the nonappearance could be due to a couple's anxiety over being in the group. Careful preparation of the couples usually prevents this problem. If it happens, the couple's concerns need to be addressed. Perhaps they need more reassurance before they feel comfortable with being in a group. We suggest that individual couples work to stem the crisis.
- Near the middle stage of a group, a couple was very dissatisfied with the group's progress. We strongly encouraged them to come into the group and raise their feelings of discomfort and dissatisfaction as a problem. This couple came close to leaving the group and would have if the issue had been handled defensively by the group and the leaders.

157

Breaking of Policies

Breaking of policies can occur at any time in the life of a group and has to be handled immediately. Letting things slide undermines the viability of the group and can lead to irreversible damage. Naturally, the types of policies that are broken differ; some are more serious than others. Breaking of a serious rule, such as breach of confidentiality, is a rare occurrence. Minor infractions, such as lateness, are more common and therapists are well served to have mechanisms in place to deal with these.

More important incidents, such as blatant socializing outside the group or refusal to finish out the group year, require more than mechanisms. The therapist must use all his or her therapeutic skill and the power of the group itself to deal with the problem. Occasionally, it is advisable to call in a consultant. In other instances—for example, if confidence has been betrayed—it may be necessary to discharge a couple from the group and from the services of that therapist. If members can apologize to the group, the relationship may be reparable, and the group would be handled like a group in a crisis. Leaders must remain aware that such crises have long-range impact on the group and are better prevented than dealt with after the fact.

Divorce Threats and Impending Divorce

Occasionally, a group contains a couple in which one or both partners verbalize thoughts or plans of divorce. What makes this an emergency is that the couple who repeatedly threatens divorce seriously undermines the morale of the group.

In many ways, a divorce in a couples group is analogous to (albeit not quite as disturbing as) a suicide in a noncouple therapy group. The marriage—which is, after all, the "primary patient" in the couples group—ceases to exist. If a couple were to go through with a divorce during the group year, it would have to leave the group.

Similarly to suicide threats, divorce threats come in two varieties: acute and chronic. The acute threat occurs at the height of a crisis, with one or both partners extremely upset and despondent. The therapist needs to verbalize that—as long as they *want* to—the partners can resolve this crisis. The full support from the group can often turn the crisis around and restore a couple's sense of competence in overcoming trouble spots. It is extremely important that the group not take sides, despite the fact that it is very tempting for its members to see the villain and the victim in a divorcing couple. Getting hooked into such a pattern is likely to antagonize one partner—or even both—and worsen the divorce threat rather than lessen it.

The chronic divorce threat is a different matter. We all know couples who utter such threats repeatedly but, somehow, no one takes them quite seriously. The group knows that these threats are a common occurrence and that neither partner is really willing or able to live without the other. In some couples, the divorce-threatening partner is always the same one and in all likelihood is using the threats as a tool of power against the other. In other couples, the partners take turns making the divorce threats, which are then part of a continuing dance of avoiding intimacy.

Diane and Dwight had been coming to the group for many years before Diane threatened divorce. Her warning came because Dwight handled a situation in a way that Diane found deeply insulting to her and her cultural background. Diane was so horrified at his racial slur that she said she would divorce him unless he remained in therapy to work out the issues. Although her threat was quite unsettling to the group, they too were horrified by the ease with which Dwight insulted his own ethnic heritage. However, no member really thought Diane would leave Dwight. There were too many positive aspects to the marriage and too many fears of divorce on both sides. What was clear was that Dwight's anger would get the best of him and he would slip into contemptuous interchanges like his parents before him, who had insulted him for poor academic achievement.

Handling the ongoing group is quite analogous to handling the routines of daily living in one's marriage, one's parenting experience, and one's career. Although the tried and true mechanisms for dealing with predictable trouble are reassuring and handy to have in place, one can never become too casual or comfortable in cavalierly handling group issues. As in life, people are sensitive to being "handled" and are likely to feel manipulated.

Skillful intervention is first and foremost done from the therapeutic stance of a genuine and caring human being. This stance, more than any of the techniques outlined previously, enables a group to survive its developmental and daily bumps.

159

10

Coordinating Clinical Diagnosis With Outcome Research

The principal area that I have to stay aware of is that my wife is not a mind reader.

—A husband who forgets that emotions are important

EVIDENCE-BASED PRACTICE IN SYSTEMS THERAPY

I am delighted to be able to report that since the publication of the first edition of this text, considerable outcome research has been done in the areas of couples therapy, group therapy, and, to a lesser extent, couples group therapy. It is important as scientist–practitioners that we be aware of scientific advances in our field, especially inasmuch as they inform clinical practice. In addition, it is important to be able to inform clients with confidence of key findings from research about the effectiveness of the treatment that they may receive. This shared knowledge is key in the spirit of ethical informed consent. With help from Dr. Seth Gillihan of the University of Pennsylvania, this chapter reviews each of these areas of the literature and goes on to report our own work in evidence-based practice on the couples groups at the Coché Center.

161

Recent Research in Couples Psychotherapy

A sizeable corpus of research shows that couples psychotherapy is effective in treating a wide range of issues, from individual clinical disturbances like mood and affective disorders to physical diagnoses like chronic pain to problematic functioning in the relationship. Although this book is concerned primarily with the quality of couples' relationship, these other important areas of the literature demonstrate the versatility and effectiveness of couples psychotherapy and will be reviewed briefly. Moreover, results from large representative national surveys have shown powerful associations between marital distress and psychological disorders (e.g., Whisman, 1999). Other research has shown that mental illness can be both cause (Ulrich-Jakubowslu, Russell, & O'Hara, 1988) and consequence (O'Leary, Christian, & Mendell, 1994; Whisman & Bruce, 1999) of relationship distress; therefore, effective couples treatment of individual distress likely will benefit both partners.

Anxiety Disorders

Many studies have found that couples therapy for anxiety disorders is an effective form of treatment. The bulk of studies have focused on panic disorder with agoraphobia (e.g., Barlow, O'Brien, & Last, 1984; Emmelkamp et al., 1992; for reviews see Byrne, Carr, & Clark, 2004; Daiuto, Baucom, Epstein, & Dutton, 1998). The partner in these studies generally acts as a "co-therapist" (e.g., Cobb, Mathews, Childs-Clarke, & Blowers, 1984) and encourages the agoraphobic person to maintain the behaviors that led to improvement in treatment. Other anxiety disorders that have been treated effectively in couples therapy include obsessive–compulsive disorder (OCD; Emmelkamp, de Haan, & Hoodguin, 1990) and posttraumatic stress disorder (PTSD; Monson, Schnurr, Stevens, & Guthrie, 2004).

Mood Disorders

Additional research has focused on the evidence base for couples therapy as treatment for mood disorders, especially major depressive disorder. Several studies have found that couples therapy leads to significant improvement in depressive symptoms (e.g., Emanuels-Zuurveen & Emmelkamp, 1996; Teichman, Bar-El, Shor, Sirota, & Elizur, 1995; for a review, see Barbato & D'Avanzo, 2008). One of the larger studies in this area found that couples therapy was as effective as antidepressant medication in treating major depressive disorder and that individuals in the couples treatment condition were much less likely to drop out of treatment (Leff et al., 2000). Importantly, the cost of couples therapy was estimated to be no greater than the cost for medication. Couples psychotherapy for depression may be particularly useful when relationship conflict is present (Barbato & D'Avanzo, 2008; Jacobson, Dobson, Fruzzetti, Schmaling, & Salusky, 1991).

Substance Abuse
Several clinical trials have examined the effectiveness of treating alcohol and other substance abuse in a couples context, with positive results (e.g., McCrady, Stout, Noel, Abrams, & Nelson, 1991; O'Farrell, Cutter, Choquette, Floyd, & Bayog, 1992; O'Farrell & Fals-Stewart, 2000). It has been shown to be effective with both male (Fals-Stewart, Bircher, & O'Farrell, 1996) and female (Winters, Fals-Stewart, O'Farrell, Birchler, & Kelley, 2002) substance abusers. A recent meta-analysis of research in this area concluded that couples therapy for drug abuse generally produces better outcomes on drug use variables as well as on relationship satisfaction (Powers, Vedel, & Emmelkamp, 2008). In addition to being more clinically effective than individually based treatment, couples therapy appears to be more cost effective (Fals-Stewart, Klostermann, Yates, O'Farrell, & Birchler, 2005).

Other Physical Concerns
The couples therapy modality has been used with a host of physical concerns too numerous to list exhaustively here; a sampling of areas for which couples therapy has proved to be beneficial includes dealing with cancer (Donnelly et al., 2000), osteoarthritis knee pain (Keefe et al., 1996), wife abuse (O'Leary, Heyman, & Neidig, 1999), orgasmic dysfunction (Everaerd & Decker, 1981), terminal illness (Mohr et al., 2003), and coronary rehabilitation (Priebe & Sinning, 2001). In short, couples therapy is a powerful therapy modality that is effective in treating a large and growing host of treatment concerns.

Relationship Satisfaction
Although couples psychotherapy has been shown to be effective in treating a single "identified patient" in the relationship, substantial work has also been done to develop effective couples treatments for addressing the relationship. Several reviews and meta-analyses have summarized this work more comprehensively than is possible here (for systematic reviews,

see Baucom, Shoham, Mueser, Daiuto, & Stickle, 1998; Christensen & Heavey, 1999; Dunn & Schwebel, 1995; Hahlweg & Markman, 1988; Johnson & Lebow, 2000; Lebow & Gurman, 1995; Sayers, Kohn, & Heavey, 1998; Shadish & Baldwin, 2003, 2005; Snyder, Castellani, & Whisman, 2006; Wood, Crane, Schaalje, & Law, 2005). Our goal is to highlight the main findings from the last three decades of research in this area, as well as to note some of the mechanisms by which couples therapy has been shown to have its effects.

In reviews of the effectiveness of couples therapy for relationship distress and satisfaction, two clear trends emerge that seem both contradictory and a bit ironic:

- Couples therapy is highly effective for treating a broad range of issues.
- Many couples fail to benefit from couples therapy (Snyder et al., 2006).

This state of affairs is similar to that of other effective treatments for psychological problems, such as the treatment of major depressive disorder with antidepressant medication; the medication is much better than placebo but fails to help a substantial proportion of depressed individuals (e.g., DeRubeis et al., 2005). As Shadish and Baldwin (2003) reported in their meta-analysis of marital and family therapies, couples therapy is better than no treatment for approximately 80% of individuals receiving couples therapy (see also Snyder et al., 2006). This number is particularly striking given that the degree to which a couple wants to work on its relationship is not predictive of changes in relationship satisfaction (Halford, Lizzio, Wilson, & Occhipinti, 2007). From these data, one can surmise that a variable that increases the likelihood of successful treatment outcome is skill intervention: Motivation alone is not predictive of success, but skillful intervention correlates highly with improved relationships.

Key Research in Behavioral Couples Therapy

The majority of studies have used behavioral couples therapy, which focuses on the patterns of actions and communication of the couple. It is generally a skills-based approach. A smaller number of studies have looked at emotion-focused couples therapy and insight-oriented couples therapy. Individual studies have demonstrated the effectiveness of behavioral (e.g., Snyder, Wills, & Grady-Fletcher, 1991), emotion-focused (e.g., Denton, Burleson, Clarke, Rodriguez, & Hobbs, 2000), and insight-oriented (e.g., Snyder et al., 1991) couples therapy approaches. The various couples treatments tend to be comparably effective—no single therapy helps every couple. Of additional concern is the fact that up to 60% of individuals who improve following couples therapy will show significant deterioration, thus emphasizing the need for relapse prevention measures (Snyder et al., 2006).

Given the effectiveness of cognitive therapy in treating a host of psychological problems, it makes sense that couples therapists have adapted principles from cognitive therapy for couples therapy. Early work in this area focused on establishing that specific thought patterns were associated with relationship distress. For example, Epstein and Eidelson (1981) confirmed that unrealistic beliefs about relationships were negatively correlated with marital satisfaction; other research has pointed to the specific kinds of attributions and beliefs associated with marital strife (Townsley, Beach, Fincham, & O'Leary, 1991; for a review, see Bradbury & Fincham, 1990). In light of these associations between cognitive variables and relationship satisfaction, additional work has examined the effect of incorporating cognitive interventions into couples therapy. In general, the results have been positive (e.g., Baucom & Lester, 1986) and typically indistinguishable from those of behavioral marital therapy (e.g., Emmelkamp et al., 1988; for a review, see Baucom et al., 1998).

Integrative Efforts in Treating Couples

In an effort to develop more effective treatments, several attempts have been made to combine or integrate different couples therapy approaches. Several studies combined behavioral with cognitive interventions for couples. Although the results were positive for the treatment overall, the addition of a cognitive component did not result in significantly better outcomes than those for behavioral therapy alone (e.g., Baucom, Sayers, & Sher, 1990; Halford, Sanders, & Behrens, 1993; for a review, see Baucom et al., 1998).

Other attempts at integration included Christensen and colleagues' (2004) "integrative behavioral couples therapy," which incorporates a strong element of emotional acceptance into a behavioral treatment. This research study tested integrative versus traditional behavioral couples therapy in a large randomized clinical trial. Contrary to their hypothesis, the integrative treatment was not significantly more effective than traditional behavioral couples therapy, although both treatments were highly effective; similar results were found in 2-year follow-up data (Christensen, Atkins, Yi, Baucom, & George, 2006). Findings from these studies underscore the difficulty involved in designing more effective couples therapies.

Key Change Variables

Other attempts to develop more effective couples therapies have sought to identify the mechanisms whereby couples therapy produces positive change. This line of inquiry is relatively new and therefore the amount of literature to date is small (for a review, see Gottman, 1998). Several studies have shown surprising and somewhat disappointing results about the presumed "active ingredients" of various couples therapies; for example, the degree of improvement in communication, a cornerstone of behavioral couples therapy, is not associated with increases in relationship satisfaction (see Snyder et al. 2006).

Nevertheless, other studies have identified factors that are significantly associated with treatment outcome. One predictive measure is that successful integrative couples psychotherapy increases acceptance between partners of one another and of the marriage (Cordova, Jacobson, & Christensen, 1998). Similarly, Bradley and Furrow (2004) found in emotion-focused couples therapy that therapists' facilitation of the couple's emotional experience was predictive of more adaptive partner behaviors. Much work remains to be done in order to identify additional mechanisms of success in couples therapy and to translate these mechanisms into more effective treatments.

Who Benefits?

Finally, efforts have been made to determine factors that predict success in couples therapy—for example, age, education, employment, length of relationship, and degree of relationship distress. Results from individual studies have been inconsistent (see Snyder et al., 2006), suggesting that we currently know more about which treatments are effective than about who is most likely to benefit from treatment. Even less is known about matching specific therapies with specific individuals. A handful of individual studies has produced results suggesting certain forms of treatment based on characteristics of the partners in the couple—for example, that couples who are sexually dissatisfied may benefit more from integrated than from traditional behavioral couples therapy (Atkins et al., 2005). The one clear finding to emerge from a meta-analysis in this area was that, for moderately distressed couples, emotion-focused couples therapy was more effective than behavioral couples therapy (Wood et al., 2005).

In our clinical practice, we long ago recognized that couples therapy, powerful as it is, would not help every couple or help every couple with every issue. We therefore broadened our thinking to consider not only various approaches in couples treatment, but also additional treatment modalities altogether. Given our strong systemic bent, we were aware of the power of psychotherapy groups to effect change in human systems (see also Feld, 1998); we now briefly review the research on the effectiveness of group interventions, before turning our attention to the integration of couples and group therapies—the couples psychotherapy group.

Group Psychotherapy

Similar to the research with couples therapy, group psychotherapy now has a large evidence base supporting its effectiveness as a therapy modality for a wide range of issues. As with couples therapy, a vast array of presenting problems have been treated successfully in a group format (for a review, see DeRubeis & Crits-Christoph, 1998), including social phobia (Hope, Heimberg, & Bruch, 1995), coping with metastatic cancer (Spiegel, Bloom, & Yalom, 1981), depression (Free, Oei, & Sanders, 1991), and obsessive–compulsive disorder (Fals-Stewart, Marks, & Schafer, 1993).

Individual Treatment Within a Group
Much of the research in this area involves adaptations of individual treatments for the group setting. In this approach, group dynamics are not employed as part of the treatment model but individuals are treated simultaneously in a room together. For example, Beutler et al. (1987) adapted cognitive therapy for depression for use in a group format and found better outcomes among members of the group treatments, including a lower rate of dropout. Similarly, Wilfley and colleagues (2002) found that both group cognitive–behavioral therapy and group interpersonal psychotherapy were effective treatments for binge-eating disorder. Many of these cognitive and behavioral groups maintain an individual approach to treating psychopathology and do not incorporate the systems perspective that we have found so useful in our group work.

Although these group treatments often have proven to be effective, we note their limitations as mental health treatment. Many clients come to group therapy not necessarily because they have an Axis I DSM-IV disorder but rather because they want to develop more effective social skills or they wish to deepen their understanding of themselves. In a group-dynamics-based treatment model, the group becomes the microcosm for the social interactions outside it, and clients learn through here-and-now work to be more socially adept and sensitive. Clients learn from experience. Groups without group dynamic expertise are more limited in the skills they can model for participants. In so doing, individual work in a group setting minimizes key healing aspects of the group modality (e.g., group cohesiveness and the microcosm of the larger world that is accessible for treatment with a knowledge of group dynamics (Yalom & Leszcz, 2005).

Satterfield's Hybrid Model

There have been attempts to integrate groups that are both empirically based and that capitalize on the dynamics of group interactions. After his internship at the Coché Center, Jason Satterfield (1994) became interested in a hybrid model that integrates cognitive–behavioral interventions and group dynamics. As Satterfield points out, there is a difference between "offering cognitive therapy through a group rather than [offering it] simply in a group setting" (p. 185). The complementarity of cognitive–behavioral techniques and systems thinking can produce a very vigorous result not unlike the "hybrid vigor" observed in plants (Birchler, Yao, & Chudalayandi, 2006).

The group dynamics can evoke member reactions that can be tested using the tools of cognitive therapy; for example, group members can encourage an individual to examine the evidence for his assumption that the group members do not care about him. The shared experience of learning the skills of cognitive therapy also may lead to enhanced group cohesion, thereby building a stronger and more productive whole. Although the complexity of our couples psychotherapy groups defies creation of a clear manual, we do incorporate cognitive and behavioral approaches into our groups. The result has been groups that are more evidence based and effective, as the following pages demonstrate. We now turn our attention to the literature on couples group therapy.

Recent Research in Couples Group Psychotherapy

The literature on couples group psychotherapy is sparse, in large part because of the relatively small numbers of clinicians who have been trained to use this modality. We have been excited to witness the growth of couples group psychotherapy practice since the publication of the first edition of this book. As we go to print, I return from day-long training of the model for over 150 colleagues nationally within the last 2 months. Given the commitment to clinical research that Dr. Erich Coché and I worked toward for 25 years, I am especially enthused about the development of a body of knowledge from evidence-based practice in couples group psychotherapy.

Couples Group Therapy for Partner Concerns

As with couples therapy, many of the existing studies have used couples groups to deliver treatments to individuals, rather than treating the couple as a system. Couples group therapy has been used to deliver effective treatment for one partner's abuse of alcohol (Bowers & Al-Redha, 1990) or drugs (Li, Armstrong, Chaim, & Shenfeld, 2007); for helping couples deal with one partner's HIV status (Gazarik & Fischman, 1995; Pomeroy, Green, & Van Laningham, 2002) or breast cancer diagnosis (Manne et al., 2005); for treating female hypoactive sexual desire (Hurlbert, White, Powell, & Apt, 1993); and for treating one partner's emotion dysregulation, such as that seen in borderline personality disorder (Kirby & Baucom, 2007). Couples groups also have been used effectively to treat the difficult issues of partner abuse (Brannen & Rubin, 1996; Stith, Rosen, McCollum, & Thomsen, 2004) and sexual deviance (e.g., exhibitionism; Risen & Althof, 1990).

Couples Group Therapy for Relationship Concerns

Many clinicians have begun to recognize the power of group couples psychotherapy not simply as a more efficient means to deliver existing treatments, but also as a treatment modality uniquely designed to address systemic issues in intrapersonal, interpersonal, intracouple, and intercouple functioning. As such, it has the power to effect change at multiple levels and to do so simultaneously and therefore efficiently. Empirical research has demonstrated the effectiveness of couples group psychotherapy to facilitate greater relationship satisfaction (for early reviews, see Bennun, 1986; Marett, 1988). Communication training in a couples group format has been shown to make couples happier and less distressed (Wilson, Bernstein, & Wilson, 1988). Other studies that have successfully used behavioral marital therapy in a group couples setting include Bennun (1985), Brady (1976), Liberman, Levine, Wheeler, Sanders, and Wallace (1976).

Although these studies consistently show the effectiveness of couples group psychotherapy, they generally do not demonstrate significant advantages in outcome for couples groups (Wilson et al., 1988). Other couples group psychotherapy approaches that have shown effectiveness at improving relationship quality include a short-term, solution-focused couples group (Zimmerman, Prest, & Wetzel, 1997), cognitive–behavioral psychoeducation (Kaiser, Hahlweg, Fehm-Wolfsdorf, & Groth, 1998), and a program emphasizing forgiveness and reconciliation (Sells, Giordano, & King, 2002). A close look at the methods of these various approaches reveals important commonalities, such as training in more effective communication, conflict resolution, and addressing issues of intimacy and sexuality.

The original edition of this text included a report of outcomes associated with couples group psychotherapy in our own practice. We do not include it in this edition because our methodology has improved and our sample is now larger. With help from Dr. Melissa Hunt and Kevin McCarthy, MA, from the University of Pennsylvania, I am pleased to report updated findings, based on data collected over the course of the past 4 years. Julia M. Hormes, MA, from the University of Pennsylvania, provided assistance in formatting and clarifying the research as presented in this chapter.

EVIDENCE-BASED PRACTICE AT THE COCHÉ CENTER

Assessments made at the beginning of group participation form the basis for later evaluations of a couple's progress and eventual success or failure in therapy (E. Coché, 1983). We continue the tradition of combining formal objective assessments with group-based evaluations of the experience. For example, we customarily bring the members' initial group goal sheet (Appendix A-i) to the progress reports that are part of the ending phase of the group. It is customary procedure for the whole group to evaluate how far a couple has come in meeting the goals the partners had set.

Modest Research Goals Address Key Questions

Using these formal and informal evaluations, Dr. Hunt, Mr. McCarthy, and I designed a small study (described next) in which we distributed questionnaires to members of a couples group. As Dr. Erich Coché and

I stated in the first edition and as Marett (1988) has pointed out, actual outcome research on couples groups remains sparse and the few existing studies still have serious methodological shortcomings. This concern provided even more impetus to try to get modest answers to modest questions. It seemed to us that something is far better than nothing. Further, we wanted to address the following questions:

- How effective are the groups?
- What aspects of couples' relationships improved as a result of therapy?
- Can we trace a connection between the overall mood of a group and change as experienced by the participants?
- What did the participants say was most effective in their groups?

A review of this study follows. Our experience is then integrated into the state of the knowledge described previously.

Evidence-Based Practice Methods in This Study

Our couples have been extraordinary in their dedication to educating colleagues about what works. Evidence-based practice produces a win for all involved in its stages. I attribute the dedication of our couples to the professional stance of our team of scientist–practitioners: We all believe that it is our privilege and obligation to try to be open about what we do so that others may benefit from our successes and learn from our failures.

Our couples make group choices, which may include the willingness to invite observers into their confidential clinical community. In 1988 they helped us make a training video tape still used widely (Coché & Coché, 1990). At each session, they are willing to fill out brief questionnaires to document process variables for evidence-based practice. In their opinion, they are the winners: Data collected benefit them directly because each couple gets a chance to sit down with PhD candidates in clinical psychology and review objective test findings. In this way, evidence-based practice both informs our treatment and provides instrumental feedback for group members.

The Tricky Process of a Modest Research Design That Works

In designing our evidence-based practice, we selected highly validated measures, which have demonstrated good results in assessing change in couples and group therapy. We selected from several relationship scales and chose the Dyadic Adjustment Scale (DAS) and the Inventory of Interpersonal Problems-32 (IIP-32). Choices were based on extensive use in the literature (DAS manual) and a comparative review of couples' assessment measures done during a clinical internship for Dr. Melissa Hunt.

We selected instruments providing information about areas requiring change by our couples. This selection process has been a great challenge for us. Many of the current instruments do not provide sufficient "meat" to generate great group discussions, yet our couples are willing to fill them out. To bolster their interest, we have added some individual measures as part of the diagnostic workup of the group. Often couples are invited to take the MIPS and the SCL-90 as well as our systemic research tools. They very much appreciate the opportunity to understand more deeply the variables that are part of their personality and their coping styles, and they applaud the testing. Although data from these individual measures are not part of the following report, they augment the treatment that couples receive.

Instruments Used in This Research

We used the Dyadic Adjustment Scale, the Inventory of Interpersonal Problems, and the Group Climate Questionnaire (GCQ) in the research we report here:

- The *DAS* is a 32-item self-report measure. It assesses couples' agreement on key areas in marriage. It also assesses level of satisfaction with their relationship. Finally, it measures the level of expression of emotion to one another, as well as couples' rating of the degree of unity of their relationship. The DAS has been shown to distinguish between distressed and nondistressed couples and is sensitive to changes in response to couples therapy (DAS manual). We collected DAS data from three of the four couples in the 2005–2006 advanced couples group; five of the five couples in the 2006–2007 group (three returning and two new couples), and all three of the couples in the 2007–2008 group (the two couples new to the 2006–2007 group and one returning couple from the previous two groups). Internal consistency for the measure for all years in our sample was good (full scale, $\alpha = .90$; consensus, $\alpha = .80$; satisfaction, $\alpha = .75$; expression, $\alpha = .69$; cohesion, $\alpha = .69$).

- The *IIP-32* is a 32-item self-report measure of difficulties that individuals have in relationships. Respondents answer two types of questions about their relationships with other people. They describe frequent unwanted behaviors and behaviors that they want to increase. The IIP is based on a circumplex model of interpersonal behavior, which maps interpersonal interactions on two dimensions: dominance and affiliativeness. It reports on selected behaviors and generates eight subscales that reflect different types of problems that people might characteristically have in relationships. A total score indicates how much interpersonal distress an individual experiences in his or her relationships. The IIP was included in the core battery approved by the American Group Psychotherapy Association Task Force on Research Designs because of its renowned psychometric properties and ease of use. We have collected data for five couples in September 2006, the same five couples in June 2007, and three of those couples who continued in the 2007–2008 group in June 2008. Internal consistency of the full IIP scale in our sample was excellent ($\alpha = .95$), as were each of the subscales (*Mdn* $\alpha = .82$).
- The *GCQ* is frequently used to measure variables defining group atmosphere that have an impact on change factors. Just as the concept of working alliance is relevant in general psychotherapy research, the concept of group climate is important in group psychotherapy research. Three subscales measure the amount of positive feelings that group members have toward each other and the group and their willingness to work (engaged), the amount of conflict and tension that the group has (conflict), and the amount that group members avoid responsibility for working toward change (avoidant).

    The engaged subscale has been consistently found to predict improvement in group members, whereas the other subscales have produced more mixed findings (e.g., Ogrodniczuk & Piper, 2003). Reliability for the GCQ in this sample was good for the engaged ($\alpha = .72$) and conflict ($\alpha = .70$) but not the avoidant ($\alpha = .04$) subscales. We added the GCQ to our data collection only for the 2006–2007 group. Every month at the end of the group, the keeper of the structure collected data. The couples did not leave until the data were collected. Although the couples joked about the need to collect the data

173

("Oh, that again!"), their real concern involved being useful in the treatment of other couples. If they could help other couples by spending 5 minutes at the end of each session, they were more than willing to assist. Group Climate Questionnaire scores were averaged across the months to produce a single estimate for each group member.

To analyze the data, we used a repeated-measures analysis of variance (ANOVA), accounting for the fact that the same individual gave outcome data at three different time points. We included "couple" as a covariate to control for the statistical dependency in scores due to the partners being in a relationship with each other. The resulting statistical model informed us about change in outcome scores on the DAS or IIP for an individual over their time in the group, irrespective of the difficulty of his or her relationship.

Results for Each Measure

Dyadic Adjustment Scale. Descriptive statistics for the full DAS and for the four subscales are given in Table 10.1. Keep in mind that these data do

Table 10.1 Means and Repeated-Measure Analysis of Variance (ANOVA) of Couple Agreement on Dyadic Adjustment Scale

DAS	2005 ($n = 6$)	2006 ($n = 8$)	2007 ($n = 10$)	2008 ($n = 6$)	$F (1, 19)$	p
Full scale	90.58 (11.98)	105.75 (13.67)	110.20 (14.57)	111.17 (12.32)	17.44	.0005
Consensus	41.83 (8.47)	47.00 (3.46)	48.70 (5.72)	49.00 (4.43)	9.55	.006
Satisfaction	31.08 (2.50)	34.88 (5.46)	36.00 (5.70)	35.83 (3.65)	7.41	.01
Expression	4.83 (2.48)	8.50 (2.82)	8.60 (2.17)	7.50 (2.59)	4.28	.05
Cohesion	12.83 (2.99)	15.38 (3.93)	16.90 (4.31)	18.83 (3.06)	5.12	.04

Notes: DAS = Dyadic Adjustment Scale. N values are the number of individuals contributing data. Column values for each year are mean scores. Column values for each year in parentheses are standard deviations.

not account for the fact that couples improved and often stayed for the next year, some couples graduated, and new couples were added, which will cause the estimates to vary. However, for all of the DAS subscales, the trend is for increases over time spent in the group, and the ANOVA statistics presented in the final columns of Table 10.1 verify this observation. For each year a couple spends in couples group therapy, it is likely to improve on its DAS full scale score an average of 5.89 points (out of a maximum 151 points), an average of 2.60 points on the consensus subscale, an average of 1.37 points on the satisfaction subscale, an average of 0.58 points on the expression subscale, and an average of 1.33 points on the cohesion subscale. The "couple" term was generally significant in each model ($p < .006$; except for the model predicting the cohesion subscale, $p < .07$), suggesting that couples in the group generally differed in the levels of relationship adjustment they reported.

Inventory of Interpersonal Problems-32. Inventory of Interpersonal Problems data were only available for two of the advanced couples groups. Descriptive statistics are given in Table 10.2, again without accounting for variation due to couples that graduated or joined the group. Although IIP scores seemed to decrease with time in couples group therapy, these changes were not statistically significant for any of the IIP subscales.

Table 10.2 Means and Repeated-Measure Analysis of Variance (ANOVA) of Interpersonal Functioning on the Inventory of Interpersonal Problems

IIP	2006 ($n = 5$)	2007 ($n = 10$)	2008 ($n = 6$)	F (1, 10)	p
Full scale	32.40 (24.36)	30.00 (19.68)	25.83 (13.73)	2.39	.15
Dominant	2.20 (2.49)	2.40 (2.95)	2.17 (1.94)	0.20	.67
Vindictive	2.40 (2.19)	2.10 (3.28)	1.50 (1.23)	0.93	.36
Cold	3.20 (5.07)	2.60 (2.68)	2.50 (3.73)	1.34	.27
Socially avoidant	4.80 (4.44)	3.90 (3.24)	3.33 (2.80)	2.07	.18
Nonassertive	6.40 (3.21)	5.70 (3.89)	5.00 (1.90)	2.04	.18
Exploitable	6.60 (3.44)	6.40 (3.66)	5.83 (3.43)	.84	.38
Overly nurturant	5.20 (3.63)	4.90 (2.02)	4.00 (2.00)	1.12	.31
Intrusive	1.60 (2.07)	2.00 (2.26)	1.50 (1.23)	0.35	.57

Notes: IIP = Inventory of Interpersonal Problems. N values are the number of individuals contributing data. Column values for each year are mean scores. Column values for each year in parentheses are standard deviations.

Of more significance is that couples did significantly vary in the levels of reported interpersonal problems they brought to the groups ($p < .05$).

Group Climate Questionnaire. Finally, we looked to see whether the group atmosphere seemed to predict changes in the group members for the 2006–2007 couples group. We used the average GCQ subscale scores to predict changes in the DAS and IIP scores. The mean level of engagement in the group was relatively high (M = 4.89; SD = 0.81; maximum GCQ subscale score possible = 6); conflict (M = 1.39; SD = 1.00) and avoidance (M = 2.64; SD = 1.00) were relatively low. However, none of the GCQ subscales predicted change in either the DAS or IIP scores for the 2006–2007 group. The following vignette provides a summary for each couple and an example to illustrate the change.

Diane and Dwight did not agree about the changes that they had made. Diane believed that they made dramatic improvement; Dwight reported both problems and improvement. Dwight was anxious to end his multiyear membership in the group, but Diane had greater need to continue. The couple graduated from the group and continued in monthly couples therapy with great success.

Margaret and Michael grew beyond their own ability to envision a good marriage. Their growth was inspirational for the other couples. Within a 2-year period of time, they moved from having mild improvement in communication and conflict resolution to graduating from the group with no need for further treatment. Improvement was dramatic.

Robyn and Spencer agree with one another that their relationship is great and has been outstanding since their marriage. Their goal in their group was to prevent trouble from developing because both were the product of divorce. They report being "soul mates," being open and in tune with each other, and having little to hide from one another. This couple holds hands, both physically and metaphorically. They have used the couples group to cement a strong foundation for marriage and children. This 2-year investment stands them in good stead for a strong future.

Holly and Trevor began with different appraisals of their marriage. Trevor began the group with concerns about the marriage, and Holly rated her marriage higher than the other couples'. Within 1 year, her appraisal of her marriage had dropped considerably and was closer to that of Trevor. The couple came together through their months of membership in the group. When Holly began the group, she was trying to minimize trouble in the marriage. As her trust in the group and in psychotherapy developed, Holly stopped minimizing difficulty so that both she and Trevor admitted the need to make some changes. At the time of their graduation from the group they were reporting successful and satisfying times together.

Antonia and Patrick exhibited a rollercoaster pattern of unhappiness and change for the better. Antonia shows a straight line of improvement, although the level of improvement is lower than that of other group members. However, after data were completed, continued changes resulted in a dramatic change pattern for Antonia during her membership in the couples group. Patrick began slowly in the group and was not too heavily invested in making changes at first. In the second year of his group membership, he became invested in his own change and showed considerable progress. At the time of writing of this book, the couple is enjoying vastly improved intimacy in sexuality, deeper levels of communication, substantial reductions in levels of depression, and general appreciation for being married to one another for the first time in over 15 years.

What Did Our Couples Say?

In addition to collecting outcome data using the measures described previously, we also invited couples to tell us, in their own words, other learnings they had gained that they believed to be worthy of mention. The following are verbatim comments broken into statements about self, about the partner, and about the marriage.

How I Have Changed
- "I am asking for what I need or deserve for the first time in my life."
- I am "controlling my temper by using other tools to address issues that come up. Better understanding of interpersonal relationships has allowed me to apply much of what I have learned to my whole life."
- I am "more secure as an individual and as part of a team together."
- "I am less judgmental. I don't blame myself."
- I have "taken a more active role in my life and what I do."

How My Partner Has Changed
It is customary for married adults to see both problems and beneficial changes in their partner more quickly than in themselves. The following

changes were observed in the partner with whom our members lived daily:

- My partner is "more relaxed around our children, less critical, having more fun."
- "My partner is dealing with issues without the anxiety he used to have."
- My partner is "helping me grow by communicating more of his feelings and sticking to his positions."
- My partner "seems more relaxed—she is—and actually enjoys lovemaking."
- My partner is "coming to grips with his/her own life—not having to 'do it all first and feel emotions second.'"

Said About the Couple
The following observations about the marriage and the quality of life between the members of the couple were made:

- "We are more responsible and more considerate of each other."
- "We are able to negotiate and compromise. We are both better listeners."
- "We work together at solving problems. We can bring problems to each other safely. We do not place blame on each other."
- There is a "happier home life for all."
- We are "more in sync on many things. More flexible as individuals and as a couple. More adaptable as individuals and as a couple."
- We have "adjusted to our sexual differences although still back-slide at times. We feel pleasure in giving pleasure at our partner's level. We are more patient and not judgmental."
- "We are able to talk more freely about below-surface stuff."
- We have a "new model for living life. We are ... seeing progress for both of us in the work we're doing."
- "We have dealt with [a tragedy] and believe we have a stronger relationship for it."

Conclusions From Our Research

In conclusion, we draw the following patterns from our results:

- Couples experienced different levels of distress when they entered the group. Regardless of level of unhappiness upon entry into the group, each couple reported significant improvement in its relationship over the period of data collection.

- Results indicate that many areas of the relationship change for the better in response to treatment.
- The couples group model does not target change at the level of overall interpersonal relationships, but rather at the level of couples' interactions. Therefore, it is not surprising that responses to interpersonal problems in general did not change as a result of membership. This means that it is likely that interchanges in the group are brought home with the couple more than they are brought into the general life space of each member. It would require specific training to generalize interpersonal improvement learned in the group beyond the level of direct couples interaction.
- Given the frequency of change reported from the GCQ, it was surprising to find that group members did not relate the climate to changes made. This may be explained by limiting data collection to 1 year of analysis. Alternate explanations might include chronic response set from month to month, or that the relationship between group climate and outcomes on other measures is more complex than was captured in the model presented here.
- Informal reports from the couples indicate that large amounts of positive change occurred in the marriages. Members reported changes for themselves and were most appreciative of change in their partners and in the relationship. As one woman said, "I feel as though my husband, for the first time in 16 years, actually desires my company. And that is awesome."

Directions for Future Research Based on Our Work

As one of our research team said about our design for evidence-based practice, "If large oaks from little acorns grow, then our tree requires a lot more nuts." Evidence-based practice is sobering. We began in 1986 to develop technology to measure ephemeral change in the space between intimate partners. A modest study in the first edition indicated that our couples benefited from the atmosphere of the group as well as the clinical interventions.

In the late 1990s, Dr. Julian Slowinski and I carried out modest clinical field research with the first couples group designed specifically to treat disorders in intimacy and sexuality (J. M. Coché et al., 2006). Our results were once again that the group was beneficial in a general way for the members and clearly better than no treatment. To date, all our modest attempts at evidence-based practice support the finding that our couples benefit more from treatment than they think they would have if they had not undergone treatment. As rewarding as it is to see the changes described previously, we need to be able to be more specific in our findings, as Burlingame concludes in his review of the field (Burlingame, Fuhriman, & Johnson, 2003; Burlingame, MacKenzie, & Strauss, 2004). Future directions become quite clear from data analysis:

- How generalizable are the data? This study did not control for potentially important variables, such as the reality that the group assessed was very advanced clinically. The degree of generalizability to other groups in this or any other practice needs to be assessed in the future.
- Couples groups conducted by other leaders in other locations need to assess further the generalizability of the results presented here.
- The study involves a relatively small sample, which results in limited analytic power. Larger sample sizes will give a better estimate of what couples groups can do to change their members.
- Measures used were specific to couples therapy, but not couples group therapy. Future research should look into the development and validation of measures specific to couples group therapy.
- Who benefits? The general tenor of the responses indicates that in the view of our respondents many couples could benefit from some work on their communications, interpersonal skills, and/ or intimacy issues. However, several couples mentioned that, in order to benefit from the group, couples need to make a commitment to work on these issues.
- How can we improve the group experience? Couples appreciate high levels of therapist involvement, including structured interventions near the beginning of a group contract and workshops to build cohesiveness.
- More workshops should be held. Couples indicated appreciation for structured interventions, psychoeducational material, and targeted workshops around themes of relevance.

Couples' Appraisal of Research Participation

Couples told us that they received their greatest learning in the areas of intimacy, communication, and the appreciation of one another's individuality. Having more fun together ranked surprisingly low. Nevertheless, many of our couples know how to have fun together and do not need to concentrate on this goal in a group. Instead, they need to reduce the torturous pain that comes from feeling misunderstood and unaccepted by a person whom they deeply love. They need to resolve conflicts successfully and learn to live peacefully together. However, our clinical goal is optimal life satisfaction for our couples, so the theme of pleasure, enjoyment, and even happiness is worth considering. We consider this in Chapter 11.

Couples rated very high that they had achieved their initial goals and later goals that they set during the course of the group. We are deeply rewarded by this finding because our goal is to help clients make changes in desired and life-enhancing directions. However, we also believe there is value in looking at those couples who gave this a low rating and those who did not respond at all.

Couples found the positive or cohesive tone of the group to be very helpful to them. However, one finding is curious: Though couples perceived the structured exercises as less helpful, they requested more structured leader interventions. Here, again, we need more data. We suspect that individuals in the couples with varying cognitive styles experience leadership differently and this seemingly contradictory set of data may, in fact, be due to subgroups responding consistently within their own experience. Group policies were not viewed as helpful to the marriages of the members, nor would we expect them to be. In the eyes of the participants, the interpersonal aspects of the group were the most important: honesty, trust, helping, and being in a group. The structure imposed by the therapists, important though it may be to the overall functioning of the group, is not paramount in the minds of the participants.

Asked how to improve the group, some couples requested greater direction and leadership by the therapists. This presents an interesting therapeutic dilemma: Should we as leaders become more directive at the risk of making the group more dependent (Bion, 1960) or should we remain faithful to our theoretical concepts and let the group search for answers, believing, as we do, that people change when there is nothing left to do? We plan to continue to invite the leadership behaviors to come from the group, even at the risk of being perceived as "wasting time" or "floundering" by members whose anxiety skyrockets at a lack of evident structure. Although we believe that each therapy team has to find its own answers to this issue, any extreme in leadership style, either too laissez-faire or too autocratic, is likely to be detrimental to the group (Lewin, 1951).

Incorporating Research Into Clinical Practice

In a presentation at a 2008 symposium for the American Group Psychotherapy Association, Kevin McCarthy mentioned reasons that clinicians might want to collect data on process and outcome in their practices. These reasons include the ethics of evidence-based practice and the value of understanding our own work (McCarthy & Coché, 2008).

As our modest research demonstrates, evidence-based practice need not be cumbersome, expensive, or esoteric, even in the complex field of couples group psychotherapy. The studies reported here were accomplished with the help of a personal computer and a simple spreadsheet. Yet the results (though limited in their generalizability) are of use to clinicians and to the couples themselves. Couples were extremely helpful to us in providing us with feedback on our work, thus enabling us to make advantageous adjustments in our treatment package. We encourage clinicians to build similar modest but viable evaluations into their clinical service delivery. The feedback loop in letting consumers know that their psychotherapists are interested in their responses more than compensates for the inconveniences in collecting the data.

11

Recent Advances in Couples Expertise
Theory, Research, and Practice

This has not made a real difference; this has made *the* difference for me … in my marriage.

—Trevor

INTRODUCTION

Future trends worth discussion need to reflect progress from the fields of relational psychoanalytic thought, cognitive behavioral couples work, educational contributions from positive psychology, behavioral finance, neurobiology, and sensory awareness. This chapter touches on recent advances that are likely to enable major contributions from these fields to the clinical execution of couples group psychotherapy. Recent trends in couples group psychotherapy that seem likely to become more important in the next decade include:

- relational psychoanalytic concepts and practice;
- the educational imperative from positive psychology;
- the world of behavioral finance;
- the neurobiology of coupling; and
- the centrality of sensory awareness.

183

RELATIONAL PSYCHOANALYTIC
CONCEPTS AND PRACTICE

Recent exposure to newer thinking in psychoanalytic work has focused my attention on a quiet expansion of interventions in the last decade. Dreams and associations, long the foundation for deep psychodynamic insight work, have been complemented by both concepts and practice that involve the dynamics of interpersonal space and action-oriented therapy. The power of the model of couples group therapy that is in these pages is a direct result of work done between 1986 and 1989 with Dr. Carl Whitaker, a psychodynamically trained creative thinker who was one of the founders of the field of family therapy.

Erich Coché and I sought out Carl because I wanted to have direct experience working with his brilliant way of utilizing psychodynamic training to get quickly to the heart of the matter in interpersonal clinical work. Hence, I was very excited when Dr. Shay focused my attention on the world of relational psychoanalysis in general (Frank, 2002; Ginot, 2007) and enactments in particular. Incorporating expertise from neurobiology and attachment theory into a psychodynamic conceptual framework, this cadre of colleagues may point the way to an integration between fields that have traditionally been considered too separate.

Enactments

An example of this kind of thinking concerns work by Frank (2002) and Ginot (2007) on enactments. The notion of enactments—interpersonal manifestations of dissociated relational styles—finds support in both attachment studies and neuroscientific research. Enactments can be viewed as the ultimate communicators of a client's neurally encoded history. They are unconsciously triggered between clients and their therapists or other clients. These internalized relational patterns can be changed by experiences both inside and outside the therapeutic setting. By making automatic and unconscious patterns conscious, therapists attempt to repair and enhance chronically dysfunctional patterns.

In personal communications from Joseph Shay, PhD, and Gil Spielberg, PhD, I have come to understand that enactments may have replaced dreams and transferential analysis as the analytic gold from which change occurs. I have been deeply affected by what seems like a recent convergence of previously divergent, almost antagonistic schools

184

of thought. In past eras, turf issues concerning various schools of therapy were overwhelmingly powerful. Recently, it has become likely that analytically and behaviorally trained mental health professionals will be able to find a common ground, despite differing languages. Perhaps a future direction for couples therapy is an integration of behavioral and analytic thinking, of verbal and nonverbal interventions, and of individual and interpersonal treatment. As long as we keep in mind that theory is a heuristic device for clinical application rather than a dogma, this integration may point the way to even better couples group work than we have been able to achieve to date.

THE EDUCATIONAL IMPERATIVE
FROM POSITIVE PSYCHOLOGY

As a PhD student in human development at Bryn Mawr in the 1970s, I gravitated toward seminal work by Fromm (1956), Rogers (1951), Erikson (1968), Sullivan (1953), Vaillant (1977), Tillich (1952), Piaget (Piaget & Inhelder, 2000), and Frankl (1963). In fact, the first edition of this work outlines a foundation for the model of couples group psychotherapy drawn from the combined fields of interpersonal systems therapy (couples therapy and group therapy), positive existential philosophy (Buber, 1958; Bugental, 1981; Frankl, 1963; Fromm, 1956; Tillich, 1952), and applied social psychology. I found these thinkers challenging to then current trends toward uncovering and treating pathology as a way of helping people live better lives. I was fond of saying that I first wanted to understand normal development; then I wanted to optimize it. If I found pathology along the way, I wanted to be able to identify, diagnose, and treat it. I wished for the day when we could legitimately state that our goal was to help couples live more vibrant lives, rather than merely to treat the underlying dysfunction between them (Figure 11.1).

Thanks to Dr. Martin Seligman and other pioneers, in the last decade positive psychology has provided legitimacy for the completely desirable trait of enjoying one's life fully. Our attention as people and as professionals is finally being drawn toward helping people behave in more positive ways in order to achieve full relationships with those they love. Founded on early work by Rogers, Vaillant, and Fromm, colleagues have developed theory and research on optimal functioning that can be applied to clinical

185

Figure 11.1 A destination retreat setting creates therapeutic ambiance during couples group psychotherapy in the Stone Harbor, New Jersey, office, 2008. (Photo courtesy of Dr. Judith Coché.)

work with individuals and couples. Dr. Jason Satterfield (in a personal communication as this book was going to print) noted:

> I do see roots [in positive psychology] in Fromm, Rogers, Horney, even Sullivan. When ideas keep resurfacing like this, I take it is as proof that we're onto something very foundational. Cognitive Behavioral Therapy got so focused on pathology, that they forgot all this terrific work. I'm glad it is re-emerging.

Recent work by Seligman (2002) and Diener and Biswas-Diener (2008) points the way to integrating concepts from ideal human development to treat interpersonal malaise. For example, Gable and Reis (2003) have demonstrated that responding actively and constructively to a partner enhances satisfaction with coupling. Behaving in an active and upbeat manner toward a primary life partner is likely to create a kind of interpersonal synergy or flow that will continue to enhance the loving satisfaction experienced by each partner over time. Success begets success. As Gottman found, we want minimally a 5:1 ratio of positive to negative behaviors in living with our partners. These positive behaviors include compassion, forgiveness, and gratitude.

Regardless of how ridiculous the behavior of a spouse may seem, the other partner has options in how to respond. Knowing this and learning skillful ways to exercise the options give each spouse a feeling of control over at least his or her part of a situation. In *Authentic Happiness,* Seligman (2002) discusses the consequences of secure attachment in romance. Similarly to earlier work by Bowlby (1990) and Susan Johnson (2005; Johnson & Greenberg, 1994), Seligman's book concludes that "securely attached people and secure romantic relationships do better. (p. 195)" Seligman describes a discouraging review of major marriage manuals, but goes on to state that positive psychology instructs in how to improve a good marriage. The strengths he proposes include kindness, gratitude, forgiveness, social intelligence, integrity, humor, fairness, self-control, and humility. His conclusions were evident to Margaret and Michael, though they did not read his work.

Margaret and Michael enjoyed the benefits of a pretty good marriage. Sex had remained enriching, growing children were healthy, finances were secure, and deep connections had been forged with both families. By most people's standards, this couple did not need couples therapy. Many couples would have felt fortunate to enjoy a percentage of the benefits that Margaret and Michael took for granted. Margaret and Michael did not enter the couples group in order to repair a broken marriage. They worked for 2 years on their marriage in order to make a good marriage even better. Anxious by nature, Margaret found it hard to claim her natural gifts: a Katherine Hepburn-like appearance, quick wit and depth of psychological insight, and the capacity to listen to another with full focus. Applying some of the tenets of positive psychology to her treatment enabled Margaret to begin to see her own gifts. Michael had no trouble claiming his gifts: classically clean-cut good looks, a quiet demeanor with a burst of humor, and the intelligence to figure out most things predisposed him to a successful career as an executive. Without pathologizing less than optimal patterns between them, couples group psychotherapy enabled them to enjoy the fruits of the marriage more fully. It also allowed the couple to dig into difficulties with mutual decision making, coparenting, and future life planning within a conceptual frame that was more developmental than pathological.

I look forward to further integration of the fields of healthy human development, social psychology, and applied mental health intervention. The gaps in skill teaching, cognitive psychotherapy, and depth psychotherapy are likely to be minimized as our increasing expertise allows us to know better when to apply which approach. To date, positive psychology and communications skills augment the world of our knowledge of couples and provide an educational foundation for needed clinical interventions. In the future, we might not be surprised to see greater integration between these approaches and clinical treatment.

THE WORLD OF BEHAVIORAL FINANCE

In the past 20 years, we have begun to take for granted that couples need to communicate effectively, that they deserve to enjoy mutual sexual pleasure, and that shared values make coupling easier. It follows logically that couples need to set the expectation that success in financial negotiations will be a key tool in their coupling venture. The emerging field of behavioral finance (Budge, 2008) focuses on the impact of the psychology of money and finance on all individuals, couples, and families. It is a field of crucial importance. All too frequently couples beginning to assess the strengths and weaknesses of their marriage completely overlook any reference to the ability to negotiate financial differences and plan successfully for a future together. In my experience, it is rare for couples to enter couples work with budgets intact and a way to talk about financial differences.

Dwight loves Diane dearly. Having raised children by herself, Diane often worries about her future financial security. Although she is too proud to ask Dwight to agree to support her from inherited funds, it would help her tremendously if he eased her discomfort by acknowledging the marriage as a financial foundation for her future. Instead, the couple gets into heated discussions about what kind of travel is affordable. Diane maintains that she would love to travel but worries about the cost. Dwight maintains that there are enough funds to go around. But neither is able to tackle the underlying ambivalence around taking inherited funds and applying them to a new marriage. Raised with the assumption that a prenuptial contract would ensure intact funds after a divorce, it simply did not occur to Dwight that his second marriage was not likely to end in divorce and therefore money might have a different meaning than in his first, failed marriage. Discussing the meaning of money and expressing his primary goal to make Diane happy and secure, Dwight was able to see that in this marriage money could have a very different meaning than at any other time in his life. During the course of their work, Dwight gifted Diane a permanent financial resource of her own, regardless of what would happen to him.

A number of key problem areas emerge when working with couples around the ideas, feelings, and behaviors involved in financial management and planning:

- Frequently, one member of a couple has larger dreams than bank accounts. Working out conflicts around finances requires skill in conflict resolution. Often it appears that members of the couple split the ambivalence about spending. In this scenario, one member of the couple takes the position that the couple should spend more, while the other champions belt-tightening. Although each member is ambivalent about spending or cutting back, splitting this ambivalence allows the partners to maintain the status quo. Partners need face none of the discomfort that change brings and can blame their partner as a default stance. Family-of-origin material, including a financial genogram, can be instrumental in giving the couple a way to think about a joint future.

- Members of a couple often feel comfortable with different levels of financial risk. Each is secure in his or her own position and the position of the other is intimidating. This dynamic encourages derisive criticism (e.g., "Yes, he'd rather leave his money under a mattress than invest it in the stock market"). Distrust surfaces when one partner intimidates the other into adopting uncomfortable investment patterns. A discussion of values clarification is often hard for a couple to manage without disintegrating into hurled attacks against one another. Therapist-facilitated interactions can be crucial in helping couples adjust to an integrated level of risk management between them.

- Earning power and financial management skills can be done by different partners. At times, the major earner believes that he or she has the right to be the major spender. "My money," rather than "our money," is the unconscious message, though the content of the discussion portrays fair distribution of assets. This sort of disrespectful conversation impedes consistency in financial management. However, therapist-facilitated interventions can help a couple to frame the differences between them in terms of their love for one another and a rich joint future together, rather than in terms of what each person deserves.

High levels of couples' satisfaction and constructive attitudes toward money and finance are deeply intertwined; yet, most couples get engaged before they are able to discuss the way in which money functions in their lives. There is no expectation for couples to unite in creating a common future that may need to embrace the differing financial values that coupling brings. A future direction for group psychotherapy with couples includes making the unconscious conscious and using mistakes from the past to inform a better future for couples who are able to process their financial dreams and behaviors as a team.

THE NEUROBIOLOGY OF COUPLING

One of the most exciting developments since the publication of the first edition of this book is the growing understanding of the neurobiological underpinnings of coupling. Dr. Seth Gillihan and I reviewed the large amount of recent original research that has been published in this area, including several reviews of this literature. For example, Lewis, Amini, and Lannon (2000) used this research as a basis for their general theory of love in a book by the same name. Esch and Stafano (2005) provided a more recent summary of the existing research in their review of "the neurobiology of love."

Couples in our practice typically express appreciation for our educating them about some of this work. For many of them, concepts from neurobiology take ideas like love and attachment out of the abstract and make them more concrete; thus, neurobiological awareness validates their subjective experiences. For example, terror at the thought of being abandoned by one's partner is easier to understand when one knows about the effects of social separation on our nervous systems. On the positive side, understanding that intimate touch has effects on specific brain regions underscores the importance of taking care of our partners' needs for human touch.

As scientists, we recognize that much of the work in this area is provisional; because it is so new, future work surely will provide refinements and likely will reveal problems with our current neurobiological models of coupling. Although the specifics may change, the general principle is sound: Our deepest experiences of love are represented in the body and brain.

In the following pages, we review some of the existing work in this area. We begin by covering some of the early work linking relationship experiences to psychophysiology. Later studies in this line of research included neuroendocrine measures such as cortisol levels, as well as the neuropeptide oxytocin. We then turn our attention to specific aspects of coupling that have been investigated, including brain activity during the sexual response, the health effects of supportive relationships, the neurobiological effects of touch, and the nature of attachment. Finally, we cover studies that have addressed the higher order construct of being in love.

Psychophysiological Effects of Couples' Interactions

More than 25 years ago, researchers demonstrated that physiological measures during couples' interactions (such as heart rate and skin conductance) could be used to predict relationship satisfaction (Levenson & Gottman, 1983). Related research showed that these same measures were predictive not only of current satisfaction, but also of longitudinal changes in satisfaction (Levenson & Gottman, 1985). The general finding was that greater physiological arousal during conflict resolution was associated with greater distress in the relationship. This finding demonstrated that conflict in our closest relationships takes a toll on both our minds and our bodies (see also Jacobson, Gottman, Waltz, Rushe, & Babcock, 1994). Likewise, spouses whose blood pressure increases around conflict resolution are less likely to initiate discussions of conflicts (Denton, Burleson, Hobbs, Von Stein, & Rodriguez, 2001).

Other related findings are of interest:

1. We find significant associations between physiological measures of arousal and marital distress (e.g., Menchaca & Dehle, 2005).
2. A correlation exists between affectionate communication and baseline physiological measures: resting heart rate and baseline cortisol (a stress hormone). Floyd et al. (2007a, b) found that individuals who reported higher levels of affectionate communication had lower resting heart rates and a smaller cortisol response to stress. These findings suggest that positive relationships have a broad protective effect that operates outside the couples' interactions.
3. Conversely, social rejection can be as painful as many types of physical pain. Poignant evidence for the relation between social and physical pain was compiled in a review by MacDonald and Leary (2005), who posit that social exclusion presented a very real physical threat in evolutionary history. They suggest that animals (including humans) are motivated to seek social ties in order to avoid pain. Powerful evidence stems from research observations that parts of the physical pain system are involved in responses to social rejection. Thus, when a person says that it "hurts" following a breakup, the meaning is literal (see also Komisaruk & Whipple, 1998).
4. The bulk of neuroendocrinologic research in this area has focused on the HPA (hypothalamic–pituitary–adrenal) axis, or the "fight or flight" response; however, more recent research has focused on a different entity altogether: oxytocin, a hormone and neurotransmitter that appears to be involved in many of the positive effects of social interaction (for a review, see Uvnäs-Moberg, Arn, & Magnusson, 2005). It has been dubbed part of the "calm and connection system" (p. 59). Though much of the research on oxytocin has been done with voles (see Curtis & Wang, 2003), it is

applicable to humans. Part of the evidence for the role of oxytocin in affiliative behavior comes from differences in the prevalence of oxytocin receptor distribution between monogamous prairie voles and polygamous montane voles (Insel & Shapiro 1992). In prairie voles, oxytocin, and vasopressin (another hormone) both appear to be involved in the development of pair-bonds; oxytocin appears to be more important in females and vasopressin in males (Young & Wang, 2004; see also Porges, 1998).

5. Some researchers have developed hypotheses about the development of pair-bonds, drawing primarily on the rodent literature. Young and Wang (2004), for example, observe that oxytocin and vasopressin are involved in helping voles to recognize individuals, which is a necessary step if stable pairs are to develop. Furthermore, they note that dopamine, a neurotransmitter that is central in the reward system, is released during mating. They therefore hypothesize that when reward (dopamine release) meets mate recognition (oxytocin/vasopressin release), the bonds between the pair are developed. They are careful to state that it is unknown to what extent the systems delineated in voles are also present in humans, but they suggest that similar processes may be at work in the formation of stable human couples (for a review and possible implications for human bonding, see Depue & Morrone-Strupinsky, 2005).

6. In humans, oxytocin is released when women breastfeed their young; thus, it may facilitate attachment between mother and child (Carter, 1998). Earlier research found that nipple stimulation per se resulted in the release of oxytocin into the bloodstream (Christensson, Nilsson, Stock, Matthiesen, & Uvnäs-Moberg, 1989).

7. Additional research on humans has demonstrated that oxytocin is released in response to many stimuli, including massage and sexual activity (Uvnäs-Moberg et al., 2005). For example, Carmichael and colleagues (1987) measured plasma oxytocin levels at baseline and while men and women privately self-stimulated to orgasm; oxytocin levels were higher for both men and women during sexual arousal and orgasm than at baseline.

8. Other research has found that oxytocin may be selectively involved in orgasm and ejaculation, with a role for vasopressin during sexual arousal, at least in men (Murphy, Seckl, Burton, Checkley, & Lightman, 1987). More recent research has found

evidence that oxytocin may play a role in increasing interpersonal trust (Kosfeld, Heinrichs, Zak, Fischbacher, & Fehr, 2005), an important element of stable relationships. Most of the specifics about the roles of oxytocin, vasopressin, and other chemicals in forming and maintaining human couples' relationships remain to be ironed out. Evidence is sufficient to suggest a role for these hormones not only in rodent species but also in our species.

In sum, clients often find it helpful to know that their relationship is based on more than feelings and abstract concepts of romantic love. In fact, it is the product of millions of years of evolution and the resulting array of powerful chemical agents that affect the mind and the body.

Brain Activity During Sexual Response

During the past three decades, a technological revolution has taken place in our ability to observe the workings of the human brain. Cognitive neuroscientists today have ready access to equipment that can produce beautifully clear images of the entire brain in a matter of a few minutes. With the advent of functional magnetic resonance imaging (fMRI), these machines can detect local fluctuations in blood flow on the order of a few seconds, with a spatial resolution as small as 2 millimeters. Clever research designs have capitalized on these machines' ability to detect differences in blood flow—which are correlated with neural activity—thus providing us with previously unavailable windows into the workings of the brain.

Following are a few highlights in this rich field of inquiry. Many of the studies in this domain have used relatively lax statistical significance criteria for the neuroimaging data, which is a particular concern when no a priori hypotheses are specified. Therefore, existing findings in this area must be considered provisional because many of the reported brain activations could be unreliable.

1. Recent cognitive neuroscience research has addressed the brain areas that are involved in the sexual response for both males and females. Cognitive neuroscience research in this area has run the gamut, using experimental methods that range from "PG" to "NC-17." Experimental manipulations have included smelling a woman's perfume (Huh et al., 2008), viewing erotic material (Arnow et al., 2002; Karama et al., 2002; Moulier et al., 2006; Mouras et al., 2003; Paul et al., 2008; Rauch et al., 1999; Redouté et al., 2000;

Walter et al., 2008), sexual stimulation of the penis (Georgiadis & Holstege, 2005), and orgasm and ejaculation (Georgiadis et al., 2006; Holstege et al., 2003).

2. Data from these various studies have implicated a vast range of brain regions in the sexual response (for a brief review, see the introduction in Walter et al., 2008). These regions include all of the major lobes of the brain (frontal, temporal, parietal, occipital) as well as subcortical regions like the thalamus, hypothalamus, basal ganglia, and cerebellum. Findings across studies, even ones that use similar designs, often are inconsistent.

3. These studies have provided objective evidence for what couples therapists have long known—that sex is complicated. As Walter et al. (2008) point out, the sexual response appears to involve at least four distinct components, which include the cognitive, motivational, autonomic, and emotional.
   a. The cognitive component involves our conscious and unconscious processes of recognizing a person as a sexual partner.
   b. The motivational component comprises our drive to engage in sexual activity.
   c. Autonomic processes are involved in the physical sexual response (e.g., quickened heart rate, engorgement of the genitals).
   d. The emotional component involves the complex array of excitement, love, pleasure, and so forth that can be a part of the sex experience.

Couples therapists can let couples with troubled sex lives know that sex is a whole brain activity, which can be an antidote for the frustrating expectation that sex should be easy (Coché et al., 2006). Given the complexity of the sexual response, it is not clear which of these various components may be reflected in the brain activations seen in many of the existing studies.

More recent studies have therefore attempted to isolate brain regions that are specifically involved in the sexual response.

1. Walter et al. (2008) designed an experiment to control for the general emotional arousal involved in the sexual response; by using an emotionally charged but nonsexual control task, they created a design to isolate sex-specific neural processing. They found that the sexual intensity of erotic material was associated specifically

with blood flow to the hypothalamus in both men and women, suggesting that this part of the brain plays a key role in the sexual response.

2. Walter et al. (2008) note that the hypothalamus appears to be involved in the initial sexual response and not in sexual performance. They also found that the subjectively rated sexual intensity of the images was associated with blood flow to the ventral striatum, a brain area that is known to be involved in the neural reward system (Yacubian et al., 2007). This latter finding is a key one.

3. Sex is a highly rewarding activity, producing an effect in the brain that is not unlike the "rush" associated with drugs of abuse such as heroin. Thus, the individual who is addicted to sex shares more in common with the drug addict than may at first be apparent. This point needs to be emphasized in therapy with couples in which one of the partners may be struggling with relationship infidelity or sex addiction (e.g., frequenting prostitutes).

In sum, the brain chemicals that underlie our sexual experiences are powerful, for both good and for ill. Without intensive treatment, it is as unlikely that the individual will stop the behavior as it is unlikely that the untreated drug addict will become clean and sober without medical treatment.

Health Effects of Supportive Relationships

Supportive relationships are good not only for our hearts and minds but also for our physical health. Conversely, bad relationships hurt our physical health (for a brief review, see Spiegel, 1999). Brief highlights in this area include:

1. Janice Kiecolt-Glaser and colleagues have done a lot of research showing that relationship conflict is connected to poorer immune function. For example, her group observed newly married couples in the laboratory for 24 hours during which the couples discussed a marital problem for 30 minutes. Couples whose conflict resolution involved more negative or hostile behavior tended to show a broad decrease in immune function, as well as longer elevations in blood pressure (Kiecolt-Glaser, Malarky, Chee, & Newton, 1993). Studies like this one began to show the mechanisms whereby poor social relationships produce negative health outcomes.

2. Subsequent research by the same group showed that prediction works in the other direction, as well: Levels of epinephrine

and norepinephrine (two stress hormones) during the first year of marriage predicted divorce 10 years later. Even among couples who stayed together, stress hormone levels predicted which marriages would be laden with conflict (Kiecolt-Glaser, Bane, Glaser, & Malarkey, 2003).

3. Related research has demonstrated an association between relationship distress and a striking array of health outcomes, including slower wound healing (Kiecolt-Glaser et al., 2005); couples with high levels of hostility actually healed at only 60% of the rate of couples with lower levels of hostility. On the positive side, husbands' positive behaviors during conflict discussions led to decreases in wives' levels of stress hormones (Robles, Shaffer, Malarkey, & Kiecolt-Glaser, 2006), again showing that a person's words and deeds affect the partner's body and brain.

Other researchers have confirmed the association between relationship quality and health. Over a 2-year period, individuals in relationships that were consistently negative showed a deterioration in physical health (Newsom, Mahan, Rook, & Krause, 2008). Floyd et al. (2007a, b) found that communicating affection is beneficial not only to the receiver of the affection but also to the giver. People who wrote an affectionate letter to a loved one experienced a faster drop in stress hormones following exposure to a stressor compared to participants who did not write a letter.

In sum, couples therapists can help clients take solace in knowing that when they care for one another's hearts, they also care for the other's body in every sense: physically, emotionally, spiritually, and metaphorically. We actually take the heart of another into our care when we couple.

Neurobiological Effects of Touch

Verbal communication is not the only pathway by which partners may influence each other's well-being, and it may not even be the primary pathway. Physical touch has powerful effects. Recent research is showing empirically what coupled people have known for ages—that being touched lovingly by our partners is good for us. Various research findings provide clinically relevant material:

1. Women who reported being hugged more often by their partners had lower blood pressure and higher levels of baseline oxytocin; the oxytocin appears to be a mechanism by which more frequent

197

hugs lead to lower blood pressure (Light, Grewen, & Amico, 2005).

2. Touch is more effective than verbal support alone at reducing the HPA stress response when women encounter social stress. Women who received a neck and shoulder massage from their partners showed a significantly lower stress response than did women who received only verbal support from their partners (Ditzen et al., 2007). Findings like this one can encourage partners that touch is not just "touchy-feely"—its effects are backed by hard science.

3. Warm contact with a partner lowers women's blood pressure, at least among women reporting high levels of partner support (Grewen, Girdler, Amico, & Light, 2005). This same study found that both men and women who reported high levels of partner support also had higher levels of oxytocin.

4. Numerous studies have observed the positive effects of massage, including on muscle pain (Law et al., 2008), on the tolerability of postoperative pain (Piotrowski et al., 2003), and on pain tolerance in rats (Lund et al., 2002).

5. Related research informs about brain regions involved in touch and the power of its impact. An early study using functional MRI (Francis et al., 1999) showed that pleasant touch (touching velvet) was associated with greater activity in the orbitofrontal cortex, a brain region that appears to be involved in process-ing emotion as well as reward and punishment (Kringelbach & Rolls, 2004). The orbitofrontal cortex also has been implicated in perceptions of beauty (Kawabata & Zeki, 2004). This same group of researchers later showed that pleasant touch and pain-ful touch involve distinct regions of the orbitofrontal cortex, as well as different parts of the anterior cingulate cortex (Rolls et al., 2003). This suggests that the cingulate activation in the pleas-ant condition may again be related to the role of this brain area in affective processes (Bush, Luu, & Posner, 2000). On the other hand, cingulate activity in the pain condition may have reflected the participants' inhibition of the urge to move their hands away from the painful stimulus.

In sum, these studies provide a glimpse into the brain processes involved in pleasant touch and suggest mechanisms whereby hugs and other physical signs of affection signal "reward" in the human brain. Although isolated findings are only the first stage of integrated research that can provide empirical foundations for clinical interventions, a beginning of central importance is available for clinical incorporation.

The Nature of Attachment

The nature of human attachment has been of central interest in related fields of human development, psychology, and psychiatry for at least half of a century. As Konner (2004) states, attachment is "one of the most important determinants of human well-being" (p. 705) and therefore worthy of scientific investigation. As I reviewed current findings, I was able to integrate these with earlier classical conclusions based largely on theoretical formulations. Individual research studies point the way to conclusions of import.

1. Hennessy (1997) observed that many but not all species experience a neuroendocrine stress response following separation from their social partners. Hennessy reasoned that the activation of the HPA stress response may prepare the separated animal to deal with ensuing threats to its safety and concluded that the key variable is whether members of the species exhibit emotional attachment to their partners.
2. Research ponders the nature of human attachment. Originally, attachment was conceived of as existing between offspring and caregivers, generally the mother. More recent theorizing posits that romantic partnering shares similarities with infant–parent attachment and suggests that successful partnering relates to earlier successful attachment. For example, securely attached infants tended to be more secure in their adult love relationships (Hazan & Shaver, 1987).
3. Research has implicated the hormones oxytocin and vasopressin in healthful attachment processes in voles. Research with humans has suggested that these hormones may play similar roles in human attachment processes. Michael Meaney has added to knowledge about the powerful effect that early attachment experiences can have. Although the research has involved primarily rats, implications for human adjustment are enormous. For example, Plotsky et al. (2005) showed that early rearing conditions—in the first 14 days of life—can have long-term effects. The experimenters varied the amount of maternal contact that the rat pups had; when the pups were later tested as adults, they showed significant differences in their stress system "set point."

4. Even more striking are the demonstrated effects of early rearing behaviors on genetic expression (Liu et al., 1997). As Meaney and his group have shown, greater maternal licking and grooming of rat pups causes differences in DNA methylation of the offspring. This difference in methylation led to differences in the chromatin structure (the combination of DNA and protein that comprise chromosomes) and gene expression, and it was associated with differences in the stress response (Weaver et al., 2004).

I have found in our work with adults that attachment across the life span may be an important therapeutic issue. Early attachment difficulties, as when a primary caregiver is neglectful or abusive, may affect later attachment to romantic partners. However, I also have worked with individuals who had weak attachments to absent parents, but vowed to do better for their children and succeeded. These individuals often have rich, fulfilling coupled relationships, underscoring the fact that early childhood events do not exert absolute control over life experiences.

1. The maternally caused DNA methylation was reversible in adulthood through the use of a chemical agent (Weaver et al., 2005). It would be fascinating to know whether similar reversals could be enacted environmentally rather than chemically, and especially to know scientifically the extent to which early attachment insults in humans can be altered by subsequent positive relationships.
2. Additional research has targeted the brain regions involved in attachment processes. As Lorberbaum et al. (1999) found, parts of the anterior cingulate and medial prefrontal cortices show increased activity when mothers hear an infant cry. The anterior cingulate is "rich in both opiate and oxytocin receptors … which are thought to be involved in social bonding" (p. 101). They also suggest that the medial prefrontal activation may be related to processing emotional information in the infants' cries. A subsequent study (Bartels & Zeki, 2004) found that viewing pictures of one's infant also led to significantly greater activity in the anterior cingulate, as well as in other brain regions that have been implicated in the reward system.
3. The neural regions that were more active when viewing pictures of their infants also tended to be more active when viewing pictures of a romantic partner (Bartels & Zeki, 2000). In their 2001 review, Insel and Young pointed out that the patterns of activation in both

maternal and romantic love shared many similarities with images of the brain experiencing a cocaine high (Breiter et al., 1997).

These results suggest that the psychodynamic processes that underlie romantic attachment are similar to those that support parent–infant attachment. The seminal work by Susan Johnson (Johnson, 2005) provides a theoretical understanding and clinical applications of these concepts. Furthermore, research points to the key role of the reward system in the development of social attachment.

Love

Although poets and artists may proclaim that love defies scientific analysis, many of our colleagues are involved in the enterprise of analyzing "love."

1. Research tries to delineate neurobiological processes involved in falling and being in love. Research approaches include neuroendocrine investigations and brain imaging. Individuals who had recently fallen in love showed significantly elevated levels of cortisol, a stress hormone, compared to individuals who were single or who were in long-standing relationships (Marazziti & Canale, 2004). I interpret this difference to the excitement and stress associated with new love, a viable explanation given the "sturm und drang" typical of a new intimate relationship.

2. Women who had recently fallen in love showed relative elevations in testosterone, but new love had the opposite effect on men's testosterone levels. The researchers speculated that "falling in love tended temporarily to eliminate some differences between the sexes, or to soften some male features in men and, in parallel, to increase them in women" (Marazziti & Canale, 2004, p. 934). Research considers the influence of falling in love on levels of neurotrophin levels; neurotrophins may be involved in emotional experience and in behavioral changes (Emanuele et al., 2006). Early stages of love were associated with significantly elevated levels of nerve growth factor, again relative to single or long-term paired individuals. For both of these studies, the differences between groups disappeared when the "in-love" participants were reevaluated beyond the acute falling-in-love period. In sum, these studies show that transient and powerful chemical changes underlie the process of falling head over heels in love

201

with a person. When clients complain that things "don't feel the same" as they did when they first fell in love with their partner, I am beginning to have a scientific explanation.

3. Other research has investigated the brain regions that may underlie the experience of love. Aron et al. (2005) used functional MRI, tracing patterns of neural activity in individuals who were "intensely in love" when they viewed pictures of the beloved. Significant activity was seen in brain areas involved in reward and motivation, including the ventral tegmental area and the caudate nucleus. Given the regions of activations, neurotransmitter dopamine very likely is involved (for a complete discussion, see Fisher, Aron, & Brown, 2006).

4. Ortigue, Bianchi-Demicheli, Hamilton, and Grafton (2007) set out to explore less conscious aspects of romantic love. They found that subliminal presentation of the loved one's name resulted in faster subsequent reaction time for deciding whether a string of letters was a word. Ortigue et al. (2007) also used functional MRI and found that subliminal presentation of the loved one's name resulted in increased neural activity in regions that included the ventral tegmental area and the caudate nucleus (as did Aron et al., 2005), in addition to other areas. These results suggest that a person who is in love does not have to be made consciously aware of having thought of his or her beloved in order to have that person affect patterns of brain activity.

5. Event-related potentials (ERPs) also have been used to study brain processes in romantic love. One such study showed pictures of romantic partners to individuals who were newly in love; the pictures evoked a pattern of electrical brain activity that has been associated with motivated attention. This pattern was significantly stronger in response to the romantic partner than to images of a friend or of an unknown beautiful person (Langeslag, Jansma, Franken, & Van Strien, 2007). Thus, this pattern of activity may reflect the "I only have eyes for you" aspect of early infatuation and love. Although these studies may shed light on the passion and intimacy inherent in the process of falling in love, less is known about the neurobiology of committed love (see Sternberg, 1986).

Most of the years of long-term relationships are not characterized by the early intense feelings of love. Thus, research on these later years may be quite informative and beneficial as it is developed. Especially important will be understanding not only how humans fall in love but also how they maintain commitment and intimacy when the flames of passion have cooled. It is only after one begins to explore and attempt to understand the unfolding expertise that neurobiology brings to the clinician that one can appreciate the centrality of nonverbal communication in the lives of all couples. We now turn to an exploration of developing theory in somatic psychology and its application to the clinical welfare of our couples.

THE CENTRALITY OF SENSORY AWARENESS

It is impossible to learn how to be better married simply by talking about it because a preponderance of couples' communication is nonverbal. Given the essential foundation of intimacy in nonverbal behavior, it is astonishing that we are only now beginning to apply understandings from neurobiology to couples' well-being. Although somatic psychology has long had interest in the relationship between mind and body, Damasio (1999) wrote about the relationship of consciousness, awareness, and self-knowledge only within the last decade. A future direction for couples group therapy involves an expansion and integration of nonverbal dimensions, including touch, movement, and sensory awareness, into a safe and powerful group therapy experience. In discussions with Dr. Suzanne Cohen (1997, in press), Kitty Holzmer, MA, and Karen Carlson, the future directions described in the following sections emerged.

Integrating Nonverbal Dimensions Into Couples Therapy

The bulk of couples' communication has always been primarily nonverbal. Early in my training, Dr. Ray Birdwhistell (1970) provoked traditionally trained psychoanalytic clinicians with Philadelphia-based research that claimed that over 70% of communication was nonverbal. During this time period, Dr. Fritz Perls was working within Gestalt psychology; Moreno (1951) was well founded in psychodrama; and Eric Berne (1966) drew attention to nonverbal aspects of psychotherapy. These thinkers suggested that clinicians need to observe how people unconsciously transmit information.

203

More recently, Dr. Daniel Goleman (1997) and Dr. Daniel Siegel (2001, 2006) have brought awareness to the public about the importance of the relationship between sensory stimulation and interpersonal functioning. Siegel stresses the necessity to promote neural integration in psychotherapy by suggesting that the clinician concentrate on attunement as the heart of therapeutic change. In order to do this, he suggests that we must SNAG (i.e., "stimulate neuronal activation and growth" within) the brain and that permanent change is possible. From his psychophysiological laboratory, Dr. John Gottman (1994) allowed us to trace our own neurological patterns and assisted us in applying our knowledge to clinical interventions with couples.

Drs. Leslie Greenberg and Susan Johnson became interested in research in psychotherapy decades before the expansion of the role of neuropsychology in clinical intervention. In their 1994 book, *The Heart of the Matter*, they review the role of emotion in intimate interactions and conclude its centrality. Susan Johnson's exemplary work in emotion-focused couples psychotherapy works with the concept of attachment from a more behavioral perspective than her neuropsychological colleagues. Furthermore, Karen Prager (1995) considers intimacy throughout the life span from a more psychodynamic perspective.

Despite varying emphases, each of these theoreticians in interpersonal psychotherapy agrees that a complex understanding of the interweaving of genetic, behavioral, and emotional factors is the only road map complex enough to help us as clinicians. Academic rigor can be packaged in delightful reading matter. Helen Fisher (1994) titillated our imaginations by comparing us to nonhuman species in our mating proclivities, and Donald Ferguson (2006) drew apt comparisons between humans in love and reptiles. In the 1990s, we began to see independent authors agreeing with one another that the days of merely talking in order to change relationships had come to a close. Suzanne Cohen (in press) agrees that most of emotional and social communication occurs on the nonverbal level (estimates are between 75 and 90%). Dr. Cohen reviews three categories of somatic therapies. She includes therapies that utilize touch as part of awareness and insight, make use of movement and expression, and focus on sensory awareness within a relationship.

To date, work in our couples groups has focused primarily on the use of touch, with some exploration of the use of movement. In the future, we also hope to draw attention to deeper levels of sensory awareness as part of intimacy. The need to train clients in nonverbal loving was obvious to me when I began to work with couples in the 1980s. Consequently, I invited trained massage therapists to teach couples shoulder and foot massage, fully clothed. Although the couples had a nice time, the massage did not seem central to their growth in therapy, in their opinions. However, since 1980, I have continually tried to help couples create a nonverbal language of intimacy in a way that feels safe in a couples group.

In some years, I have invited specialists in sex therapy, couples massage, and Pilates to co-design and co-lead parts of working sessions within the couples group. The couples are enthusiastic about these special events because they are introduced to nonverbal ways of improving and the days create enjoyable learnings to take home, such as massage skills. Couples rate the effectiveness of the intervention at the end of each meeting. In spite of the initial enthusiasm, high energy, and stimulating material created through these guest appearances, the couples who were continuing for another contract period at the end of the 2006–2007 group agreed that they preferred the safety and depth of their ongoing clinical community to the variety and anxiety created through having guest leaders.

For this reason, in 2007, Dr. Juliette Galbraith and I became the ongoing co-leads for these couples, as mentioned in Chapter 8. In 2007, couples growth was rated as very high and satisfaction with the group as equally high. The conclusion that we draw from this clinical experiment is that, as in any high-functioning family, the safety created by an ongoing emotional bond between members, and between members and the leaders, exceeds the possibility for new learning through guest leadership. Future groups may invite the occasional guest leader to provide variety if the group is highly stable and needs to be charged with new energy, but the ongoing model of a solo lead or consistent co-lead seems more satisfying to all involved.

Each leader needs to wrestle with the balance between practicality and expertise in designing special interventions. Our couples prefer highly trained experts to general skills imparted by leaders who may have less training than the specialists.

Deepening Levels of Coupling Through Movement and Massage

My interest in nonverbal healing arts and exercise forms led me to examine contributions from the fields of sensory awareness, touch, and movement. Group dynamics training encourages concentration on all aspects of client participation, including body posture, patterns of movement, and

205

capacity for retaining attention within the group. This combination of cognitive association patterns and body sensations forms a powerful matrix that underlies interpersonal functioning within a couple and a group. In order to create opportunity for this richness to unfold within a group setting, I turned to work by Karen Carlson and Kitty Holzmer. Karen's work with experiential anatomy provided a brief, structured exercise during 2006 and 2007. Kitty's expertise in human sexuality and therapeutic massage enriched couples' skills during a full day of work together.

Karen is a master Pilates trainer, who refers to herself as an "experiential anatomist." Working from ideas developed in part by Dr. Joan Borysenko (1988), Karen understands that a tight body does not feel. In 2006 and 2007, Karen and I spent hours designing movement segments for our couples. We crossed our fingers nervously that they would be willing to go along with what might feel to them like outlandish ideas. To our delight, all but one person reported immediate benefit from Karen's deceptively relaxed movement exercises.

Inviting us to her studio in 2007, Karen led the couples through a graduated series of increasingly self-disclosing, nonverbal communication segments between partners consisting of safe, expressive movements that demonstrated how couples felt about another interpersonally without touching. Most couples smiled. They enjoyed moving through space to music. The couples returned to our offices that afternoon to discuss the exercises and ways of applying them to being more intimate in their marriages.

Margaret and Michael enjoy one another's company tremendously. They dress to go out to dinner to celebrate events and feel powerfully safe in the company of one another without words. When Karen invited them to move together to music, they were only too happy to accept her invitation. First one and then the other intuited how far to stand from one another, how closely to mirror hands that did not touch each other, and how to create a sense of being coupled without touching. As I watched them playfully following Karen's verbal directions, the level of quiet and deep human intimacy was evident. In all ways possible, Margaret and Michael touched one another.

Troubled couples have bodies tightened by suppressed rage, contempt, and confusion. Sensuality feels less safe for couples in chronic pain. For this reason, it was very difficult to design a way to teach the basics of sensual and/or erotic massage to our group of couples. Some had little interest because they thought they did not need the work. Others had little interest because they thought they were already so skillful that no training was needed. Everyone felt uncomfortable at the thought of being expressively nonverbal together, as though the expressions on their faces and the ways they walked together did not convey information to all that bothered to notice. However, it seemed crucial to tackle this task.

As we looked at the five couples, each had its concerns:

- Holly and Trevor did not feel the need for further education in this area.
- Spencer and Robyn, married 3 months, were ecstatic with their level of nonverbal communication.
- Margaret and Michael felt safe and comfortable with one another nonverbally and a bit reticent about sharing this area of their lives with other people.
- Dwight and Diane were very different from one another in non-verbal intimacy needs and habits: Diane wanted to snuggle and make love nearly every night, while Dwight's dynamics predisposed him to avoid nonverbal intimacy.
- Patrick and Antonia also shared extremely different comfort levels at this point in their couples work: Patrick enjoyed many kinds of sensuality, but Antonia found this area painful.

Nevertheless, the contract underlying marriage includes nonverbal affection, so it was not an option to leave this area untouched.

With a master's degree in sexuality and decades of clinical practice in various forms of mind–body work, Kitty had impressed me with her intuitive grasp and gentle way of approaching the space between people. Kitty and I spent at least 15 hours, together and apart, planning this one workshop day. Given that we had more than a quarter of a century of experience between us, the level of detail of our planning could only be caused by our worry that we might offend one of the members, as well as by our tenacity in deciding that couples could and needed to learn to enjoy each other more.

Kitty brought complimentary vials of body oil and pots of therapeutic oils smelling of vanilla and eucalyptus and fresh fruit scents. She invited members to make a tiny pot of their own olfactory preference and told them they were welcome to use this during their massage. She made it clear that all work was to be done at the level of comfort, but it surprised me that the couples seemed to take great pleasure in creating little pots of their own aromatic choice. It was safe to have a class project on which to concentrate and fun to have a souvenir of the day.

After a verbal lead into a shoulder massage, Kitty invited five couples to spread out on mats and towels and get comfortable with tank tops or t-shirts and work-out pants. She then gently and delicately walked couples through how to give one another a foot massage. The room became quiet as couples began to share nonverbal energy. To their surprise, the couples found the exercise was both harmless and enriching, so, after a quick lunch, they were ready to do something a bit more ambitious. Kitty and I were fearful that teaching the couples shoulder massage might prove too challenging for two of our couples. We were especially concerned about Patrick and Antonia, who had sex at that point in time somewhere between once a month and once every 3 months, depending on whose report one believed. However, our couples are good students and they were prepared to learn the assignment of the day.

They stretched out, one sitting cross-legged at the shoulders of the other. Each person was to give a shoulder massage to as well as receive one from his or her partner, with verbal instructions by Kitty. The person giving the massage was given step-by-step instructions on how to knead the back and shoulders of the partner. The goal was to induce pleasure and relaxation. As I watched, I could see the partner getting the massage visibly relax into the experience as the pleasure conveyed through the hands of his or her partner allowed him or her to enter a slightly altered state of consciousness. Four couples looked relaxed and were clearly occupying a pleasant zone together. Patrick was stretched out on his stomach, as instructed, and seemed to be steadfastly relaxed, while Antonia collected herself around his shoulders and massaged his neck and back as instructed. This would not have riveted my attention had Antonia's face not streamed tears onto the top of Patrick's head as she massaged his shoulders. I wondered quietly what could be eliciting the depth of her emotionality and credited Patrick with deep caring in his capacity not to notice that his massage was interrupted by his wife's tears. I found myself admiring Antonia's courage in moving into an area that was clearly so deeply troubling. I made a mental note to invite discussion after the massage was over.

Each couple went home that day with some instructive material; the tiny vial of custom-designed, scented body oil; and a deeper sense of nonverbal interpersonal comfort. In the discussion that followed the massage exercise,

> *Patrick said that he really wanted to make everything OK for Antonia and for them as a couple but was not sure how to do that. It was clear that he would have done anything asked of him. Antonia simply stated that the experience felt sad to her, but that she wished it had not felt so sad. The couple seemed determined to relearn physical touching together and went on to massage each other's toes at home after the workshop. Toe massage in socks later progressed to a deeper level of nonverbal intimacy as the couple's marital health improved and, at this writing, sex is better than ever before in the marriage.*

As I reflect on the complexities and the richness in expanding couples group work to include planned attention to nonverbal interaction, I am certain that the benefits far outweighed the delicacy necessary for the design. I have often joked that "psychotherapy is the application of a science that has not yet been developed." It is clear that, while theoreticians and researchers in neurobiology and attachment theory were examining coupling in various species, I was moving toward a way to apply knowledge that was not yet fully developed. As we now turn attention to the use of DVDs and books, we move to more familiar ground in helping couples learn through visual stimulation.

Sensuality and Sexuality: A Couples' Smorgasbord

In our workbook for couples titled *Intimacy and Sexuality*, Dr. Julian Slowinski and I present an exercise about love play. We distinguish between intercourse and "outercourse" and describe what we think of as "love play" to replace earlier ways of thinking of this as foreplay. We likewise refer to erotic enhancements as part of value-added sex. Dr. Slowinski considers four *T*s essential to promoting intimacy and greater sexual satisfaction:

- Couples need TIME to be together in today's busy world, which conspires against our sex lives.
- Couples need to TALK about their lives as well as about their sexual needs and interests, to create a fertile environment for love play to flourish.
- TRUST between partners is essential for the safety needed for sexual openness. Criticism and exploitation are enemies of sexual pleasure.
- TOUCH is magical in and out of the bedroom. It bonds partners together in a safe and respectful partnership.

I often think of sensuality and sexuality as kind of a smorgasbord for couples. Many nurturing and nourishing items create pleasure and enjoyment. One member may prefer massage and a Jacuzzi, while another prefers reading erotic poetry aloud in bed. As in a smorgasbord, it is possible for partners to taste various pleasures—some at one point in time and others later. It is also possible for these partners to have staples, which they go to time after time. It goes without saying that individual partners have different preferences. The world of sensuality and sexuality is open to partners at all ages and stages of coupling and can be enhanced through respect for one another's individual differences (J. M. Coché, 2002b, pp. 46, 47).

The Paradoxical Safety of Group Work Involving Sexuality

Although the shyness that once pervaded honest discussions about sexuality has been greatly reduced since 1990, many couples feel reticent about beginning to discuss explicitly sexual concerns, even with a professional advisor. Humiliation and shame can be tightly interwoven in the attitude toward sexual pleasure and in its practices. Because a group can be tremendously supportive in helping people move toward desired goals, it seemed sensible, but unlikely, that couples would relish the opportunity to discuss openly sexual concerns in a group with one another.

Dr. Julian Slowinski and I began to ask colleagues who had guided couples groups toward explicitly sexual material how we might successfully get people talking. We found that many opportunities invite sexual education and sexual awareness. When we asked colleagues about treating sexual dysfunction as part of a group, however, we learned that few if any shared clinical experiences with us. For the most part, they did not think it feasible to discuss sexual dysfunctions with other couples. Nevertheless, we persevered. We began a group for couples who, despite initial reticence, educated us about the value of plain talk about sex in group. As mentioned before, in order to minimize the shame and humiliation around these discussions, we encourage couples to shift their language from talking about "foreplay" to "love play." We encourage them to "keep the erotic pot bubbling" by touching each other, expressing affection, and enjoying one another casually from day to day.

We have found that members of a couple differ greatly from one another in the way they work sexually. For this reason, we work on helping couples edit their sexual scripts and enjoy the riches of "outercourse" (Klein, 2002). We encourage couples to enhance sexual enjoyment by doing show and tell with varieties of dildos and other sex toys from local adult stores. We invite them to become acquainted with Web sites like www.goodvibrations.com, which provide resources for a variety of healthy sexual activities. Helping couples with sex as part of permanent coupling requires creative problem solving around individual differences and working through emotional blocks between the members. The variables that contribute to the power of a group are in full play when sexuality is discussed: Sharing of common experiences diffuses the depth of concern for the members, and members can take home the insight and support of other couples as they go to bed each night.

As we know, reducing the humiliation and secrecy of sexual dysfunction lessens the anxiety for both partners. Because the major sexual organ is the brain and the major sexual dysfunction is anxiety, it seems natural that couples would benefit from sharing this level of their marriage with a highly trusted small group. Most of our couples, however, are not sexually dysfunctional. They are sexually disinterested or show imbalance in their level of appetite and interest in variety in sexual pleasure. On entering treatment, many are unable to connect with one another on such fundamental levels that the likelihood of sexual intimacy seems quite low. As Karen Prager (1997) says, many seemingly sexual dysfunctions require treatment for disturbances in attachment and intimacy.

Antonia and Patrick disagreed how frequently they had sex with one another. Antonia reported more frequent sexual activity than her husband remembered. Despite chronic lack of sexual interest in her partner, Antonia intuited that improving the marriage might revive sexual interest. In the final year of treatment, Patrick became more assertive while Antonia lost weight, began dressing in a feminine style, and catapulted to a new level of success in her own career. This new infusion of energy created vibrancy and novelty in a marriage that had become chronically disabled. As she had predicted, Antonia's new presentation of herself led to a feeling of arousal, which surprised group members, group leaders, and her husband. Although Patrick enjoyed the change, he had to adapt to the challenge of a wife who became more interested in sex than he was.

In conclusion, as we consider contributions from recent advances in positive psychology, neurobiology, the meaning of money, relational

211

psychoanalysis, and sensory psychology, I am struck by how key dimensions in coupling remain unchanged over time. No need is more fundamental than the human need for emotional attachment. When we couple, we attach to another person at the cellular level—a level of functioning that influences our health, our financial security, and our well-being.

As theoreticians, it is our prerogative to decide which array of ideas before us seems most useful in working with couples. As practitioners, it is our responsibility to absorb the evidence and creativity in our field and to apply these learnings to the couples we serve. As people, we must hold ourselves accountable to the forces within us as we use our training to influence the lives of family after family. Couples group psychotherapy requires us to meet a theoretical challenge, a clinical complexity, and continued accountability to that part of all of us that needs and wants to couple.

CONCLUDING THOUGHTS

We have taken the reader through the background, the inception, the literature, and the clinical practice of a unique model in couples group psychotherapy. The trip has been an adventuresome one for us as mental health professionals. It has enabled us to integrate theory, research, and practice from disciplines too often seen as unrelated and even, at times, in contradiction with one another. Yet, we believe that this marriage of ideas enriches the model in a manner that would be hard to replicate using one pathway alone. As marital partners, we found the experience of developing this model stimulating and creative, even when fraught with the inevitable differences of opinions that partnership brings. I am reminded of an inscription from a couple, both mental health professionals, in a book that they gave my husband and me at our wedding: "We wish for you, in your marriage, many levels of creativity." In conclusion, we wish our colleagues many levels of their own creativity as they work with couples in groups.

Section IV

Appendices

APPENDIX A: GROUP THERAPY FORMS AND POLICIES

APPENDIX A-I: INITIAL GROUP GOALS

Format: hand out in first meeting and discuss.

Name:
Date:
Name of group:
Leader(s):

Please complete the following statements:

- Here are my top goals for my time in this group:

- Here is the progress that I hope to make to get to my goals:

- Here is how I will know that I have progressed:

- This is who will be most affected by any changes that I make:

APPENDIX A-II: GROUP THERAPY PROGRESS REPORT

- My major goal for this year was:

- The progress I have made toward this goal is:

- The changes that I still need to make are:

- The ways in which I think I can make these changes are:

- Changes that others have seen in me this year are:

Date: Name:

APPENDIX A-III: GROUP PSYCHOTHERAPY POLICIES

Group Psychotherapy Policies at the
Coché Center (revised Fall 2003)

Introduction
The following policies have been adopted from those suggested by the American Group Psychotherapy Association and provide a foundation by which group psychotherapy at the Coché Center can function with maximum power. All are accepted and effective methods in handling psychotherapy in groups. We thank you in advance for honoring and respecting the points discussed below.

Written Confidentiality Agreement Within the Group
All information discussed in group psychotherapy meetings is to remain in the room. Names of other group members are not to be brought home to family or friends, and issues involving the lives of other group members are to be held in the strictest of confidence. In order to discuss one's own psychotherapy work, the best method is to relate the situation germane to yourself, pulling in other members anonymously and only as auxiliaries.

Confidentiality Between Members of a Family
Members of the same family who are concomitantly in group psychotherapy and other forms (couples or family therapy) are not to discuss the happenings of the group in the other form of psychotherapy. Confidentiality between family members is left to the discretion of the psychotherapist. Confidentiality about the families of the group members which is gained through prior or simultaneous psychotherapy will be handled on a case-by-case basis.

Goal Assessments
Each member is requested to write what his or her goals are during the course of the upcoming clinical year. Reports on the progress of the client become part of the group work and are used in planning for the potential leave-taking or continuation of the member the following year.

Absences From the Group

The group takes place unless there is a holiday or both psychotherapists are out of the city. An attempt to reschedule the group for that week will be made. We assume that members will be absent from the group between two and four times in an 11-month period due to illness, vacation, or business conflicts. Lateness and superficial absences are dealt with by the working group.

Socializing

We request that during your membership in a group, you limit your social contact with other members. Please do not invite others for coffee, for social gatherings, or to celebratory events. The group can plan ways to celebrate the accomplishments of its members as part of the group experience. We expect that after group sessions members may engage in social conversation on their way out of the building. We ask that the discussion remain on the level of social conversation. Thus, group psychotherapy issues are restricted to the time and location of the group meeting.

Special Workshop

A special workshop may be held as part of the ongoing group experience. The topic is chosen at the request of the group members.

Adjunctive Individual, Couples, and Family Therapy

Although there may be very infrequent meetings with the therapist outside the group times, it is necessary to have another form of therapy (couple, family, individual) available as a foundation. Group psychotherapy is a very lively opportunity to raise a number of issues, but time limitations may prevent dealing with issues in depth. Individual sessions are scheduled as decided by the outside therapist and the group member.

Fees

The monthly charge is payable on the first day of the month, for the month to come. Invoices are sent to each member at the end of the month for insurance and tax purposes. Because financial management is important in psychotherapy, tardiness in payment will be discussed within the group as needed.

The Group Therapy Contract
Group psychotherapy in a group in which members begin and end together is based on members' trust in one another that each will honor the full time and financial commitments. A breach of this contract against professional advice releases the Coché Center from further responsibility to the client.

How to Work in a Group
Because of the richness of the experience, members will benefit from the group whether they sit back and listen or actively pursue issues of importance. It is our experience that the greatest benefit can be obtained by being as honest as possible as quickly as possible and by talking up. Group therapists assist in forming a cohesive and trusting atmosphere so that maximum benefit can be obtained.

Alumni Contacts
A natural outgrowth of membership in a Coché Center group can be to develop an interest in outside friendships once previous members are no longer active group participants. We ask that confidentiality be maintained about current group members and that "alumni" activities be reported to the Group psychotherapy director. Current group members must limit social activity to one alum at a time, in order to avoid problems for other group members who also want to participate in alumni group activities. If a member is "taking time off" and may choose to return to a group at a later time, minimal socializing with members ensures the likelihood of a successful reentry into a current psychotherapy group.

Training Function
Co-therapy is provided by trained professionals at a postgraduate level. Co-therapists are clinical associates, clinical consultants, or postgraduate interns doing advanced training in group psychotherapy. Each group has a consistent team of the same two professionals for each clinical year. We thank you for your cooperation with these policies and encourage you to discuss any questions or disagreements with the psychotherapists who are heading your group.

Judith Coché, PhD
Diplomate (clinical), American Board of Professional Psychology fellow, American Group Psychotherapy Association

Clinical supervisor, American Association of Marriage and Family Therapy
Certified group psychotherapist

APPENDIX A-IV: GROUP CONTRACT

The Coché Center, L.L.C.
Group Psychotherapy Contract
The Coché Center agrees that _____ will be a member of the _____ group for the period _____.

The group member agrees to the following:

1. I have read the group psychotherapy policies and have asked necessary questions so that I understand and agree to the group psychotherapy policies.
2. I understand and agree that auxiliary individual, couples, and/ or family psychotherapy, about once every 3 weeks, is necessary unless decided otherwise by the Coché Center and myself. I agree to schedule and keep the necessary appointments.
3. I understand and agree that my financial responsibility for this group is due on the first day of the month for the month to come. I agree to pay my fee.
4. I understand and agree that my membership is for the full duration that this group meets, unless otherwise agreed upon by the Coché Center and myself. I agree to attend the group for its duration.
5. Should the need arise, I agree that I will initiate discussions of any necessary deviations from this contract with my group and its leader(s).

_____, clinician, the Coché Center
_____, group member
_____ date

APPENDIX B: STRUCTURED EXERCISES FOR MEMBERS

APPENDIX B-I: USING GUIDED IMAGERY IN COUPLES GROUP THERAPY

Following are examples of various types of structured exercises, along with responses by actual group members to the exercises, where applicable.

Guided Imagery: The False Alarm

The following exercise was presented to the workshop participants at the American Association of Marriage and Family Therapy workshop in San Francisco, October 1989. The workshop was held at the annual conference, which took place 6 days after a major earthquake hit the San Francisco Bay area. The exercise is exactly what we would have done in a couples group that week, had there been one in San Francisco. It represents a multi-level healing way to deal with the existential disaster that the earthquake presented.

Sit comfortably so that your feet are supported by the floor and your arms and hands are supported by your body. Rest your head on a back or head rest or on the muscles of your neck by letting it hang forward slightly. Breathe deeply, concentrating on the wonder of your breath as it enters and leaves your body. Close your eyes as I take you on a special journey ... a journey to a place inside you where meaning occurs ... where people are important ... where what is most important becomes clear and graspable.

As you concentrate on the sound of my voice and on your breathing, you may drift in and out of a slightly different way of being in the world. Your fingers may tingle. You may seem to be dozing off. Allow yourself to know that you are safe with us here to explore yourself. You will remember everything that happens and it can guide you to being more in touch with what is so important to you and to those you love.

Imagine that you are sitting comfortably at the kitchen or dinner table with someone you love ... your spouse, your children, your lover, your friend, your parents, your brother or sister. It is a typical family meal for you ... you are sitting in the presence of those you love.... If you live alone, imagine that you have invited someone to dine with you ... someone you love and value. Take a moment to look at the faces of those at the table. How old are they? How are they dressed? What do their faces tell you of how they are feeling during this normal dinner-time conversation? What are they talking about? What is the mood at the table? Are people seriously involved with one another? Is all attention focused on one person? Take a moment to notice, to be aware of how you feel toward these people with whom you share your evening meal.

Suddenly all is not well. Imagine a threat to your well-being ... a hurricane approaches suddenly, a fire breaks out in an electric wire, a refrigerator emits poisonous gas, an earthquake tremor is suspected, a burglar seem to appear from nowhere with a gun. Suddenly, something occurs that grips you in terror and in shock—a sudden danger to the well-being of those you love and to the well-being of yourself and your belongings. Look now at the faces at the table and let yourself seek the threat of disaster. As you look at those who are at the table with you, allow yourself to feel the threat of loss, of death, of destruction, of property ... the threat of an unknown terror. Take a moment now to let yourself know how much it means to you to cherish the friendship, or the love, of those with you. Think of what you would miss the most if the disaster were to strike. Now, just as you are coming to know the threat of loss, imagine that this was, after all, a false alarm.

The false alarm becomes clear to you now as you sit with your loved ones. The burglar was just a neighbor, the fire gets doused, the tremor passes, the hurricane misses your house, and the fire department is called for the gas leak. All is safe. Imagine the threat lifting as you imagine how your disaster turns into merely a false alarm.

Now, with new vision, look at the faces of those with you. Imagine that you can touch, embrace, and hug those near you. Imagine that you can tell your friend, your lover, and your family about the pain of the imagined loss and the relief of the false alarm. Imagine that you have become aware, through the threat of disaster, of the treasured relationships in your life.

Finally, before you come back to be with us in this big room, promise yourself, when you go home from this remarkable journey that you have had this day in San Francisco ... promise yourself that you will take the time to let those whom you love know that you took the time to notice how much they meant to you. Promise yourself that, from this threat of loss, you can become more intensely aware and more expressively appreciative of yourself, your home, your work, and your beloved friends and family ... of how much this gives you every single day of your life.

As I count backward, come back into the room slowly: 9, 8, 7, 6—begin to attend to cues in the room; 5, 4, 3—wiggle your toes and fingers; 2, 1—slowly open your eyes. Hello, everyone.

Discussion: It is imperative to have a chance to debrief after an intense experience like this. People will feel energized by talking or by listening to others talk if time does not permit participation by everyone. Enable participants to discuss whatever they choose about their experience in the fantasy.

APPENDIX B-II: ROLE PLAYING AFTER IMAGERY

Often, guided imagery is an introduction to role playing by group members with one another. In the following example, I guided couples through imagery and invited them to use other members to enact the themes of their imagery. The dialogue that follows is from the 1990 video of couples working with their issues. In the videotape, *Techniques in Couples Group Psychotherapy* (Coché and Coché, 1990), Will uses other members to sculpt a theme.

The exercise begins by an introduction of the work:

"Now that your eyes are closed ... everybody close your eyes ... and your bodies are in a relaxed state, I want you to pay full attention to my voice as I take you on a personal adventure. What you experience will be safe and will help you to know yourself and your marriage better. Think of your marriage and of the problems that brought you to the couples group. I would like you to choose one problem which interferes with the level of intimacy you want to experience with your spouse. I want you to think for a moment now about how you feel about your problem. Think of one problem which gets in the way of intimacy with your spouse. And think about how you feel about this problem. After you have chosen your problem, and you know how you feel about it, you are commissioned to sculpt the level of intimacy of one of the couples in this group. I would like you to think now of a couple that reminds you most of your

own marriage. If you were a sculptor, how might you sculpt this marriage? How would you position the partners in a relation to one another?"
    Will chooses to work.

    JC: *Okay which couple did you choose?*

    Will: *Ah, Erik and Nan.*

    JC: *Okay, if you like, you can include Erik's mother in your sculpture, if you believe that she is really central to their marriage.*

    Will: *Okay, do you want me to talk about it, or just to like … I, I did picture her.*

    JC: *You did picture her. Why don't you choose people to represent Erik and Nan. Just go ahead and sculpt. Do you need us to move the furniture at all?*

    Will: *Yeah, I think we will, because I pictured it as a scene at the dining room table with Nan and Erik.*

    JC: *Okay. Who's who?*

    Will: *Denise will be Nan, and Nate … Nate, you'll be Erik and Dale will be Erik's mother. What I'd like you to do, um, bring your chair over here. Erik and Nan, you might want to watch really carefully. Now bring your chair into here. This is the dining room table. And, um, Nate we need you in the middle. And Nan's in the middle and mother and Erik are in … Bring your chair in a little more. Nan's in the middle. What I want you to do is, I want you to … this is a formal, you know, formal dinner. It's not in the new kitchen, it's in the dining room, okay? It's very formal, you know; there are mirrors and you just look at this room and kind of get, you know. And, um [to Nate] you have to really be resisting talking to Nan and considering her opinion. You're really looking at your mother and, um, you're not really happy, okay, but you're engaged in a conversation. [To Denise] You are having your third scotch. You are not talking. You are really depressed. I mean you are depressed. You are very, just, you're not a part of it. And can only … [To Dale] you're confused in a way. You're delighted to be there. You know, it's your dining room and everything, but you're not … you're no … you're not sparkling because you're dining with this couple. And you have to really be, you know, you're kind of putting up with the situation 'cause you don't really know what to do. It's not your place to really call this one. And, um, you're reluctant to … You don't give her any view. You know. Okay, I want you to get into this now.*

Nate: So, mother, how was the trip to the store today, the grocery store?

Dale: Oh, it was just fine. It was nice to get out. I had a good time.

Denise: That's great!

Dale: What I was wondering about was how the garden was coming in the back, whether you've worked on that section that we talked about, with the rose bushes or not.

Nate: Ah, um, not, I haven't, but I'll have the men come over and they'll be working on it next week.

Dale: I was wondering what the design looked like for that section that we talked about the other night. Because I saw these wonderful roses at the nursery near the store where I was and I just wondered what you were planning for that section.

Nate: I have some preliminary sketches. I'll be happy to show them to you.

Denise: Did you think about my idea for the garden?

Nate: Well, mother and I had already talked about what we were going to do back in that corner, so ...

In this way, themes from Will's own life and marriage had an impact on all members of the group.

APPENDIX B-III: WRITING EXERCISES

Writing Exercises: The Meaning of Marriage

Instructions: Take a pencil and paper and write your quick response to the following question. You have about five minutes to write, before we discuss this together. For you as an individual, what does it mean to be married? Or, what would you like it to mean to be married?

The couples' responses were initially reported in the first edition of this text. Their responses are repeated for the reader:

Karl and Randy

Karl: To take the whole package ... because of the other person's good points and even because of the bad. To take care of each other. To be ever entwined with the other.

Randy: I would like it to mean constancy, planning together. Knowing we were making plans with the ground point assumption of continuing being together.

Skip and Nell

Nell: To be accepted as you are and then to be able to flex, to bend and to change, to blend more harmoniously with your partner's personality. To be able to share joy, pain and sorrow, without worrying about how you sound. To build a life together that is interesting to both. To care for each other and meet each other's needs. To forgive each other for hurtful indiscretions. To express love physically. To give each other room to grow as individuals. This is what I'd like marriage to be.

Skip: [wrote nothing]

APPENDIX C: EDUCATING COUPLES ABOUT COMMUNICATION

TEACHING NECESSARY SKILLS TO COUPLES

Couples are often surprised when we inform them that they need to do some skills training. They are pleased to know that skills training is not psychotherapy and will cost less than half the rate of therapy. Once they begin to understand that skills training will save them time and money in therapy, they also begin to understand that learning skills can allow us to work more creatively in treatment. The combination of educational skills at modest cost and couples group therapy allows couples maximum educational and clinical intervention at affordable prices. Communication skills can be taught to one couple or 20 couples. Because I wrote a workbook, *The Communication Workbook* (J. M. Coché, 2004), people can extend the skills to use in their homes. The skills appeal to partners who like clarity and structure. There are many approaches to couples' skills. In order to help couples be more comfortable learning these skills, I often use the example of Olympic tennis. The interchange goes something like this:

JC: *If you were an Olympic tennis player, would you go into an Olympic tennis match without lessons?*

Michael (looking slightly insulted): *Don't be silly.*

JC: *But marriage is an Olympic sport for many of us and, yet, we routinely get married without any lessons. Maybe we can teach you and Margaret how to love more skillfully. Would you like that?*

Michael: *Yes.*

His eyes told me that he understood.

When I do training for colleagues, I am frequently asked how and whether to teach psychoeducational skills to couples. Colleagues have strong and differing opinions about the wisdom of augmenting couples' psychotherapy with psychoeducationally based communications skills. Colleagues who are in agreement about the wisdom of teaching skills whenever possible can still be in disagreement about which skills are important for whom and why.

Detailed handling of the theoretical and research foundations of couples' skills is beyond the scope of the present work. Nevertheless, colleagues frequently ask me to consult on my educational skill package with them and I am happy to do that. I know that it can be overwhelming for colleagues who are unaccustomed to training couples in skills to sift through literature in which competent experts present slightly different skill packages from one another. Fortunately, many of these programs are easily available through books and online. I suggest that clinicians review their preferences from among the experts who have spent decades developing products to educate couples. Halford et al. (2003), and Gordon (1993) are among a host of authors to consult.

How Did I Develop the Skills We Use?

In the 1980s, I began to know that we needed to teach skills to couples. When Dr. Erich Coché died in 1991, funds were donated to a small cache that allowed me to read all the available literature, apply my knowledge from developmental and social psychology, and put together an original set of skills based on my research. I chose skills from Carl Rogers (1951), George Spivack and Myrna Shure (1974), and the Harvard Business School because these made good sense and had been well used by others for many decades.

Little knowledge existed about the neurobiology of coupling in these early years, but I knew this area was crucial, so I concocted a simple list of feelings and taught what I called "the feelings primer" to those unaccustomed to valuing and accessing emotionality in expression. In 2004, I created a small workbook called *The Couples Communication Workbook* and made it available to couples in order to make the skill steps clear. That workbook also contains the latest research in coupling, and this combination equips our clients to save as much therapy time as possible by augmenting treatment with bibliotherapy and psychoeducation.

Why Teach Skills?

I would like to see school children routinely learn to communicate effectively as part of their basic education in fluency. We all need to be emotionally articulate, and the time to learn emotional fluency is during our period of most intense cognitive development. Thus, I am one of many who hope for the day when communication skills training is part of most curricula for children between the ages of 9 and 13. Until that day, however, we can save expensive therapy time by setting the expectation that our clients will do their part to learn to communicate effectively with one another. For example, we teach four skills in sets of two that seem common sense to most people when they first hear about them.

The Intimacy Loop

Two skills are grouped together to form what we call the "intimacy loop." Stated very simply, this set of skills has two steps. First, one person talks about how he or she feels (the "feelings primer") and the other person engages in active listening. Then the two partners reverse roles: The talker listens and the listener talks. The result is always that the members of a couple can feel closer to one another.

The Business of Coupling

A second set of skills comprises the "business of coupling." All committed couples have to use two skills borrowed from cognitive and social psychology: They must problem-solve and negotiate on a daily basis in order to live their lives together. To this end, we teach interpersonal problem solving (Spivack & Shure, 1977) and negotiation skills as taught by the Harvard Business School (Fisher & Ury, 1981).

Which Skill When?

We teach couples when to use which skill and we console them when they realize that mastering these skills is far from easy. We know that the skills are easy to learn in a vacuum, much as beginning French is not hard to memorize when one sits in a high school class in the United States. However, we explain that the more emotional the topic is, the harder a couple may find it to apply the skills that they believe they have mastered. A couple who needs to discuss bankruptcy, terminal illness, infertility, the illness of a child, and other welfare-threatening topics may find themselves stumbling over the very skills that they thought they had mastered.

We want couples to understand that the neurobiology of coupling may necessitate that they calm down before they can listen to each other. It helps couples to understand this rational learning pattern, and they customarily appreciate the ability to use the skills at home.

What Is the Difference Between Skill-Teaching and Psychotherapy?

Education paves the way to deeper learning. Psychotherapy is necessary where skill-teaching leaves off. Most couples can master skills easily but find it much harder to integrate the skills into their conflict-filled lives. It is hard for them to know when to use which skill. The self-discipline needed to remain calm when one feels angry is hard to practice. However, the skills are worth the investment. A couple that has learned to use basic communication skills in difficult and conflicted times has most likely attained an advanced level of fluency in interpersonal communications. This articulate status can often significantly diminish the amount of time and energy needed in psychotherapy.

Much like tooth brushing can prevent later decay and slow down potential gum disease, a couple who learns the skills and practices them in their lives can slow down marital decay and prevent damage to the marital foundation. Customarily, skills learned in a clinical setting fall apart as tension builds and personal unhappiness takes charge of the emotionality between the members of a couple. Therapy becomes necessary to target clinical interventions to the personalities of each member of the couple and the dynamics between them. After a bit of therapy about the right to be furious after partner mistreatment and the right to be heard by the partner, many clients are ready to practice the skill of remaining calm. In this way, skill-building forms the foundation for a greater depth experience as part of couples psychotherapy. Some couples attend programs at church. Others go to a weekend course at a university. Still others prefer to work with us. How the skills are learned is less important than that the learning occurs.

Holly was certain that she did not need further communications skill training because part of her professional expertise is within the arena of interpersonal communication: She trains others. However, once she understood that it is valuable to learn the language of coupling at the same time as one's partner, she became an enthusiastic consumer of couples' skill training. Highly versed in the capacity for active listening, Holly found it harder to discuss the depth of feelings that she knew she had. She did not want to burden anybody else or make them uncomfortable by making them listen to how she felt. She would hold feelings in and allow them to seep out in quiet, highly intellectual sentences directed toward her partner. Due to her discomfort, these statements were not particularly easy to comprehend. "I wish you wouldn't do that" was a disguise for "I can't stand it when you talk to me that way." Her partner, Trevor, had been raised as "the man of the house" and had quickly learned to hold everything in until he felt like he would explode. When he met Holly, he did not want to endanger her love for him so he disciplined himself to try to handle his reaction internally all of the time. At times, this caused him to go numb from the pile-up of emotionality that had to remain inside. At irregular intervals, however, his face would get red, the veins on his neck would pop out, and he would sound vituperative for 75 seconds. After his explosion, he would mope for days. Trevor was a quick learner and Holly already understood the foundations for most of the skills, so the couple was able to absorb needed communication training within a few hours. Much to their surprise, they both found the experience invaluable in getting through problematic interchanges that previously would have disabled them as a couple for days at a time. A few hours of skill training probably saved them unnecessary hardship and a substantial amount of time and money in psychotherapy. They went on to use the couples group to work at the level of pain that they could not address alone.

Examples of Couples' Skill-Training

Numerous experts in couples therapy have developed evidence-based programs in skill-training, including the following:

- Howard Markman and Scott Stanley put the field of couples' communication on the map when they began to do granted research to teach professionals how to teach couples' communication and developed an approach that they call PREP (prevention and relationship enhancement program). They assume that good marriages take work. They have skills for handling conflicts, dealing with core issues, and enhancing a committed relationship. These skills overlap with those that we use—namely, the speaker–listener technique, problem solving, and communicating clearly and safely (Markman, Stanley, & Blumberg, *Fighting for Your Marriage*, 1994).

- Lori Gordon stresses the mechanics of emotion, taking a daily temperature reading, the art of talking, the art of listening, and the art of fighting fair among other areas of couples' skills. Her style is clear and her examples are highly clinical (Gordon, *Passage to Intimacy*, 1993).

Each of these approaches has its own strengths. It is wise for clinicians to match their own therapeutic road map with the skills they choose and the way in which they are taught. Either spend time integrating these skills into your own framework or look through these masterful and well-designed approaches to couples' skill training and choose one that fits your clinical need and therapeutic style.

APPENDIX D: A WHO'S WHO OF OUR COUPLES

The stars of this volume are five women married to five men. These 10 people share their lives, their hopes, their dreams, their passions, their terrors, and their futures with one another, and with you, the reader. To make it easier for you to follow, I give you a capsule description of each couple. Significant details have been altered to protect the identity of each person.

In 2006, all five of the couples described here became part of a new couples group. Diane and Dwight and Antonia and Patrick had been members of previous couples groups in earlier years. At the end of the contract period for the 2006–2007 group, Diane and Dwight and Margaret and Michael graduated from the group. The other couples (Robyn and Spencer, Holly and Trevor, and Antonia and Patrick) returned to a group of three couples in 2007–2008. The three returning couples requested that the group remain closed to new members so that they could move deeply and quickly. All three couples graduated at the end of 2008.

ANTONIA AND PATRICK

Antonia has Mensa-level intelligence, which she uses to create the best world that is humanly possible for her two children, as well as to build a sizable career in the field of technical engineering. She can seem overbearing to anyone who gets into a path that she sees as critical to achieving a goal. She has a history of feeling ashamed of her body, which is medium frame and somewhat athletic. Wholesome and attractive, Antonia has hidden her body through amply sized clothing and has deflected her beauty through a refusal to wear makeup. In addition to her work in the couples group, Antonia has done individual depth psychotherapy as well as participating in an individual psychotherapy group for women. Her high intelligence and tenacity have enabled her to make sweeping and transformational changes throughout the course of her treatment.

Patrick is a fluidly moving, tall man with a quietly impish demeanor. A one-woman man, he has endured more than a decade of inadequate sex in order to remain married to Antonia, who lost interest in sexual activity with her husband. Gentle and passive, Patrick was encouraged as part of his treatment to learn to speak up more assertively than was his custom. Combining extremely high mechanical intelligence with facets of a learning disability, Patrick thought of himself as not very intelligent during the first 35 years of his life. Deeply compassionate and caring, Patrick is beloved by most who know him, making the tragedy of his wife's disinterest even starker than it otherwise might be.

Antonia and Patrick have been married for 22 years. Religion and a value system centered around marriage and children prevent them from finalizing what others have often felt to be a functional divorce within an ongoing marriage. To the group, it feels like they are almost always on the verge of divorce. This precipice marriage keeps the anxiety high for both the adults and the adolescent son and daughter in this family. The couple joined one of the very early couples groups in the 1980s and benefited from it. They left psychotherapy for 15 years and returned to be part of this group. They were in this group for 3 years.

ROBYN AND SPENCER

Robyn is British, outgoing yet prone to depression. Most of the time, Robyn wears a smile as big as her face, drawing those who know her into a sense of pleasure in conversing with her. Robyn is stately and attracts attention with her bright colors and her naturally bright coloring. With blonde hair and blue eyes, she captures attention when she walks into a room. Robyn loves to laugh and loves to help others to laugh. Having her as a member of a group is a lot like having a sunny day in the treatment room. This makes it all the more dramatic when Robyn's depression comes to the surface and her big smile turns into a flood of pain and tears. She has used medication successfully and wants nothing more than to be happily married and raise children.

Spencer learned how high his intelligence was by taking an intelligence test at the Coché Center. Growing up with parental inattention to his unusual ability with technology and information processing, Spencer took a job in retail sales at a large warehouse and remained at that job for a decade. His first wife divorced him, partially due to his underachievement.

Pleasing to the point of nonassertion, Spencer feared making inroads at work, which froze his place on a career ladder and froze his salary at a place far too low for his intelligence. After his first wife divorced him, Spencer had some concerns about homosexuality and was unsure that he would feel comfortable with a heterosexual marriage and children, which had been his life goal.

Robyn and Spencer decided to do the couples group at this point in their marriage as a kind of preemptive strike. Each wanted this to be the last marriage in his and her life, and each had had enough psychotherapy to absorb the necessity to work through dysfunctional interpersonal patterns before remarrying. Newlyweds during their 3 years in the group, they moved from a state of pure joy to very deep work around depression and sexuality. Miscarriages had been part of both first marriages, and the couple was jubilant when pregnancy occurred during their membership in the couples group. Their baby attended couples group therapy for the first few months of her life.

DIANE AND DWIGHT

Diane became the widowed mother of two active children in her early 40s. Struggling with depression and anxiety, Diane used psychotherapy to keep herself and her family in balance during the extremely difficult years of raising her children alone. Simultaneously to this necessity to shepherd young children, Diane undertook completion of a PhD degree in contemporary American history. She has engaged in individual depth therapy as well as ongoing group psychotherapy to help her through her husband's death, her widowhood, her recoupling, and the raising of her children. Perky and smiling by nature, Diane lights up a room with her effervescent warmth, unless she is anxious.

Dwight is intelligent and feels more comfortable remaining cognitive at all times. With a history of underachievement and a potential learning disability, Dwight found it difficult to meet the demands of his highly successful family. A bachelor for 25 years after his divorce, Dwight dedicated himself to raising his two daughters and never expected to marry again. Captivated by Diane's beautiful personality, Dwight agreed to do anything necessary in order to share his life with her. This included joining a couples group. This group challenged Dwight to become less intellectual and more emotionally articulate. In the early years, Dwight would repeat phrases anxiously as a way of trying to remember what was said, and tried to take notes to hold onto some of the emotionally laden material.

Diane and Dwight married a decade before this book was written. They had been members of an earlier couples group and used their couples group work to resolve deep issues in depression, anxiety, and anger. Early phases of treatment revolved around expressing anger quietly and directly rather than passively and sarcastically. The couple was tireless in its willingness to do whatever it took in order to be successfully married to one another. Despite the seemingly unending treatment, they were an inspiration for the other couples because of the extensive changes they were able to make. Diane and Dwight did not return for the third year of this group.

MARGARET AND MICHAEL

Margaret is petite, with a natural level of classic beauty that creates an aura of elegance even when she is simply dressed. She possesses a quick wit and a ready smile, and her face can move from being closed and anxious to being wide open as she connects easily to the other members of the group. Extremely perceptive, she is able to nail the dynamics of the other members more quickly than she is able to discuss her own dynamics. Unfortunately, Margaret is unaware of her beauty and often battles with feeling self-conscious.

A superb craftswoman, Margaret is able to create sophisticated costumes and design the patterns to go with them. Although she does this as a volunteer and sews the clothing for her children, it would never occur to her to open a shop. Margaret invests heavily in natural foods, yoga, and psychotherapy. She was part of a small women's group with Antonia. Her mother-in-law has been her employer for some time, in a retail shop, and she handles this through a quiet, passive anger that makes it hard for her to think straight. During the course of her treatment, she was frequently overwhelmed by the need to parent two girls and two boys almost on her own, due to her husband's business hours.

Although Michael is not a bank president, he carries himself as though he might be. He has engineered a very successful career in technology at the corporate level. He is tall, strident, and engaging, and his confidence is clear as soon as he speaks. For this reason, it never occurred to him that he was being abusive in his handling of anger and that the people he loved the most were being damaged. After all, he came to this style of anger management through his own growing-up years. In order to support his brood, Michael agreed to an executive position that required 5 hours for daily travel. For this reason, he had to leave most of the child rearing to Margaret, and he missed out on parenting his children during their growing years. Like Margaret, he finds it difficult to get along with his mother, but his value system requires that he be tenaciously loyal to her.

Margaret and Michael are the love of one another's life. Inspirational to the other couples, they speak glowingly of their early marriage years and the work they did with one another to keep sex and love alive while they were raising their children. Michael finds Margaret beautiful and Margaret finds Michael handsome. They enjoy deeply satisfying sex with one another despite Margaret's concerns about her appearance. Within 2 years, this attractive and loving couple made huge strides in the couples group and graduated with no need to return for a third year.

HOLLY AND TREVOR

Holly is a petite and brilliant graduate with a PhD in organizational development from Columbia University. Unfortunately, Holly would prefer to spend her time in crafts as Margaret does. Although Holly has earned hundreds of thousands of dollars annually, she chafes under corporate schedules and becomes angry and resentful. Her skill in interpersonal communication creates an occupational hazard for her as a member of the couples group; it is sometimes easier for her to help others rather than to help herself. Waiting until her mid-30s to get married, Holly wanted to "get it right" and implored Trevor to do the couples group as part of their early marriage. During their 3 years in the couples group, Holly left corporate America, had a miscarriage, had a baby, and brought her baby to the couples group for the first year of his life. Accustomed to affluence, Holly has had to make adjustments in her expectations as her need for freedom has propelled her to stop earning money.

Trevor has a Humphrey Bogart quickness and a direct and unforgettable way of engaging others. His brilliance catches others off guard as he darts intellectually from discussing football to the economic analysis that is part of his career. Although Trevor is extremely skillful, he is not particular confident about his own ability; psychotherapy has given him the gift of his own intelligence and he now earns hundreds of thousands of dollars annually to support his wife and baby. He has found it exceptionally difficult to speak up to Holly's assertive stance in relation to what she wants. This has caused them deep issues around money and work, which could have been prevented if Trevor had been more assertive.

Holly and Trevor married around the time of the beginning of this couples group and remained in the group for 3 years. Trevor did deep work very quickly because of his ability to make changes. He developed confidence, became assertive in relation to his wife, and began to understand that duplicity was not going to succeed in his marriage. Completely devoted to her partner, Holly actually contemplated divorce at one point unless Trevor made needed changes. Instead, at the time of this writing, the couple is more together than ever before and their baby has had the benefit of one year of couples psychotherapy.

REFERENCES

Abraham. L. (2007, August 12). Can this marriage be saved? *New York Times Magazine,* pp. 30–35, 53–55.

Abraham, L. (2007, October 28). Just the few of us. *Stella, the Sunday Telegraph,* pp. 58–63.

Agazarian, Y. (1997). *Systems-centered therapy for groups.* New York, NY: Guilford Press.

Agazarian, Y., & Peters, R. (1981). *The visible and invisible group: Two perspectives on group psychotherapy and group process.* London, England: Routledge & Kegan Paul.

American Group Psychotherapy Association (2007). Practice guidelines for group psychotherapy: Preparation and pre-group training. Retrieved September 2, 2008, from http://www.agpa.org/guidelines/preparation.html

Arnow, B. A., Desmond, J. E., Banner, L. L., Glover, G. H., Solomon, A., Polan, M. L., et al. (2002). Brain activation and sexual arousal in healthy, heterosexual males. *Brain, 125,* 1014–1023.

Aron, A., Fisher, H., Mashek, D. J., Strong, G., Li, H., & Brown, L. L. (2005). Reward, motivation, and emotion systems associated with early stage intense romantic love. *Journal of Neurophysiology, 94,* 327–337.

Atkins, D. C., Eldridge, K. A., Baucom, D. H., & Christensen, A. (2005). Infidelity and behavioral couple therapy: Optimism in the face of betrayal. *Journal of Consulting and Clinical Psychology, 73,* 144–150.

Bader, E., & Pearson, P. T. (1988). *In quest of the mythical mate: A developmental approach to diagnosis and treatment in couples therapy.* New York, NY: Brunner/Mazel.

Barbato, A., & D'Avanzo, B. (2008). Efficacy of couple therapy as a treatment for depression: A meta-analysis. *Psychiatric Quarterly, 79,* 121–132.

Barlow, D. H., O'Brien, G. T., & Last, C. G. (1984). Couples treatment of agoraphobia. *Behavior Therapy, 15,* 41–58.

Bartels, A., & Zeki, S. (2000). The neural basis of romantic love. *Neuroreport, 11,* 3829–3834.

Bartels, A., & Zeki, S. (2004). The neural correlates of maternal and romantic love. *Neuroimage, 21,* 1155–1166.

Baucom, D. H., & Lester, G. W. (1986). The usefulness of cognitive restructuring as an adjunct to behavioral marital therapy. *Behavior Therapy, 17,* 385–403.

Baucom, D. H., Shoham, V., Mueser, K. T., Daiuto, A. D., & Stickle, T. R. (1998). Empirically supported couple and family interventions for marital distress and adult mental health problems. *Journal of Consulting and Clinical Psychology, 66,* 53–88.

Beck, A. T. (1979). *Cognitive therapy and emotional disorders.* New York, NY: New American Library.

Bennis, W., & Shephard, H. (1956). A theory of group development. *Human Relations, 9,* 415–437.

Bennun, I. (1985). Behavioral marital therapy: An outcome evaluation of conjoint, group and one spouse treatment. *Scandinavian Journal of Behaviour Therapy, 14,* 157–168.

Bennun, I. (1986). Group marital therapy: A review. *Journal of Sexual and Marital Therapy, 1,* 61–74.

Berne, E. (1966). *Group treatment.* New York, NY: Grove Press.

Better Sex Video Series. Chapel Hill, NC: Sinclair Intimacy Institute.

Beutler, L., Scogin, F., Kirkish, P., Schretlen, D., Corbishley, A., Hamblin, D., et al. (1987). Group cognitive therapy and alprazolam in the treatment of depression in older adults. *Journal of Consulting and Clinical Psychology, 55,* 550–556.

Bion, W. R. (1960). *Experiences in groups.* New York, NY: Basic Books.

Birchler, J. A., Yao, H., & Chudalayandi, S. (2006). Unraveling the genetic basis of hybrid vigor. *Proceedings of the National Academy of Sciences, 103,* 12957–12958.

Birdwhistell, R. (1970). *Kinesics and context: Essays on body motion communication.* Philadelphia, PA: University of Pennsylvania Press.

Bloch, S., Browning, S., & McGrath, G. (1983). Humor in group psychotherapy. *British Journal of Medical Psychology, 56,* 89–97.

Blue, V. (Ed.) (2003a). *The ultimate guide to adult videos: How to watch adult videos and make your sex life sizzle.* San Francisco, CA: Cleis Press, Inc.

Blue, V. (Ed.) (2003b). *Sweet life 2: Erotic fantasies for couples.* San Francisco, CA: Cleis Press, Inc.

Bogdanoff, M., & Elbaum, P. (1978). Role lock: Dealing with monopolizers, mistrusters, isolates, "helpful Hannahs," and other assorted characters of group psychotherapy. *International Journal of Group Psychotherapy, 28,* 247–262.

Borriello, J. F. (1979). Intervention foci in group psychotherapy. In L. R. Wolberg & M. L. Aronson (Eds.), *Group psychotherapy, 1979.* New York, NY: Stratton Intercontinental.

Borysenko, J. (1988). *Minding the body, mending the mind.* New York, NY: Bantam.

Bowers, T. G., & Al-Redha, M. R. (1990). A comparison of outcome with group/marital and standard/individual therapies with alcoholics. *Journal of Studies on Alcohol, 51,* 301–309.

Bowlby, J. (1990). *A secure base: Parent–child attachment and healthy human development.* New York, NY: Basic Books.

Bradbury, T. N., & Fincham, F. D. (1990). Attributions in marriage: Review and critique. *Psychological Bulletin, 107,* 3–33.

Bradley, B., & Furrow, J. L. (2004). Toward a minitheory of the blamer softening event: Tracking the moment-by-moment process. *Journal of Marital and Family Therapy, 30,* 233–246.

Brady, J. P. (1976). An empirical study of behavioral marital therapy in groups. *Behavior Therapy, 8,* 512–513.

Brannen, S. J., & Rubin, A. (1996). Comparing the effectiveness of gender-specific and couples groups in a court-mandated spouse abuse treatment program. *Research on Social Work Practice, 6,* 405–424.

Breiter, H. C., Gollub, R. L., Weisskoff, R. M., Kennedy, D. N., Makris, N., Berke, J. D., et al. (1997). Acute effects of cocaine on human brain activity and emotion. *Neuron, 19,* 591–611.

Buber, M. (1958). *I and thou* (2nd ed., R. G. Smith, Trans.). New York, NY: Charles Scribner's Sons.

Budge, G. S. (2008). *The new financial advisor: Strategies for successful family wealth management.* New York, NY: John Wiley & Sons.

Budman, S. H., Soldz, S., Demby, A., Davis, M., & Merry, J. (1993). What is cohesiveness? An empirical examination. *Small Group Research, 24,* 199–216.

Budman, S. H., Soldz, S., Demby, A., Feldstein, M., Springer, T., & Davis, M. S. (1989). Cohesion, alliance and outcome in group psychotherapy. *Psychiatry, 52,* 339–350.

Bugental, J. F. T. (1981). *The search for authenticity: An existential-analytic approach to psychotherapy.* New York, NY: Irvington Publishers.

Bugental, J. F. T. (1984). *The art of the psychotherapist: Evoking the healing/growth potential.* Santa Rosa, CA: Psychology Corporation.

Burlingame, G. M., Fuhriman, A., & Johnson, J. (2003). Process and outcome in group counseling and psychotherapy. In J. L. DeLucia-Waack, D. A. Gerrity, C. R. Kalodner, & M. Riva (Eds.), *Group counseling and psychotherapy* (pp. 49–61). Thousand Oaks, CA: Sage.

Burlingame, G. M., MacKenzie, K. R., & Strauss, B. (2004). Small group treatment: Evidence for effectiveness and mechanisms of change. In M. J. Lambert (Ed.), *Bergin & Garfield handbook of psychotherapy and behavior change* (5th ed., pp. 647–696). New York, NY: John Wiley & Sons.

Bush, G., Luu, P., & Posner, M. I. (2000). Cognitive and emotional influences in anterior cingulate cortex. *Trends in Cognitive Sciences, 4,* 215–222.

Butler, M. H., & Wampler, K. S. (1999). A meta-analytic update of research on the couple communication program. *American Journal of Family Therapy, 27,* 223–237.

Byrne, M., Carr, A., & Clark, M. (2004). The efficacy of couples-based interventions for panic disorder with agoraphobia. *Journal of Family Therapy, 26,* 105–125.

Carmichael, M. S., Humbert, R., Dixen, J., Palmisano, G., Greenleaf, W., & Davidson, J. M. (1987). Plasma oxytocin increases in the human sexual response. *Journal of Clinical Endocrinology and Metabolism, 64,* 27–31.

Carter, C. S. (1998). Neuroendocrine perspectives on social attachment and love. *Psychoneuroendocrinology, 23,* 779–818.

Caughlin, J. P., & Huston, T. L. (2002). A contextual analysis of the association between demand/withdraw and marital satisfaction. *Personal Relationships, 9,* 95–119.

241

Christensen, A., Atkins, D. C., Berns, S., Wheeler, J., Baucom, D. H., & Simpson, L. E. (2004). Traditional versus integrative behavioral couple therapy for significantly and chronically distressed married couples. *Journal of Consulting and Clinical Psychology, 72,* 176–191.

Christensen, A., Atkins, D. C., Yi, J., Baucom, D. H., & George, W. H. (2006). Couple and individual adjustment for 2 years following a randomized clinical trial comparing traditional versus integrative couple therapy. *Journal of Consulting and Clinical Psychology, 74,* 1180–1191.

Christensen, A., Eldridge, K., Catta-Preta, A. B., Lim, V. R., & Santagata, R. (2006). Cross-cultural consistency of the demand/withdraw interaction pattern in couples. *Journal of Marriage and the Family, 68,* 1029–1044.

Christensen, A., & Heavey, C. L. (1999). Interventions for couples. *Annual Review of Psychology, 50,* 165–190.

Christensson, K., Nilsson, B. A., Stock, S., Matthiesen, A. S., & Uvnäs-Moberg, K. (1989). Effect of nipple stimulation on uterine activity and on plasma levels of oxytocin in full term, healthy, pregnant women. *Acta Obstetricia et Gynecologica Scandinavica, 68,* 205–210.

Cividini, E., & Klain, E. (1973). Psychotherapy in the cotherapeutic group. *Socijalna-Psihijatrija, 1,* 65–74.

Cobb, J. P., Mathews, A. M., Childs-Clarke, A., & Blowers, C. M. (1984). The spouse as co-therapist in the treatment of agoraphobia. *British Journal of Psychiatry, 144,* 282–287.

Coché, E. (1983). Change measures and clinical practice in group psychotherapy. In R. R. Dies & K. R. MacKenzie (Eds.), *Advances in group psychotherapy* (pp. 79–99). New York, NY: International Universities Press.

Coché, E., & Dies, R. R. (1981). Integrating research findings into the practice of group psychotherapy. *Psychotherapy: Theory, Research and Practice, 18,* 410–416.

Coché, E., Polikoff, B., & Cooper, J. (1980). Participant self-disclosure in group therapy. *Group, 4,* 28–35.

Coché, J. M. (1980). Social roles and family interaction in collaborative work. In E. A. Pepitone (Ed.), *Children in cooperation and competition: Toward a developmental social psychology* (pp. 389–411). Lexington, MA: Lexington Books.

Coché, J. M. (1984). Psychotherapy with women therapists. In F. W. Kaslow (Ed.), *Psychotherapy with psychotherapists* (pp. 151–169). New York, NY: Haworth Press.

Coché, J. M. (1990). Resistance in existential-strategic marital therapy. *Journal of Family Psychology, 3,* 236–250.

Coché, J. M. (2004). *The communications workbook* (4th ed.). Self-published.

Coché, J. M. with Allen, D. (2002a). *The couples money school primer.* Self-published

Coché, J. M., & Coché, E. (1986). Group psychotherapy: The severely disturbed patient in hospital. *Carrier Foundation Newsletter, 113,* 1–7.

Coché, J. M., & Coché, E. (1990). *Couples group psychotherapy: A clinical practice model.* NY: Brunner/Mazel, Inc.

Coché, J. M., & Satterfield, J. M. (1993). Couples group psychotherapy. In H. J. Kaplam & B. J. Saddock (Eds.), *Comprehensive group psychotherapy* (3rd ed., pp. 283–292). Baltimore, MD: Williams & Wilkins.

Coché, J. M. with Slowinski, J. (2002b). *The couples sex school primer.* Self-published.

Coché, J. M., Slowinski, J., McCarthy, K. S., & Galbraith, J. (2006). Couples group psychotherapy for sexuality and intimacy: Intensive treatment for lifelong change. *Group, 30,* 25–39.

Cohen, S. (1997). Working with resistance to experiencing and expressing emotions in group therapy. *International Journal of Group Psychotherapy, 47*(4), 443–458.

Collins, V. F. (1998). *Couples and money: A couples' guide updated for the new millennium.* Sherman Oaks, CA: Gabriel Publication.

Cooper, L. (1976). Co-therapy relationships in groups. *Small Group Behavior, 7,* 473–498.

Cordova, J. V., Jacobson, N. S., & Christensen, A. (1998). Acceptance versus change interventions in behavioral couple therapy: Impact on couples' in-session communication. *Journal of Marital and Family Therapy, 24,* 437–455.

Curtis, J. T., & Wang, Z. (2003). The neurochemistry of pair bonding. *Current Directions in Psychological Science, 12,* 49–53.

Damasio, A. (1999). *The feeling of what happens: Body and emotion in the making of consciousness.* San Diego, CA: Harcourt.

Daiuto, A. D., Baucom, D. H., Epstein, N., & Dutton, S. S. (1998). The application of behavioral couples therapy to the assessment and the treatment of agoraphobia: Implications of empirical research. *Clinical Psychology Review, 18,* 663–687.

Davis, K. L., & Meara, N. M. (1982). So you think it is a secret. *Journal for Specialists in Group Work, 7,* 149–153.

Denton, W. H., Burleson, B. R., Clarke, T. E., Rodriguez, C. P., & Hobbs, B. V. (2000). A randomized trial of emotion-focused therapy for couples in a training clinic. *Journal of Marital and Family Therapy, 26,* 65–78.

Denton, W. H., Burleson, B. R., Hobbs, B. V., Von Stein, M., & Rodriguez, C. P. (2001). Cardiovascular reactivity and initiate/avoid patterns of marital communication: A test of Gottman's psychophysiologic model of marital interaction. *Journal of Behavioral Medicine, 24,* 401–421.

Depue, R. A., & Morrone-Strupinsky, J. V. (2005). A neurobehavioral model of affiliative bonding: Implications for conceptualizing a human trait of affiliation. *Behavioral and Brain Sciences, 28,* 313–350.

Derogatis, L. R. (1994). *SCL-90-R: Administration scoring and procedures manual.* Minneapolis, MN: National Computer Systems.

DeRubeis, R. J., & Crits-Cristoph, P. (1998). Empirically supported individual and group psychological treatments for adult mental disorders. *Journal of Consulting and Clinical Psychology, 66,* 37–52.

DeRubeis, R. J., Hollon, S. D., Amsterdam, J. D., Shelton, R. C., Young, P. R., Salomon, R. M., et al. (2005). Cognitive therapy vs. medications in the treatment of moderate to severe depression. *Archives of General Psychiatry, 62,* 409–416.

243

Dicks, H. V. (1967). *Marital tensions: Clinical studies towards a psychological theory of interaction.* New York, NY: Basic Books, Inc.

Diener, E., & Biswas-Diener, R. (2008). *Happiness: Unlocking the mysteries of psychological health.* New York, NY: Wiley–Blackwell.

Ditzen, B., Neumann, I. D., Bodenmann, G., von Dawans, B., Turner, R. A., Ehlert, U., et al. (2007). Effects of different kinds of couple interaction on cortisol and heart rate responses to stress in women. *Psychoneuroendocrinology, 32,* 565–574.

Donnelly, J. M., Kornblith, A. B., Fleishman, S., Zuckerman, A., Raptis, G., Hudis, C. A., et al. (2000). A pilot study of interpersonal psychotherapy by telephone with cancer patients and their partners. *Psycho-Oncology, 9,* 44–56.

Donovan, J. M. (1995). Short-term couples group psychotherapy: A tale of four fights. *Psychotherapy: Theory, Research, Practice, Training, 32,* 608–617.

Doss, B. D., Atkins, D. C., & Christensen, A. (2003). Who's dragging their feet? Husbands and wives seeking marital therapy. *Journal of Marital and Family Therapy, 29,* 165–177.

Dunn, R. L., & Schwebel, A. I. (1995). Meta-analytic review of marital therapy outcome research. *Journal of Family Psychology, 9,* 58–68.

Emanuele, E., Politi, P., Bianchi, M., Minoretti, P., Bertona, M., & Geroldi, D. (2006). Raised plasma nerve growth factor levels associated with early stage romantic love. *Psychoneuroendocrinology, 31,* 288–294.

Emanuels-Zuurveen, L., & Emmelkamp, P. M. G. (1996). Individual behavioral–cognitive therapy v. marital therapy for depression in maritally distressed couples. *British Journal of Psychiatry, 169,* 181–188.

Emmelkamp, P. M. G., de Haan, E., & Hoodguin, C. A. L. (1990). Marital adjustment and obsessive–compulsive disorder. *British Journal of Psychiatry, 156,* 55–60.

Emmelkamp, P. M. G., Van Dyck, R., Bitter, M., Heins, R., Onstein, E. J., & Eisen, B. (1992). Spouse-aided therapy with agoraphobics. *British Journal of Psychiatry, 160,* 51–56.

Emmelkamp, P. M. G., van Linden van den Heuvell, C., Ruphan, M., Sanderman, R., Scholing, A., & Stroink, F. (1988). Cognitive and behavioral interventions: A comparative evaluation with clinically distressed couples. *Journal of Family Psychology, 1,* 365–377.

Epstein, N., & Eidelson, R. J. (1981). Unrealistic beliefs of clinical couples: Their relationship to expectations, goals and satisfaction. *American Journal of Family Therapy, 9,* 13–22.

Erikson, E. H. (1968). *Identity: Youth and crisis.* New York, NY: W. W. Norton & Company.

Esch, T., & Stefano, G. B. (2005). The neurobiology of love. *Neuroendocrinology Letters, 26,* 175–192.

Evans, C. R., & Dion, K. L. (1991). Group cohesion and performance: A meta-analysis. *Small Group Research, 22,* 175–186.

Evans, P. (2003). *The verbally abusive relationship: How to recognize it and how to respond.* Cincinnati, OH: Adams Media.

Everaerd, W., & Dekker, J. (1981). A comparison of sex therapy and communication therapy: Couples complaining of orgasmic dysfunction. *Journal of Sex and Marital Therapy, 7,* 278–289.

Fals-Stewart, W., Birchler, G. R., & O'Farrell, T. J. (1996). Behavioral couples therapy for male substance-abusing patients: Effects on relationship adjustment and drug-using behavior. *Journal of Consulting and Clinical Psychology, 64,* 959–972.

Fals-Stewart, W., Klostermann, K., Yates, B. T., O'Farrell, T. J., & Birchler, G. R. (2005). Brief relationship therapy for alcoholism: A randomized clinical trial examining clinical efficacy and cost effectiveness. *Psychology of Addictive Behaviors, 19,* 363–371.

Fals-Stewart, W., Marks, A., & Schafer, B. (1993). A comparison of behavioral group therapy and individual behavior therapy in treating obsessive–compulsive disorder. *Journal of Nervous and Mental Disease, 181,* 189–193.

Feld, B. G. (1997). An object relations perspective on couples group therapy. *International Journal of Group Psychotherapy, 47,* 315–332.

Feld, B. G. (1998). Initiating a couples group. *Group, 22,* 245–259.

Feld, B. G. (2003). Phases of couples group therapy: A consideration of therapeutic action. *Group, 27,* 5–19.

Feld, B. G., & Urman-Klein, P. (1993). Gender: A critical factor in a couples group. *Group, 17,* 3–12.

Ferguson, D. (2006). *Reptiles in love: Ending destructive fights and evolving toward more loving relationships.* San Francisco, CA: Jossey–Bass.

Fisher, H. (1994). *Anatomy of love: A natural history of mating, marriage, and why we stray.* New York, NY: Ballantine Books.

Fisher, H. (2004). *Why we love: The nature and chemistry of romantic love.* New York, NY: Henry Holt & Company.

Fisher, H. E., Aron, A., & Brown, L. L. (2006). Romantic love: A mammalian brain system for mate choice. *Philosophical Transactions of the Royal Society B, 361,* 2173–2186.

Fisher, R., & Ury W. (1981). *Getting to yes: Negotiating agreement without giving in.* New York, NY: Penguin Books.

Flapan, D. (1981). Interventions of the group therapist. *Issues in Ego Psychology, 4,* 19–31.

Flapan, D., & Fenchel, G. H. (1983). Group member contacts without the group therapist. *Group, 7(4),* 3–16.

Floyd, K., Mikkelson, A. C., Tafoya, M. A., Farinelli, L., La Valley, A. G., Judd, J., et al. (2007a). Human affection exchange: XIII. Affectionate communication accelerates neuroendocrine stress recovery. *Health Communication, 22,* 123–132.

Floyd, K., Mikkelson, A. C., Tafoya, M. A., Farinelli, L., La Valley, A. G., Judd, J., et al. (2007b). Human affection exchange: XIV. Relational affection predicts resting heart rate and free cortisol secretion during acute stress. *Behavioral Medicine, 32,* 151–156.

245

France, D. G., & Dugo, J. M. (1985). Pretherapy orientation as preparation for open psychotherapy groups. *Psychotherapy, 22,* 256–261.

Francis, S., Rolls, E. T., Bowtell, R., McGlone, F., O'Doherty, J., Browning, A., et al. (1999). The representation of pleasant touch in the brain and its relationship with taste and olfactory areas. *NeuroReport, 10,* 453–459.

Frank, K. A. (2002). The "ins and outs" of enactment: A relational bridge for psychotherapy integration. *Journal of Psychotherapy Integration, 12*(3), 267–286.

Frankl, V. E. (1963). *Man's search for meaning: An introduction to logotherapy.* New York, NY: Washington Square Press.

Free, M., Oei, T., & Sanders, M. (1991). Treatment outcome of a group cognitive therapy program for depression. *International Journal of Group Psychotherapy, 41,* 533–547.

Fromm, E. (1956). *The art of loving.* New York, NY: Harper & Row.

Gable, S., Reis, H., & Downey, G. (2003). He said, she said: A quasi-signal detection analysis of daily interactions between close relationship partners. *Psychological Science, 14,* 100–105.

Garrison, J. E. (1978). Written vs. verbal preparation of patients for group psychotherapy. *Psychotherapy, 15,* 130–134.

Gazarik, R., & Fischman, D. (1995). A time-limited group for patients with HIV infection and their partners. *Group, 19,* 173–182.

Georgiadis, J. R., & Holstege, G. (2005). Human brain activation during sexual stimulation of the penis. *Journal of Comparative Neurology, 493,* 33–38.

Georgiadis, J. R., Kortekaas, R., Kuipers, R., Nieuwenburg, A., Pruim, J., Reinders, A. A., et al. (2006). Regional cerebral blood flow changes associated with clitorally induced orgasm in healthy women. *European Journal of Neuroscience, 24,* 3305–3316.

Gilligan, C. (1982). *In a different voice: Psychological theory and women's development.* Cambridge, MA: Harvard University Press.

Ginot, E. (2007). Intersubjectivity and neuroscience: Understanding enactments and their therapeutic significance within emerging paradigms. *Psychoanalytic Psychology, 24*(2), 317–332.

Glass, S. (2004). *Not "just friends:" Rebuilding trust and recovering your sanity after infidelity.* Florence, MA: Free Press.

Goleman, D. (1997). *Emotional intelligence: Why it can matter more than IQ.* New York, NY: Bantam Books.

Gordon, L. (1993). *Passage to intimacy.* New York, NY: Simon & Schuster.

Gottman, J. M. (1993). The roles of conflict engagement, escalation or avoidance in marital interaction: A longitudinal view of five types of couples. *Journal of Consulting and Clinical Psychology, 61,* 6–15.

Gottman, J. M. (1994). *What predicts divorce: The relationship between marital processes and marital outcomes.* Hillsdale, NJ: Lawrence Erlbaum Associates.

Gottman, J. M. (1998). Psychology and the study of marital processes. *Annual Review of Psychology, 49,* 169–197.

Gottman, J. M. (1999). *The seven principles for making marriage work*. New York, NY: Crown Publishers.

Gottman, J. M., Coan, J., Carrère, S., & Swanson, C. (1998). Predicting marital happiness and stability from newlywed interactions. *Journal of Marriage and the Family, 60,* 5–22.

Gottman, J. M., & Krokoff, L. J. (1989). Marital interaction and satisfaction: A longitudinal view. *Journal of Consulting and Clinical Psychology, 57,* 47–52.

Gottman, J. M., & Levenson, R. W. (2002). A two-factor model for predicting when a couple will divorce: Exploratory analyses using 14-year longitudinal data. *Family Process, 41,* 83–96.

Greeff, A. P., & de Bruyne, T. (2000). Conflict management style and marital satisfaction. *Journal of Sex and Marital Therapy, 26,* 321–334.

Grewen, K. M., Girder, S. S., Amico, J., & Light, K. C. (2005). Effects of partner support on resting oxytocin, cortisol, norepinephrine, and blood pressure before and after warm partner contact. *Psychosomatic Medicine, 67,* 531–538.

Hahlweg, K., & Markman, H. J. (1988). Effectiveness of behavioral marital therapy: Empirical status of behavioral techniques in preventing and alleviating marital distress. *Journal of Consulting and Clinical Psychology, 56,* 440–447.

Halford, W. K., Lizzio, A., Wilson, K. L., & Occhipinti, S. (2007). Does working at your marriage help? Couple relationship self-regulation and satisfaction in the first 4 years of marriage. *Journal of Family Psychology, 21,* 185–194.

Halford, W. K., Markman, H. J., Kline, G. H., & Stanley, S. M. (2003). Best practice in couple relationship education. *Journal of Marital and Family Therapy, 29,* 385–406.

Halford, K. W., Sanders, M. R., & Behrens, B. C. (1993). A comparison of the generalization of behavioral marital therapy and enhanced behavioral marital therapy. *Journal of Consulting and Clinical Psychology, 61,* 51–60.

Hazan, C., & Shaver, P. (1987). Romantic love conceptualized as an attachment process. *Journal of Personality and Social Psychology, 52,* 511–524.

Heavey, C. L., Christensen, A., & Malaniuth, N. M. (1995). The longitudinal impact of demand and withdrawal during marital conflict. *Journal of Consulting and Clinical Psychology, 63,* 797–801.

Hellwig, K., & Memmott, R. J. (1974). Co-therapy: The balancing act. *Small Group Behavior, 5,* 175–181.

Hendrix, C. C., Fournier, D. G., & Briggs, K. (2001). Impact of co-therapy teams on client outcomes and therapist training in marriage and family therapy. *Contemporary Family Therapy, 23,* 63–82.

Hennessy, M. B. (1997). Hypothalamic–pituitary–adrenal responses to brief social separation. *Neuroscience and Biobehavioral Reviews, 21,* 11–29.

Heyman, R. E. (2001). Observation of couple conflicts: Clinical assessment applications, stubborn truths, and shaky foundations. *Psychological Assessment, 13,* 5–35.

Holstege, G., Georgiadis, J. R., Panns, A. M. J., Meiners, L. C., van der Graaf, F. H. C. E., & Reinders, A. A. T. S. (2003). Brain activation during male ejaculation. *Journal of Neuroscience, 23,* 9185–9193.

Hope, D. A., Heimberg, R. G., & Bruch, M. A. (1995). Dismantling cognitive-behavioral group therapy for social phobia. *Behaviour Research and Therapy, 33,* 637–650.

Huh, J., Park, K., Hwang, I. S., Jung, S. I., Kim, H-J., Chung, T.-W., et al. (2008). Brain activation areas of sexual arousal with olfactory stimulation in men: A preliminary study using functional MRI. *Journal of Sexual Medicine, 5,* 619–625.

Hunsley, J., & Lee, C. M. (1995). The marital effects of individually oriented psychotherapy: Is there evidence for the deterioration hypothesis? *Clinical Psychology Review, 25,* 1–21.

Hurlbert, D. F., White, L. C., Powell, R. D., & Apt, C. (1993). Orgasm consistency training in the treatment of women reporting hypoactive sexual desire: An outcome comparison of women-only groups and couples-only groups. *Journal of Behavior Therapy and Experimental Psychiatry, 24,* 3–13.

Insel, T. R., & Shapiro, L. E. (1992). Oxytocin receptor distribution reflects social organization in monogamous and polygamous voles. *Proceedings of the National Academy of Sciences, 89,* 5981–5985.

Insel, T. R., & Young, L. J. (2001). The neurobiology of attachment. *Nature Reviews Neuroscience, 2,* 129–136.

Jacobson, N. S., Dobson, K., Fruzzetti, A. E., Schmaling, K. B., & Salusky, S. (1991). Marital therapy as a treatment for depression. *Journal of Consulting and Clinical Psychology, 59,* 547–557.

Jacobson, N. S., Gottman, J. M., Waltz, J., Rushe, R., & Babcock, J. (1994). Affect, verbal content, and psychophysiology in the arguments of couples with a violent husband. *Journal of Consulting and Clinical Psychology, 62,* 982–988.

Jacobson, N. S., & Gurman, A. S. (Eds.). (1986). *Clinical handbook of marital therapy.* New York, NY: Guilford Press.

Johnson, S., & Lebow, J. (2000). The "coming of age" of couple therapy: A decade review. *Journal of Marital and Family Therapy, 26,* 23–38.

Johnson, S. M. (2005). *Attachment processes in couple and family therapy.* New York, NY: Guilford Press.

Johnson, S. M., & Greenberg, L. S. (1994). *The heart of the matter: Perspective on emotion in marital therapy.* New York, NY: Brunner/Mazel.

Joyce, A. S., Piper, W. E., & Ogrodniczuk, J. S. (2007). Therapeutic alliance and cohesion variables as predictors of outcome in short-term group psychotherapy. *International Journal of Group Psychotherapy, 57,* 269–296.

Kaiser, A., Hahlweg, K., Fehm-Wolfsdorf, G., & Groth, T. (1998). The efficacy of a compact psychoeducational group training program for married couples. *Journal of Consulting and Clinical Psychology, 66,* 753–760.

Karama, S., Lecours, A. R., Leroux, J. M., Bourgouin, P., Beaudoin, G., Joubert, S., et al. (2002). Areas of brain activation in males and females during viewing of erotic film excerpts. *Human Brain Mapping, 16,* 1–13.

Kaufmann, W. (1975). *Existentialism from Dostoevsky to Sartre.* New York, NY: Meridian.

Kawabata, H., & Zeki, S. (2004). Neural correlates of beauty. *Journal of Neurophysiology, 91,* 1699–1705.

Keefe, F. J., Caldwell, D. S., Baucom, D., Salley, A., Robinson, E., Timmons, K., et al. (1996). Spouse-assisted coping skills training in the management of knee pain in osteoarthritis: Long-term follow-up results. *Arthritis Care and Research, 12,* 101–111.

Keeney, B. P., & Ross, J. M. (1985). *Mind in therapy: Constructing systemic family therapies.* New York, NY: Basic Books.

Keeney, B. P., & Silverstein, O. (1986). *The therapeutic voice of Olga Silverstein.* New York, NY: Guilford Press.

Kiecolt-Glaser, J. K., Bane, C., Glaser, R., & Malarkey, W. B. (2003). Love, marriage, and divorce: Newlyweds' stress hormones foreshadow relationship changes. *Journal of Consulting and Clinical Psychology, 71,* 176–188.

Kiecolt-Glaser, J. K., Loving, T. J., Stowell, J. R., Malarkey, W. B., Lemeshow, S., Dickinson, S. L., et al. (2005). Hostile marital interactions, proinflammatory cytokine production, and wound healing. *Archives of General Psychiatry, 62,* 1377–1384.

Kiecolt-Glaser, J. K., Malarky, W. B., Chee, M., & Newton, T. (1993). Negative behavior during marital conflict is associated with immunological down-regulation. *Psychosomatic Medicine, 55,* 395–409.

Kim, H. K., Capaldi, D. M., & Crosby, L. (2007). Generalizability of Gottman and colleagues' affective process models of couples' relationship outcomes. *Journal of Marriage and Family, 69,* 55–72.

Kirby, J. S., & Baucom, D. H. (2007). Treating emotion dysregulation in a couples context: A pilot study of a couples skills group intervention. *Journal of Marital and Family Therapy 33,* 375–391.

Kiresuk, T., & Sherman, R. (1968). Goal attainment scaling: a general method of evaluating comprehensive mental health programs. *Community Mental Health Journal, 4,* 443–453.

Kirschenbaum, M. J., & Glinder, M. G. (1972). Growth processes in married-couples group therapy. *Family Therapy, 1,* 85–104.

Kirshner, B. J., Dies, R. R., & Brown, R. A. (1978). Effects of experimental manipulation of self-disclosure on group cohesiveness. *Journal of Consulting and Clinical Psychology, 46,* 1171–1177.

Kivlighan, D. M., Jauquet, C. A., Hardie, A. W., Francis, A. M., & Hershberger, B. (1993). Training group members to set session agendas: Effects on in-session behavior and member outcome. *Journal of Counseling Psychology, 40,* 182–187.

Klein, M. (2002). *Beyond orgasm: Dare to be honest about the sex you really want.* Berkely, CA: Ten Speed Press.

Kluge, P. (1974). Group psychotherapy for married couples. *Psychotherapie und Medizinische Psychologie, 24,* 132–137.

Komisaruk, B. R., & Whipple, B. (1998). Love as sensory stimulation: Physiological consequences of its deprivation and expression. *Psychoneuroendocrinology, 23,* 927–944.

Konner, M. (2004). The ties that bind: Attachment: The nature of the bonds between humans are becoming accessible to scientific investigation. *Nature, 429,* 705.

Kosfeld, M., Heinrichs, M., Zak, P. J., Fischbacher, U., & Fehr, E. (2005). Oxytocin increases trust in humans. *Nature, 435,* 673–676.

Kringelbach, M. L., & Rolls, E. T. (2004). The functional neuroanatomy of the human orbitofrontal cortex: Evidence from neuroimaging and neuropsychology. *Progress in Neurobiology, 72,* 341–372.

Kutash, I. L., & Wolf, A. (1983). Recent advances in psychoanalysis in groups. In H. I. Kaplan & B. J. Sadock (Eds.), *Comprehensive group psychotherapy* (pp. 132–138). Baltimore, MD: Williams & Wilkins.

Langeslag, S. J. E., Jansma, B. A., Franken, I. H. A., & Van Strien, J. W. (2007). Event-related potential responses to love-related facial stimuli. *Biological Psychology, 76,* 109–115.

Langley, D. M., & Langley, G. E. (1983). *Dramatherapy and psychiatry.* London, England: Croom Helm.

Law, L. A. F., Evans, S., Knudtson, J., Nus, S., Scholl, K., & Sluka, K. A. (2008). Massage reduces pain perception and hyperalgesia in experimental muscle pain: A randomized, controlled trial. *Journal of Pain, 9,* 714–721.

Lazarus, A. A. (1971). *Behavior therapy and beyond.* New York, NY: McGraw–Hill.

Lebow, J. L., & Gurman, A. S. (1995). Research assessing couple and family therapy. *Annual Review of Psychology, 46,* 27–57.

Leff, J., Vearnals, S., Brewin, C. R., Wolff, G., Alexander, B., Asen, E., et al. (2000). The London Depression Intervention Trial: Randomized controlled trial of antidepressants v. couple therapy in the treatment and maintenance of people with depression living with a partner: Clinical outcome and costs. *British Journal of Psychiatry, 177,* 95–100.

Leuner, H. (1969). Guided affective imagery: A method of intensive psychotherapy. *American Journal of Psychotherapy, 23,* 4–22.

Levenson, R. W., & Gottman, J. M. (1983). Marital interaction: Physiological linkage and affective exchange. *Journal of Personality and Social Psychology, 45,* 587–597.

Levenson, R. W., & Gottman, J. M. (1985). Physiological and affective predictors of change in relationship satisfaction. *Journal of Personality and Social Psychology, 49,* 85–94.

Levinson, D. J., Darrow, C. N., Klein, E. B., Levinson, M. H., & McKee, B. (1978). *The seasons of a man's life.* New York, NY: Alfred A. Knopf.

Lewin, K. (1951). *Field theory in social science: Selected theoretical papers.* Chicago, IL: The University of Chicago Press.

Lewis, T., Amini, F., & Lannon, R. (2000). *A general theory of love.* NY: Vintage Books.

Li, S., Armstrong, M. S., Chaim, G., & Shenfeld, J. (2007). Group and individual couple treatment for substance abuse clients: A pilot study. *American Journal of Family Therapy, 35,* 221–233.

Liberman, R., Levine, J., Wheeler, E., Sanders, N., & Wallace, C. J. (1976). Marital therapy in groups: A comparative evaluation of behavioral and interaction formats. *Acta Psychiatrica Scandinavica, 266,* 1–34.

Light, K. C., Grewen, K. M., & Amico, J. A. (2005). More frequent partner hugs and higher oxytocin levels are linked to lower blood pressure and heart rate in premenopausal women. *Biological Psychology, 69,* 5–21.

Litzinger, S., & Gordon, K. C. (2005). Exploring relationships among communication, sexual satisfaction, and marital satisfaction. *Journal of Sex and Marital Therapy, 31,* 409–424.

Liu, D., Diorio, J., Tannenbaum, B., Caldji, C., Francis, A., Freedman, S., et al. (1997). Maternal care, hippocampal glucocorticoid receptors, and hypothalamic-pituitary-adrenal responses to stress. *Science, 277,* 1659–1662.

LoPiccolo, J., Heiman, J. R., Hogan, D. R., & Roberts, C. W. (1985). Effectiveness of single therapists versus cotherapy teams in sex therapy. *Journal of Consulting and Clinical Psychology, 53,* 287–294.

Lorberbaum, J. P., Newman, J. D., Dubno, J. R., Horwitz, A. R., Nahas, Z., Teneback, C. C., et al. (1999). Feasibility of using fMRI to study mothers responding to infant cries. *Depression and Anxiety, 10,* 99–104.

Low, P., & Low, M. (1975). Treatment of married couples in a group run by a husband and wife. *International Journal of Group Psychotherapy, 25,* 54–66.

Lund, I., Yu, L. C., Uvnas-Moberg, K., Wang, J., Yu, C., Kurosawa, M., et al. (2002). Repeated massage-like stimulation induces long-term effects on nociception: Contribution of oxytocinergic mechanisms. *European Journal of Neuroscience, 16,* 330–338.

MacDonald, G., & Leary, M. R. (2005). Why does social exclusion hurt? The relationship between social and physical pain. *Psychological Bulletin, 131,* 202–223.

MacKenzie, K. R., & Livesley, W. J. (1983). A developmental model for brief group therapy. In R. R. Dies & K. R. MacKenzie (Eds.), *Advances in group psychotherapy* (pp. 101–116). New York, NY: International Universities Press.

Manne, S. L., Ostroff, J. S., Winkel, G., Fox, K., Grana, G., Miller, E., et al. (2005). Couple-focused group intervention for women with early stage breast cancer. *Journal of Consulting and Clinical Psychology, 73,* 634–646.

Marazziti, D., & Canale, D. (2004). Hormonal changes when falling in love. *Psychoneuroendocrinology, 29,* 931–936.

Marett, K. M. (1988). A substantive and methodological review of couples group therapy outcome research. *Group, 12,* 241–246.

Markman, H. J., Renick, M. J., Floyd, F., Stanley, S., & Clements, M. (1993). Preventing marital distress through communication and conflict management training: A four- and five-year follow-up. *Journal of Consulting and Clinical Psychology, 62,* 1–8.

251

Markman, H. J., Stanley, S. M., & Blumberg, S. L. (1994). *Fighting for your marriage.* San Francisco, CA: Jossey–Bass Inc.

Marmarosh, C., Holtz, A., & Schottenbauer, M. (2005). Group cohesiveness, group-derived collective self-esteem, group-derived hope, and the well-being of group therapy members. *Group Dynamics: Theory, Research, and Practice, 9,* 32–44.

Marziali, E., Munroe-Blum, H., & McCleary, L. (1997). The contribution of group cohesion and group alliance to the outcome of group psychotherapy. *International Journal of Group Psychotherapy, 47,* 475–497.

Mayerson, N. H. (1984). Preparing clients for group therapy: A critical review and theoretical formulation. *Clinical Psychology Review, 4,* 191–213.

McArthur, H., Jr., & Russell, C. D. (2003). When marital interaction and intervention researchers arrive at different points of view: The active listening controversy. *Journal of Family Therapy, 25,* 4–14.

McCarthy, K. S., & Coché, J. M. (2008). *Making an evidence base from practice: Good intentions, complications, and recommendations for group psychotherapists.* Paper presented at the annual meeting for the American Group Psychotherapy Association, Washington, DC.

McCrady, B., Stout, R., Noel, N., Abrams, D., & Nelson, H. (1991). Comparison of depressive symptomatology? *Journal of Social and Clinical Psychology, 7,* 312–318.

McGoldrick, M., Anderson, C. M., & Walsh, F. (Eds.). (1989). *Women in families: a framework for family therapy.* New York, NY: W. W. Norton & Company.

Meadow, D. (1988). Preparation of individuals for participation in a treatment group: Development and empirical testing of a model. *International Journal of Group Psychotherapy, 38,* 367–385.

Mehlman, S. K., Baucom, D. H., & Anderson, D. (1983). Effectiveness of cotherapists versus single therapists and immediate versus delayed treatment in behavioral marital therapy. *Journal of Consulting and Clinical Psychology, 51,* 258–266.

Menchaca, D., & Dehle, C. (2005). Marital quality and physiological arousal: How do I love thee? Let my heartbeat count the ways. *American Journal of Family Therapy, 33,* 117–130.

Miller, J. B. (1976). *Toward a new psychology of women.* Boston, MA: Beacon Press.

Milsten, R., & Slowinski, J. (1999). *The sexual male: Problems and solutions.* New York, NY: W. W. Norton & Company.

Mitchell, S. A. (2002). *Can love last? The fate of romance over time.* New York, NY: W. W. Norton.

Mohr, D. C., Moran, P. J., Kohn, C., Hart, S., Armstrong, K., Dias, R., et al. (2003). Couple therapy at the end of life. *Psycho-Oncology, 12,* 620–627.

Monson, C. M., Schnurr, P. P., Stevens, S. P., & Guthrie, K. A. (2004). Cognitive–behavioral couple's treatment for posttraumatic stress disorder: Initial findings. *Journal of Traumatic Stress, 17,* 341–344.

Moreno, J. L. (1951). *Sodometry, experimental method, and the science of society.* Beacon, NY: Beacon House.

Moreno, J. L., & Moreno, Z. T. (1959). *Psychodrama*. Beacon, NY: Beacon House.

Moulier, V., Mouras, H., Pélégrini-Isaac, M., Glutron, D., Rouxel, R., Grandjean, B., et al. (2006). Neuroanatomical correlates of penile erection evoked by photographic stimuli in human males. *Neuroimage, 33*, 689–699.

Mouras, H., Stoleru, S., Bittoun, J., Glutron, D., Pélégrini-Isaac, M., Paradis, A. L., et al. (2003). Brain processing of visual sexual stimuli in healthy men: A functional magnetic resonance imaging study. *Neuroimage, 20*, 855–869.

Moynehan, J., & Adams, J. (2007). What's the problem? A look at men in marital therapy. *American Journal of Family Therapy, 35*, 41–51.

Murphy, M. R., Seckl, J. R., Burton, S., Checkley, S. A., & Lightman, S. L. (1987). Changes in oxytocin and vasopressin secretion during sexual activity in men. *Journal of Clinical Endocrinology and Metabolism, 65*, 738–741.

Napier, A. Y., & Whitaker, C. A. (1978). *The family crucible: One family's therapy—An experience that illuminates all our lives*. New York, NY: Bantam Books.

Neill, J. R., & Kniskern, D. P. (Eds.). (1982). *From psyche to system: The evolving therapy of Carl Whitaker*. New York, NY: Guilford Press.

Newsom, J. T., Mahan, T. L., Rook, K. S., & Krause, N. (2008). Stable negative social exchanges and health. *Health Psychology, 27*, 78–86.

Nichols, K. A. (1976). Preparation for membership in a group. *Bulletin of the British Psychological Society, 29*, 353–359.

Nietzsche, F. (1960). *Also Sprach Zarathustra: Ein Buch fur Alle und Keinen*. Munich, Germany: Goldmann.

Nobler, H. (1986). When group doesn't work: An examination of the types and causes of individual, group, and leader failures. *Group, 10*, 103–110.

O'Farrell, T. J., Cutter, H. S. G., Choquette, K. A., Floyd, F. J., & Bayog, R. D. (1992). Behavioral marital therapy for male alcoholics: Marital and drinking adjustment during the two years after treatment. *Behavior Therapy, 23*, 529–549.

O'Farrell, T. J., & Fals-Stewart, W. (2000). Behavioral couples therapy for alcoholism and drug abuse. *Journal of Substance Abuse Treatment, 18*, 51–54.

Ogrodniczuk, J. S., Joyce, A. S., & Piper, W. E. (2005). Strategies for reducing patient-initiated premature termination of psychotherapy. *Harvard Review of Psychiatry, 13*, 57–70.

Ogrodniczuk, J. S., & Piper, W. E. (2003). The effect of group climate on outcome in two forms of short-term group therapy. *Group Dynamics: Theory, Research, and Practice, 7*, 64–76.

O'Leary, K. D., Christian, J. L., & Mendell, N. R. (1994). A closer look at the link between marital discord and depressive symptomatology. *Journal of Social and Clinical Psychology, 13*, 33–41.

O'Leary, K. D., Heyman, R. E., & Neidig, P. H. (1999). Treatment of wife abuse: A comparison of gender-specific and conjoint approaches. *Behavior Therapy, 30*, 475–505.

Ormont, L. R. (1981). Principles and practice of conjoint psychoanalytic treatment. *American Journal of Psychiatry, 138*, 69–73.

Ortigue, S., Bianchi-Demicheli, F., Hamilton, A. F. D. C., & Grafton, S. T. (2007). The neural basis of love as a subliminal prime: An event-related functional magnetic resonance imaging study. *Journal of Cognitive Neuroscience, 19,* 1218–1230.

Palmer, K. D., Baker, R. C., & McGee, T. F. (1997). The effects of pretraining on group psychotherapy for incest-related issues. *International Journal of Group Psychotherapy, 47,* 71–89.

Papp, P. (1976). Family choreography. In P. J. Guerin (Ed.), *Family therapy: Theory and practice.* New York, NY: Gardner Press.

Papp, P. (1982). Staging reciprocal metaphors in a couples group. *Family Process, 21,* 453–467.

Pasolini, U., & Cattaneo, P. (1997). *The full monty* [Motion Picture]. United Kingdom: Fox Searchlight Pictures.

Paul, T., Schiffer, B., Zwarg, T., Krüger, T. H., Karama, S., Schedlowski, M., et al. (2008). Brain response to visual sexual stimuli in heterosexual and homo-sexual males. *Human Brain Mapping, 29,* 726–735.

Perel, E. (2006). *Mating in captivity.* New York, NY: Harper & Collins.

Piaget, J., & Inhelder, B. (2000). *The psychology of the child.* New York, NY: Basic Books.

Piotrowski, M. M., Paterson, C., Mitchinson, A., Kim, H. M., Kirsh, M., & Hinshaw, D. B. (2003). Massage as adjuvant therapy in the management of acute post-operative pain: A preliminary study in men. *Journal of the American College of Surgery, 197,* 1037–1046.

Piper, W. E., Debbane, E. G., Garant, J., & Bienvenu, J. P. (1979). Pretraining for group psychotherapy: A cognitive-experiential approach. *Archives of General Psychiatry, 36,* 1250–1258.

Pittman, F. (1989). *Private lies: Infidelity and the betrayal of intimacy.* New York, NY: W. W. Norton & Company.

Plotsky, P. M., Thrivikraman, K. V., Nemeroff, C. B., Caldji, C., Sharma, S., & Meaney, M. J. (2005). Long-term consequences of neonatal rearing on central corticotrophin-releasing factor systems in adult male rat offspring. *Neuropsychopharmacology, 30,* 2192–2204.

Pomeroy, E. C., Green, D. L., & Van Laningham, L. (2002). Couples who care: The effectiveness of a psychoeducational group intervention for HIV serodiscordant couples. *Research on Social Work Practice, 12,* 238–252.

Porges, S. W. (1998). Love: An emergent property of the mammalian autonomic nervous system. *Psychoneuroendocrinology, 23,* 837–861.

Powers, M. B., Vedel, E., & Emmelkamp, P. M. G. (2008). Behavioral couples therapy for alcohol drug use disorders: A meta-analysis. *Clinical Psychology Review, 28,* 952–962.

Prager, K. J. (1995). *The psychology of intimacy.* New York, NY: Guilford Press.

Priebe, S., & Sinning, U. (2001). Effects of a brief couple's therapy intervention in coronary rehabilitation: A controlled study. *Psychotherapie Psychosomatik Medizinische Psychologie, 51,* 276–280.

Rauch, S. L., Shin, L. M., Dougherty, D. D., Alpert, N. M., Orr, S. P., Lasko, M., et al. (1999). Neural activation during sexual and competitive arousal in healthy men. *Psychiatry Research, 91,* 1–10.

Redouté, J., Stoléru, S., Grégorie, M.-C., Costes, N., Cinotti, N., Lavenne, F., et al. (2000). Brain processing of visual sexual stimuli in human males. *Human Brain Mapping, 11,* 162–177.

Richman, J. (1979). A couples therapy group on a geriatric service. *Journal of Geriatric Psychiatry, 12,* 203–213.

Risen, C. B., & Althof, S. E. (1990). Couples group psychotherapy: Rebuilding the marital relationship following disclosure of sexual deviance. *Psychotherapy: Theory, Research, Practice, Training, 27,* 458–463.

Roback, H. B., & Smith, M. (1987). Patient attrition in dynamically oriented treatment groups. *American Journal of Psychiatry, 144,* 426–431.

Roberts, L. J. (2000). Fire and ice in marital communication: Hostile and distancing behaviors as predictors of marital distress. *Journal of Marriage and the Family, 62,* 693–707.

Robles, T. F., Shaffer, V. A., Malarkey, W. B., & Kiecolt-Glaser, J. K. (2006). Positive behaviors during marital conflict: Influences on stress hormones. *Journal of Social and Personal Relationships, 23,* 305–325.

Rogers, C. R. (1951). *Client-centered therapy: Its current practice, implications, and theory.* Boston, MA: Houghton Mifflin Company.

Rogers, C. R. (1957). The necessary and sufficient conditions of therapeutic personality change. *Journal of Consulting Psychology, 21,* 95–103.

Rolls, E. T., O'Doherty, J., Kringelbach, M. L., Francis, S., Bowtell, R., & McGlone, F. (2003). Representations of pleasant and painful touch in the human orbitofrontal and cingulate cortices. *Cerebral Cortex, 13,* 308–317.

Rutan, J. S., Alonso, A., & Molin, R. (1984). Handling the absence of group leaders: To meet or not to meet. *International Journal of Group Psychotherapy, 34,* 273–287.

Rutan, J. S., & Stone, W. N. (1984). *Psychodynamic group psychotherapy.* New York, NY: Macmillan Publishing Company.

Rutan, J. S., Stone, W. N., & Shay, J. J. (2007). *Psychodynamic group psychotherapy.* New York, NY: Macmillan Publishing Company.

Salvendy, J. T. (1980). Group psychotherapy training: A quest for standards. Canadian Journal of Psychiatry, 25, 394–402.

Sanders, F. M. (1996). Couples group therapy conducted via computer-mediated communication: A preliminary case study. *Computers in Human Behavior, 12,* 301–312.

Santarsiero, L. J., Baker, R. C., & McGee, T. F. (1995). The effects of cognitive pretraining on cohesion and self-disclosure in small groups: An analog study. *Journal of Clinical Psychology, 51,* 403–409.

Sartre, J. P. (1948a). *Intimacy* (L. Alexander, Trans.). New York, NY: Avon Publications, Inc.

Sartre, J. P. (1948b). *Existentialism and humanism.* London, England: Methuen & Co., Ltd.

Satir, V. (1967). *Conjoint family therapy* (rev. ed.). Palo Alto, CA: Science and Behavior Books, Inc.

Satir, V. (1988). *The new peoplemaking*. Mountain View, CA: Science and Behavior Books, Inc.

Satterfield, J. M. (1994). Integrating group dynamics and cognitive-behavioral groups: A hybrid model. *Clinical Psychology: Science and Practice, 1,* 185–196.

Sayers, S. L., Kohn, C. S., & Heavey, C. L. (1998). Prevention of marital dysfunction: Behavioral approaches and beyond. *Clinical Psychology Review, 18,* 713–744.

Schein, E. H., & Bennis, W. G. (1965). *Personal and organizational change through group methods*. New York, NY: John Wiley & Sons.

Schilling, E. A., Baucom, D. H., Burnett, C. K., Allen, E. S., & Ragland, L. (2003). Altering the course of marriage: The effect of PREP communication skills acquisition on couples' risk of becoming maritally distressed. *Journal of Family Psychology, 17,* 41–53.

Schnarch, D. (1998). *Passionate marriage: Keeping love and intimacy alive in a committed relationship*. New York, NY: Holt Paperbacks.

Seligman, M. E. P. (2002). *Authentic happiness*. New York, NY: Free Press.

Sells, J. N., Giordano, F. G., & King, L. (2002). A pilot study in marital group therapy: Process and outcome. *The Family Journal, 10,* 156–166.

Selvini-Palazzoli, M., Boscolo, L., Cecchin, G. F., & Prata, G. (1980). Hypothesizing–circularity–neutrality: Three guidelines for the conductor of the session. *Family Process, 19,* 3–12.

Sevier, M., Eldridge, K., Jones, J., Doss, B. D., & Christensen, A. (2008). Observed communication and associations with satisfaction during traditional and integrative behavioral couple therapy. *Behavior Therapy, 39,* 137–150.

Shadish, W. R., & Baldwin, S. A. (2003). Meta-analysis of MFT interventions. *Journal of Marital and Family Therapy, 29,* 547–570.

Shadish, W. R., & Baldwin, S. A. (2005). Effects of behavioral marital therapy: A meta-analysis of randomized controlled trials. *Journal of Consulting and Clinical Psychology, 73,* 6–14.

Sherif, M., & Sherif, C. W. (1969). *Social psychology*. New York, NY: Harper & Row.

Siegel, D. (2001). *The developing brain*. New York, NY: Guilford Press.

Siegel, D. J. (2006). *Toward an interpersonal neurobiology of psychotherapy*. Paper presented at the American Group Psychotherapy Association Annual Meeting, Austin, TX, March 8, 2006.

Singer, J. L., & Pope, K. S. (1978). *The power of human imagination*. New York, NY: Plenum Press.

Slavin, R. L. (1993). The significance of here-and-now disclosure in promoting cohesion in group psychotherapy. *Group, 17,* 143–150.

Snyder, D. K. (1981). *Marital Satisfaction Inventory (MSI)—Manual*. Los Angeles, CA: Western Psychological Services.

Snyder, D. K., Castellani, A. M., & Whisman, M. A. (2006). Current status and future directions in couple therapy. *Annual Review of Psychology, 57,* 317–344.

Snyder, D. K., Heyman, R. E., & Haynes, S. N. (2005). Evidence-based approaches to assessing couple distress. *Psychological Assessment, 17,* 288–307.

Snyder, D. K., Wills, R. M., & Grady-Fletcher, A. (1991). Long-term effectiveness of behavioral versus insight-oriented marital therapy: A 4-year follow-up study. *Journal of Consulting and Clinical Psychology, 59,* 138–141.

Spanier, G. B. (1976). Measuring dyadic adjustment: New scales for assessing the quality of marriage and similar dyads. *Journal of Marriage and the Family, 38,* 15–28.

Spanier, G. B., & Thompson, L. (1982). A confirmatory analysis of the Dyadic Adjustment Scale. *Journal of Marriage and the Family, 44,* 731–738.

Spiegel, D. (1999). Healing words: Emotional expression and disease outcome. *Journal of the American Medical Association, 281,* 1328–1329.

Spiegel, D., Bloom, J. R., & Yalom, I. (1981). Group support for patients with metastatic cancer: A randomized prospective outcome study. *Archives of General Psychiatry, 38,* 527–533.

Spitz, H. I. (1979). Group approaches in treating marital problems. *Psychiatric Annals, 9,* 318–330.

Spivack, G., & Shure, M. B. (1977). *Problem solving approach to adjustment.* New York, NY: Jossey–Bass, Inc.

Stanley, S. M. (2005). *The power of commitment: A guide to achieving lifelong love.* San Francisco, CA: Jossey–Bass.

Stanley, S. M., Bradbury, T. N., & Markman, H. J. (2000). Structural flaws in the bridge from basic research on marriage to interventions for couples. *Journal of Marriage and the Family, 62,* 256–264.

Stanley, S. M., Markman, H. J., & Whitton, S.W. (2002). Communication, conflict, and commitment: Insight on the foundations of relationship success from a national survey. *Family Process, 41,* 659–675.

Sternberg, R. J. (1986). A triangular theory of love. *Psychological Review, 93,* 119–135.

Stith, S. M., Rosen, K. H., McCollum, E. E., & Thomsen, C. J. (2004). Treating intimate partner violence within intact couple relationships: Outcomes of multi-couple versus individual couple therapy. *Journal of Marital and Family Therapy, 30,* 305–318.

Stokes, J. P., Fuehrer, A., & Childs, L. (1983). Group members self-disclosures: Relations to perceived cohesion. *Small Group Behavior, 14,* 63–76.

Stone, E. (1988). *Black sheep and kissing cousins: How our family stories shape us.* New York, NY: Times Books.

Stosny, S. (2005). *You don't have to take it anymore: Turn your resentful, angry, or emotionally abusive relationship into a compassionate, loving one.* Florence, MA: Free Press.

Sullivan, H. S. (1953). *The interpersonal theory of psychiatry.* New York, NY: Routledge.

Teichman, Y., Bar-El, Z., Shor, H., Sirota, P., & Elizur, A. (1995). A comparison of two modalities of cognitive therapy (individual and marital) in treating depression. *Psychiatry, 58,* 136–148.

Thelen, H. (1954). *Dynamics of groups at work.* Chicago, IL: University of Chicago Press.

Tillich, P. (1952). *The courage to be.* New Haven, CT: Yale University Press.

Townsley, R. M., Beach, S. R. H., Fincham, F. D., & O'Leary, K. D. (1991). Cognitive specificity for marital discord and depression: What types of cognition influence discord. *Behavior Therapy, 22,* 519–530.

Truax, C. B., & Carkhuff, R. R. (1967). *Towards effective counseling and psychotherapy: Training and practice.* Chicago, IL: Aldine.

Ulrich-Jakubowslu, D., Russell, D. W., & O'Hara, M. W. (1988). Marital adjustment difficulties: Cause or consequence. *Journal of Social and Clinical Psychology, 7,* 312–318.

Unger, R. (1989). Selection and composition criteria in group psychotherapy. *Journal for Specialists in Group Work, 14,* 151–157.

Uvnäs-Moberg, K., Arn, I., & Magnusson, D. (2005). The psychobiology of emotion: The role of oxytocin. *International Journal of Behavioral Medicine, 12,* 59–65.

Vaillant, G. E. (1977). *Adaptation to life: How the best and the brightest came of age.* Boston, MA: Little, Brown and Company.

von Bertalanffy, L. (1968). General System Theory: Foundations, development, applications. New York, NY: Braziller.

Walitzer, K. S., Derman, K. H., & Connors, G. J. (1999). Strategies for preparing clients for treatment: A review. *Behavior Modification, 23,* 129–151.

Wall Street Journal. (2009). No joke: Group therapy offers savings in numbers (March 24).

Walter, M., Bermpohl, F., Mouras, H., Schiltz, K., Tempelmann, C., Rotte, M., et al. (2008). Distinguishing specific sexual and general emotional effects in fMRI: Subcortical and cortical arousal during erotic picture viewing. *Neuroimage, 40,* 1482–1494.

Walters, M., Carter, B., Papp, P., & Silverstein, O. (1988). *The invisible web: Gender patterns in family relationships.* New York, NY: Guilford Press.

Watzlawick, P. (1978). *The language of change: Elements of therapeutic communication.* New York, NY: Basic Books.

Watzlawick, P. (1983). *The situation is hopeless, but not serious: The pursuit of unhappiness.* New York, NY: W. W. Norton & Company.

Watzlawick, P. (Ed.). (1984). *The invented reality: How do I know what we believe I know?* New York, NY: W. W. Norton & Company.

Watzlawick, P., Weakland, J. H., & Fisch, R. (1974). *Change: Principles of problem formation and problem resolution.* New York, NY: W. W. Norton & Company.

Weaver, I. C. G., Cervoni, N., Champagne, F. A., D'Alessio, A. C., Sharma, S., Seckl, J. R., et al. (2004). Epigenetic programming by maternal behavior. *Nature Neuroscience, 7,* 847–854.

Weaver, I. C. G., Champagne, F. A., Brown, S. E., Dymov, S., Sharma, S., Meaney, M. J., et al. (2005). Reversal of maternal programming of stress response in adult offspring through methyl supplementation: Altering epigenetic marking later in life. *Journal of Neuroscience, 25,* 11045–11054.

Wells, J. (1985). The group-as-a-whole perspective and its theoretical roots. In A. D. Colman & M. Giller (Eds.), *Group relations reader 2* (pp. 109–126). Washington, DC: A. K. Rice Institution.

Wexler, D. A., & Rice, L. N. (Eds.). (1974). *Innovations in client-centered therapy.* New York, NY: John Wiley & Sons.

Whisman, M. A. (1999). Marital dissatisfaction and psychiatric disorders: Results from the National Comorbidity Survey. *Journal of Abnormal Psychology, 108,* 701–706.

Whisman, M. A., & Bruce, M. L. (1999). Marital dissatisfaction and incidence of major depressive episode in a community sample. *Journal of Abnormal Psychology, 108,* 674–678.

Whisman, M. A., & Uebelacker, L. A. (1999). Integrating couple therapy with individual therapies and antidepressant medications in the treatment of depression. *Clinical Psychology: Science and Practice, 6,* 415–429.

Whitaker, C. (1989). *Midnight musings of a family therapist.* New York, NY: W. W. Norton & Company.

Whitaker, C. A., & Bumberry, W. M. (1988). *Dancing with the family: A symbolic-experiential approach.* New York, NY: Brunner/Mazel.

Whitaker, C. A., & Keith, D. V. (1981). Symbolic-experiential family therapy. In A. S. Gurman & D. P. Kniskern (Eds.), *Handbook of family therapy* (pp. 187–225). New York, NY: Brunner/Mazel.

Whitton, S. W., Waldinger, R. J., Schulz, M. S., Allen, J. P., Crowell, J. A., & Hauser, S. T. (2008). Prospective associations from family-of-origin interactions to adult marital interactions and relationship adjustment. *Journal of Family Psychology, 22,* 274–286.

Wilfley, D. E., Welch, R. R., Stein, R., Spurrell, E. B., Cohen, L. R., Saelens, B. E., et al. (2002). A randomized comparison of group cognitive–behavioral therapy and group interpersonal psychotherapy for the treatment of overweight individuals with binge-eating disorder. *Archives of General Psychiatry, 59,* 713–721.

Wilson, G. L., Bernstein, P. H., & Wilson, L. J. (1988). Treatment of relationship dysfunction: An empirical evaluation of group and conjoint behavioral marital therapy. *Journal of Consulting and Clinical Psychology, 56,* 929–931.

Winters, J., Fals-Stewart, W., O'Farrell, T. J., Birchler, G. R., & Kelley, M. L. (2002). Behavioral couples therapy for female substance-abusing patients: Effects on substance use and relationship adjustment. *Journal of Consulting and Clinical Psychology, 70,* 344–355.

Wolf, A. (1983). Psychoanalysis in groups. In H. I. Kaplan & B. J. Sadock (Eds.), *Comprehensive group psychotherapy* (pp. 113–131). Baltimore, MD: Williams & Wilkins.

Wood, N. D., Crane, D. R., Schaalje, G. B., & Law, D. (2005). What works for whom: A meta-analytic review of marital and couples therapy in reference to marital distress. *American Journal of Family Therapy, 33,* 273–287.

Yacubian, J., Sommer, T., Schroeder, K., Glascher, J., Braus, D. F., & Buchel, C. (2007). Subregions of the ventral striatum show preferential coding of reward magnitude and probability. *Neuroimage, 38,* 557–563.

Yalom, I. D. (1975). *The theory and practice of group psychotherapy.* New York, NY: Basic Books.

Yalom, I. D., & Leszcz, M. (2005). *The theory and practice of group psychotherapy* (5th ed.). New York, NY: Basic Books.

Young, J. E. & Klosko, J. S. (1994). *Reinventing your life: The breakthrough program to end negative behavior and feel great again.* New York, NY: Penguin Putnam Inc.

Young, L. J., & Wang, Z. X. (2004). The neurobiology of pair bonding. *Nature Neuroscience, 7,* 1048–1054.

Zimmerman, T. S., Prest, L. A., & Wetzel, B. E. (1997). Solution-focused couples therapy groups: An empirical study. *Journal of Family Therapy, 19,* 125–144.

COUPLES INDEX

AUTHOR INDEX

267

269

SUBJECT INDEX